CLOSER THAN A BROTHER

*Daily Moments
in the Life of Christ*

CLOSER
THAN A
BROTHER

*Daily Moments
in the Life of Christ*

J.R. MILLER

Edited and Introduced by James S. Bell, Jr.

MOODY PRESS
CHICAGO

Originally published as: *Come Ye Apart*
Daily Readings In The Life of Christ
by Thomas Nelson and Sons
Edinburgh 1912

© 1995 by
JAMES S. BELL, JR.

ISBN: 0-8024-1390-0

1 3 5 7 9 10 8 6 4 2

Printed in the United States of America

To my friend Rich Baker, a man whose daily walk with Christ impacts his calling.

---◇---
ACKNOWLEDGMENTS
---◇---

The library of Ned Curley, my cherished father-in-law, who in his last days believed Romans 10:13, "Everyone who calls on the name of the Lord will be saved" (NIV).

The Evangelical Library of Chiltern Street, London, England. To Terence Crosby, librarian, who graciously allowed *Jesus and I Are Friends* to become overdue. This biography by John T. Faris provides an overview of the life of J.R. Miller as well as a listing of his works.

To Margaret, Rosheen, Brendan, Brigit, and Caitlin who suffered the loss of me for much of the Christmas holidays.

INTRODUCTION

Among His parables of the kingdom of God, Jesus described those who were teachers of the law. He compared them to a homeowner who pulls out of storage "new treasures as well as old." All of us may not be called to be teachers, but each one should desire to grow deeper in Christ. Dusting off and putting into functional order the "old treasures" that only seem to get better with age is a sure means of better knowing the timeless Christ.

We think we have salvaged all the old treasures of the last couple of centuries for present consumption, those of major or even minor stature who affected perhaps millions of readers. Alas, it is not so, as I discovered when editing *Devotional Prayers* by Henry Thornton and *Who Owns The Mountains?* by Henry van Dyke. Similar to van Dyke, James Russell Miller wrote more than fifty Christian works that shaped the spiritual lives of past generations. In fact, one British publication said it sold at least a million copies of his works in Britain alone. Upon discovering several volumes among the remains of my father-in-law's library in Ireland, I was told that throughout the British Isles his vast works remain on the bookshelves of older Christians who received them from their parents (Miller wrote from 1880 to 1913).

Interestingly, J. R. Miller, who influenced Britain far more than the United States, was an American from Pennsylvania, born and bred. As with the great E. M. Bounds, J. R. Miller met the physical and spiritual needs of soldiers during the Civil War, while still enrolled at Allegheny Seminary. He later took pastorates in Pennsylvania and Illinois. In 1880 he undertook editorial work for the Presbyterian Board of Publication in Philadelphia. At the same time, he became pastor of an inner-city mission, continuing various forms of pastoral duties throughout his life. Yet his role as Editorial Superintendent of the Board is where he had greatest influence, and it became the fulcrum for his writing for more than thirty years. His numerous devotional works received such note that even Gladstone, the Prime Minister of Great Britain, wrote in thanks of Miller's *The Building of Character.*

Miller's ministry was directed primarily toward the believer's growth in Christ. Though he never underemphasized absolute surrender and self-denial, he focused on the positive side of reconciliation, comfort, blessings, and especially the friendship we have in Christ. In fact, John T. Faris, his biographer, entitled his volume on Miller, *Jesus and I Are Friends.* Miller felt a strong calling to a letter-writing ministry to Christians who had deep questions, trials, and need for encouragement. He stressed the practical outworking of our faith and progress in Christ-like character rather than doctrinal disputes among Christian factions. Miller wished evangelicals would agree and move forward on the common essentials toward an effective, mature church that would be a witness to the world.

The author of *Come Ye Apart* (original title of this volume) held that more of Christ was the answer to every need in the life of the committed disciple. Miller was not Christocentric to the exclusion of the Father or Holy Spirit, but he recognized that all things in heaven and earth would be "summed up" in Christ. If we are to be in deep fellowship with the Lord Jesus, the place to know Him is in His life and words—or to phrase it another way, His actions and teaching.

The best vehicle for this systematic growth is daily reading from the four Gospels. Miller selects the crucial verses throughout Matthew, Mark, Luke, and John that best demonstrate the personality, purposes, and performance of our Lord Jesus Christ. Rather than using large chunks of Scripture or even exegetical commentary, the author takes a pivotal verse and explores its many lessons and the need for our response. His devotional style points toward practice over theory, concrete choices and character development in contrast to mere cognitive knowledge.

Whether it is a miracle, a parable, a confrontation, or a dramatic event, each daily portion helps us to better comprehend the overwhelming significance of the Son of God's life on earth on our behalf. The author quickens the meaning of each teaching, or the lives of others encountering Christ, as they relate personally to us in order to change our lives here and now. As you read these selections, you will sense the living Christ, relating His life with yours, and enabling you to become more like Him. They contain a view of Christ we don't often hear. In *The Book of Comfort*, Miller states, "Christ is our Friend. That means everything we need. No want can be unsupplied. No sorrow can be uncomforted. No evil can overmaster us. For time and eternity we are safe." In another book, he further discussed Christ's friendship in a chapter relating to that role: "All the experiences of our lives have their part in making us what Christ will have us become, in bringing out the possibilities that He sees in us when we first come to Him." He is the kind of friend whom we describe as "closer than a brother"—and thus, so the volume is renamed.

As we are challenged and respond to this daily excursion through the four Gospels, Christ's powerful life given for us indeed opens new possibilities as we encounter Him each day.

A Christ whose mission and legacy relates merely to a historic personage of the past is not the Christ of J. R. Miller. His devotional on Matthew 16:15 ("But whom say ye that I am?") under August 7th sums up the purpose of this volume. He challenges us: "What is Christ to you personally? Is He only in your creed? Is He only a person about whom you believe a great many blessed and glorious things? . . . Is He your Savior, your Friend, your Helper? These are the questions that tell just where we stand with regard to Christ and eternal life. Opinions about Christ, though perhaps true and orthodox, are not enough; only living faith in Him saves."

Having finished this portion of Christ's glorious life I came away with a richer comprehension of what He taught and lived. Far more important, I sensed what Miller's ministry strives for—a sense of comfort. I experienced the essence of Christ's love and compassion for me personally. I was motivated to emulate Him but only through the realization that He indeed is not only my Lord and Savior but my Friend—a Friend who can daily change me to resemble Him. It is my prayer that through these daily readings He will do the same for you.

James S. Bell, Jr., 1995

January 1

IN THE BEGINNING

In the beginning was the Word,
and the Word was with God, and the Word was God.
John 1:1

Life is full of beginnings. We are now at the beginning of a year. But here is a beginning that takes us back through all the years, all important events of history, all imaginable periods of time, before the beginnings of Creation itself. Christ existed then. What an immense stretch of existence these words imply to Him who is our Savior! We cannot fathom this span, but we can find security and comfort in it when we think of Christ, and when we rest in Him as our hope and salvation. We trust in human friends, and their comfort is very assuring, yet we can never forget that they are but creatures for a brief time, and that we cannot be sure of having them around even for tomorrow. But we trust in Christ, and know that from eternity to eternity He is the same, and, therefore, our confidence is forever sure and strong.

Our trust is still more stable and firm when we read on and find who this Person is in whom we are confiding. "The Word was God." This language is straightforward. No explaining away can remove the truth of Christ's divinity from this brief clause. The Savior, into whose hands you have committed your life, is the eternal God. Earthly trusts are never secure, for everything human is mortal; but those who commit themselves to the care of Christ are safe forever. It is very assuring to think of Christ's humanity. It brings Him near to us. He is like one of us. He is our own brother, with tender sympathies and warm affections. We study the gospel and learn the graciousness of His character as seen in His compassion, His tears, His love. Then when we know that behind these qualities are the divine attributes, and that He is the true God, what glorious confidence it gives us! Let us set this glorious truth at the gate of the New Year; it is a shining point from which to start.

January 2
◇

A PLAN FOR EACH LIFE
◇

There was a man sent from God.
John 1:6

John the Baptist had his commission from God. He came as God's messenger on God's business. But each one of us is also "sent from God" into this world. When we are sent from God, it is on some definite mission. God has a plan, a purpose, for each life. No immortal soul ever came by accident into this world, and none ever came without a mission. We ought to think of this. People sometimes suppose that such men as Moses and John the Baptist and Paul were exceptions. They had their own specific mission; God sent them on very definite errands. But surely we ordinary Christians are not sent from God in the same sense. We never saw God in a burning bush, nor received our commission directly from His lips. No angel came before our birth to announce what we were to be and to do in this world. We had no revelation of bright glory smiting us down in blindness.

Yet nevertheless we are "sent from God," every one of us, and have as definite a work allotted to us as had Moses or John or Paul. Are we living out God's plan for us, what He had in view when He made us and sent us here? Are we doing in this world what He wants us to do? These are important questions; and we should not stop short of honest answers to them, for we shall have to account to God at the end of our lives for the way we have fulfilled our mission. Any life is a failure which does not accomplish that which God sent it into the world to do. We find our work and our mission by simple obedience to God and submission to Him. He first prepares us for the calling He is preparing for us, and then at the right time He leads us into it. We can, indeed, avoid our mission in this world, but only by insisting on our own way rather than God's way.

BEARING WITNESS TO CHRIST

He was not that Light, but was sent to bear witness of that Light.
John 1:8

The mission of every Christian is to bear witness to the Light. The Bible says that the spirit of man is the candle of the Lord; but in our natural, unregenerate state the candle is not lit. It is capable of being lit; but until the divine Spirit touches it with heavenly fire and sets it ablaze, it is dead and dark. When the candle is lit, however, it shines within us and makes us full of light. This is how we bear witness of the Light; it is Christ in us that shines; our light is but a small portion of His light breaking through our dim souls. Everyone who sees us sees in us a few gleams of the true Light.

There is another way also in which we may bear witness of the Light. We cannot alone light the path of anyone to heaven; we cannot save any perishing person, nor give life to any dead soul. But we can point lost and dying individuals to Christ, who is the great and true Light. We can tell others, in their experiences of need and sorrow, of the fullness there is in Christ.

We should bear this witness to Christ in many ways. We can do it by our words, telling what He has done for us. This certainly is great honor for Christ, and also great blessing for others, as we testify for Christ. If a physician heals us, we speak his praise among all our friends. Why should we not bear witness in this way for Christ? We can bear witness, too, by our lives, showing in ourselves what Christ can do for others who will come to Him. We should all be consistent witnesses, true representatives, never giving any wrong impression of our Master either by word or by act. It would be regrettable if anyone observing us should get a wrong idea about Christ. We need to be more careful that we never in any way misrepresent Him.

REFLECTING CHRIST

He came unto his own, and his own received him not.
John 1:11

The verse represents Christ coming with infinite grace to those He loved, and to His own people, only to be rejected by them and turned away from their doors. This was one of the most difficult aspects of the Savior's mission to this world. He was the God of glory and of life; He came to bring heaven to earth: but when He stood at men's doors and knocked, the doors were kept closed to Him. He had to turn and leave, bearing back in His hands the precious gifts and blessings He had brought and wished to leave.

We say the Jews, "His own," were very ungrateful to treat their Messiah in this way, and also that their rejection was a great harm to themselves because they threw away in Christ the most glorious things of heaven and eternity. But how is it with us? Christ comes to us; He is continually coming. His hands are full of blessings; He has eternal life to give. Do we receive Him? Is it not true of us also that He comes unto His own, and His own receive Him not? Do we really take from the hand of Christ all that He offers us? Do we not daily grieve Him and rob ourselves of blessings by declining what He offers? Do we especially reject Christ when He comes to us in the garb of pain and sorrow?

Many times these kinds of blessings He brings to us are the very richest and the most precious in all His storehouse. But how many of us receive Christ just as gladly, and take the gifts from His hand just as cheerfully and gratefully, when He comes in grief or suffering, as when He comes in the garb of joy or worldly prosperity? Why should we not do so? Can we not trust His love and wisdom? He never sends pain unless pain is best for us. He never chastens unless there is a blessing in this discipline.

January 5

◇

ACCEPTING CHRIST

◇

As many as received him, to them gave
he power to become the sons of God.
John 1:12

The people who shut their doors on Christ always shut out great blessings; those who open their hearts to Him let heaven's love and joy into their lives. Some say it does not matter whether they receive Christ or not; they believe in God's mercy and love and do not see why they need to accept Christ. Here it is made very plain that the only way to receive God's love and mercy is by receiving Christ. They, and they only, who accept Him become God's children. Christ is the only way to God, the only door into the Father's house. To refuse Christ is to refuse adoption into the family of God.

Some people are puzzled as to how to become Christians. Here the way is surely made as plain as a clear pathway full of light. Christ comes to us as the one Mediator, the Son of God, the divine Savior; and we have only to receive Him, to accept Him with our hearts, and commit ourselves to Him. "But there is that mystery of the new birth; I can't understand that," says a seeker. You have nothing whatever to do with that; for does not this verse say that if we receive Christ by faith we become children of God?

The same passage goes on to say that those who receive Christ are born again; but it says clearly that this change is not their own act, not the act of any man, but is divinely accomplished—they are born of God (v. 13). All that depends on us is simply to receive Christ. We have nothing whatever to do with the mystery of the new birth. That is God's work, and He is able to bring it about. Our part is the acceptance of Christ; God will change our hearts. If we accept God's Son as our Savior, the new life will at once flow into our hearts, and we shall become children of God, not by any creation of a mere name, but by the communication of divine life.

◇

THE INCARNATION

◇

The Word was made flesh, and dwelt among us.
John 1:14

We here notice that it is the same Person who was in the beginning, who was God, and who made all things, who is here said to have become flesh. The Jesus of the gospel story is the God of eternity, the Jehovah of the Old Testament. The reason for the Incarnation was the salvation of man. The Good Shepherd came to seek and to save His sheep which were lost. He came in human form that He might get nearer to the sinner.

A Moravian missionary went to preach the gospel to the slaves in the West Indies. Failing as a free man to reach them, he became a slave himself, and went with them to their toils in the field and into all their hardships and sufferings, thus getting close to them. Then they listened to him. This illustrates Christ's humiliation to save the world. We could not understand God in His invisible glory; but Emmanuel came, and in human form lived out the divine life, showing us God's thoughts and character and feelings, especially God's grace and His love for sinners. This was an important purpose of the Incarnation—it revealed in a way which men could understand the invisible nature of God.

Christ became man also that He might live our life by actual earthly experience, and thus be made to be our Savior, and to sympathize with us in all our experiences of temptation, struggle, and sorrow. We are sure now, when we come to Christ in any need, that He understands our condition and knows how to help us. We have a high priest in heaven who can be touched with the feeling of our infirmities, because He was tried in all points as we are. Christ became man so that He might taste death for every man, thus abolishing death for His people. He remembers what He suffered because He was tempted; and when He sees His people in their struggles, He remembers when He endured the same, and He is ready to sympathize with and help them.

GOD REVEALED IN CHRIST

No man hath seen God at any time; the
only begotten Son . . . hath declared him.
John 1:18

We can never know God except through His Son; there is no other possible revelation of Him. There is no ladder by which to ascend to God's blessedness but the ladder of Christ's incarnation. Christ came in lowly form and appeared to His friends as a man; but when they came to know Him, they found that He was God Himself. This is one of the most precious truths about the Incarnation; and we understand its meaning only when we see in every act and word of Christ a manifestation of the divine heart and life.

When we find Him at a wedding feast, we see God putting His sanction again upon the sacred ordinance of marriage, and upon innocent human gladness and festivities. When we see Him taking little children in His arms, laying His hands upon their heads and blessing them, we learn how God feels toward children, and that He wants parents now to bring their infants to Him. When we see Him moved with compassion in the presence of pain or of sin, we have a glimpse of divine compassion toward their suffering and pain. When we look at Him receiving the outcast and the fallen, treating them with kindness, forgiving them, and transforming their lives into beauty, we see how God feels toward sinners, and what He is ready to do for the worst of them. When we see Him going at last to the cross in voluntary sacrifice, giving His life for the lost, we see how God loves sinners.

Thus the whole of the Incarnation is a manifesting of the invisible God in acts and expressions which we can understand. It is literally true, as Jesus said, "He that hath seen me hath seen the Father" (John 14:9). If we possibly see God, and know Him, and enter into His family, we must receive Christ. To reject Him is to shut ourselves forever away from the vision of God.

A True And Holy Life

*There was in the days of Herod, the king of
Judea, a certain priest . . . and his wife.*
Luke 1:5

It makes a great deal of difference in what times and amid what circumstances and influences a man lives. In godly days, when piety pervades all life, it is not remarkable that one should live righteously; but when the times are ungodly, and the prevailing spirit is unrighteous, the life that is holy and devout shines with rare splendor, like a lamp in the darkness. Such were the times and the spirit of "the days of Herod"; and such were the lives of the blameless old people who are here mentioned. Amid the almost universal corruption of the priesthood and hypocrisy of the Pharisees, these people lived in piety and godly simplicity.

The lesson is that it is not necessary for us to be like other people, if other people are not what they ought to be. The prevalent standard of living should not satisfy us, if the prevalent standard is not God's. No matter how corrupt the times, we should strive to live righteous and godly lives. And this is not impossible. God is able and willing to give us all the grace we need to enable us to live true and holy lives in the most unfavoring circumstances; and He will do so if it's He that has truly placed us in these circumstances.

God makes no mistakes in planting people where they are. He does not put any of us in a spiritual climate in which we cannot grow in beauty and strength; and wherever He plants us, He sends streams of grace to refresh us. So whatever our circumstances may be, it is possible for us to live godly lives. The darker the night of sin about us, the clearer and steadier should be the light that streams from our life and conduct. Anyone should be able to live well in the midst of friendly influences and favoring circumstances; but it is doubly important that we be loyal and true to Christ when surrounded by those who care not for Him.

THE TEST OF LIFE
◇

And they were both righteous before God.
Luke 1:6

This is a great thing to have said of Zacharias and Elisabeth. Yet, after all, righteousness is the test which every life must endure. It is not enough to have human commendation. How do we stand before God? How does our life appear to Him? No matter how men praise and commend us, if God sees us as wrong, we are. The Pharisees were righteous before men; but if you want to see how they stood in God's eyes, read the twenty-third chapter of Matthew. We are in reality just what we are as sensed before God—nothing less, nothing more. The question always to be asked is, "What will God think of this action or thought?" If we would meet His approval, we must first have our hearts right, and then we must be true in every area of our lives.

One of the old artists was chiseling with great pains on the back of his marble block. "Why do you carve so carefully the tresses on the head of your statue?" asked one. "It will stand so high in its niche against a wall, and no one will ever see its back."

"The gods will see it," was the reply.

We should learn a lesson from the old heathen artist. We should do our work just as honestly where it will be covered up and never seen by human eyes, as where it is to be open to the scrutiny of the world. God will see it regardless of circumstances. We should live just as purely and beautifully in secret as in the glare of the world's noon light. There really is no such thing as secrecy in this world. We believe that no eye is looking when we are not in the presence of people, but really we always have spectators—we are living all our lives in the presence of angels and of God Himself. We should train ourselves, therefore, to work under the divine eye in all that we do, that our work may withstand the divine inspection, and that we may have the approval and commendation of God.

January 10
GOD LOOKS ON THE HEART

*Walking in all the commandments
and ordinances of the Lord blameless.*
Luke 1:6

Of course, this does not mean that Zacharias and Elisabeth were absolutely faultless, but that their lives were so righteous, so sincere and faithful, that God saw less in them to blame or rebuke than to praise. This truth is very clearly illustrated in one of Mrs. Herrick Johnson's little poems. A mother is sitting at her work, her mind perplexed as she thinks of her poor sinful life. She had longed to serve the Master, and had tried to do so; but it seemed to her that she had utterly failed. Just then she turned the garment she was mending, and her eye "caught an odd little bungle of mending and patchwork" done by some other hand. Her heart grew soft as the truth flashed over her. Her little daughter had wanted to help her. To be sure, she had made a mess of it; but the mother knew it was the best she could do, and she felt a strong endearment for her child. Then a voice whispered, "Are you tenderer toward the little child than I am tender for thee?" She understood this all in a flash, and her perplexed faith brightened into peace.

> For I thought, when the Master-Builder
> Comes down His temple to view,—
> To see what rents must be mended,
> And what must be builded anew,—
> Perhaps, as he looks o'er the building,
> He will bring my poor work to the light,
> And seeing the marring and bungling,
> And how far it all is from right,
> He will feel as I felt for my darling,
> And say as I said for her:
> "Dear child! She wanted to help me,
> And love for me was the spur;
> And for the true love that is in it,
> The work shall seem perfect as mine;
> And because it was willing service,
> I will crown it with plaudit divine."

January 11

MESSENGERS FROM GOD

And when Zacharias saw him,
he was troubled, and fear fell upon him.
Luke 1:12

The angel had come on an errand of love, had come to announce to Zacharias tidings which would fill his heart with great joy. It is often so. All through the Bible we find that people were afraid of God's angels. Their very glory startled and terrified those to whom they appeared. It is oftentimes the same with us. When God's messengers come to us on errands of grace and peace, we are terrified, as if they were the messengers of wrath. Angels do not appear to us in these days in their heavenly garb. They come no less truly and no less frequently than in the Bible days; but they wear other and different forms. Sometimes they appear in robes of gladness and light, but oftentimes with darker tidings. Yet our faith in our Father's love should make us confident that every messenger that He sends to us, whatever the garb, brings something good to us.

All God's angels come to us disguised,—
Sorrow and sickness, poverty and death,
One after other lift their frowning masks,
And we behold the seraph's face beneath,
All radiant with the glory and the calm
Of having looked upon the face of God.

The things which we call trials and adversities are really God's messengers, though they seem terrible to us; and if we will only quiet our hearts and wait, we shall find that they are messengers from heaven, and that they have brought blessings to us from God. They have come to tell us of some new joy that is to be granted—some spiritual joy, perhaps, to be carried as earthly sorrow, some strange and sweet surprise of love that is waiting for us. We want to learn to trust God so perfectly that no messenger He ever sends shall alarm us.

MAGNIFICAT

And Mary said, My soul doth magnify the Lord.
Luke 1:46

No wonder that Mary sang that day. At the closed gate of the garden of Eden there was a promise given of a Savior, a Savior who would be "the seed of the woman" (Genesis 3:15). After that, throughout the covenant, many women hoped that they might be the mother of this Savior. Centuries passed, and generations of disappointed hearts saw their hopes fade. Finally one day a heavenly messenger came to this lowly Nazarene maiden and announced to her that she would be the mother of this long-expected Messiah. What a glorious honor! No wonder she rejoiced. One line of her long song was, "My soul doth magnify the Lord." We cannot make God any greater; He needs nothing from us. Can the candle add to the glory of the sun's noonday splendor? Yet we can tell others of God so that He will seem magnified to them. It was said in praise of a distinguished preacher that in his sermons he made God appear very great. We can declare God's goodness and grace. Then we can live in a way ourselves to honor Him, and magnify His name.

Retzsch, a German sculptor, made a wonderful statue of the Redeemer. For eight years it was his dream by night, his thought by day. He first made a clay model and set it before a child five or six years old. There were none of the usual symbolic marks around the figure—no cross, no crown, nothing by which to identify it. Yet when the child saw it he said, "The Redeemer! The Redeemer!" This was a wonderful triumph of art. We should exhibit in our lives and character such a reproduction of the nobleness and beauty of Christ that everyone who looks upon us may instinctively recognize the features, and say, "That is the image of our Redeemer!" There is no other way of magnifying the Lord that so impresses the world.

THE CHRISTIAN'S JOY

My spirit hath rejoiced in God my Saviour.
Luke 1:47

This is another line of Mary's song, and it has for us the secret of all deep Christian joy. We have no real and lasting joy till we are in God's family, and in God as the refuge of our souls. One of the old prophets says, "Let the inhabitants of the rocks sing!" None can sing with lasting gladness but the inhabitants of the Rock—those who are in the shelter of the Rock of Ages. The world's songs soon change to cries of terror.

During the battle of Gettysburg, there was a little bird on a tree that would sing a few notes every time there was a lull in the awful roar of battle; but when the crash began again, its song would cease. That is the same way with the world's joy. It sings a few strains now and then in the pauses of life's struggle and discontent. When the waves of sorrow break, its voice is drowned; it cannot sing in loss, in bereavement, in the hour of dying. But one who rejoices in God has a joy that sings on through all the roar of battle, through all the darkness of night. Troubles come to the Christian, but they do not rob him of his joy. He may be in deep sorrow, but all the while there is a fountain of joy welling up in his heart.

Sometimes there is a fresh water spring by the seashore. Twice every day the salt tides roll over it, but the spring never ceases to flow; and when the salt waves have rolled back, the waters of the spring are still sweet as ever. That is the way with the Christian's joy. It is a living well in his heart. Even in his sorrow he has a deep peace in his soul. Then when the sorrow is past, the joy springs fresh as ever. The permanence of all joy depends upon the source from which it comes. If it be in God that we rejoice, then the world has no power to take from us our gladness.

January 14

CHRIST IS MINE

My spirit hath rejoiced in God my Saviour.
Luke 1:47

I t is a great thing when anyone can say, "My Savior!" Many people can talk about Christ very eloquently. They can linger upon the story of His life and speak with tender words of His sufferings and death. They can paint the beauties of His character and tell of the salvation which He has provided. Yet they cannot say, "He is my Savior." And what good does all this knowledge of Christ do them if they are not saved by Him?

I saw a picture of two little beggar children standing on the pavement before a beautiful house, looking in at the windows, where they viewed a happy family gathered around the table at their evening meal. There were evidences of luxury and great comfort within the house. It was winter, the night without was bleak, and the snow was falling. The poor children outside saw all the brightness and beauty that were within; they could describe it, but they could not call it their own. And while they looked in upon the happy scene, the storm swept about them, and they shivered in their thin rags and felt the gnawings of unsatisfied hunger. So it is with those who know of Christ and His salvation by hearing only, but who cannot say, "He is my Savior." They see the deep joy of others in times of trouble, but around them the storm still breaks. They look at others feeding upon Christ and witness their satisfaction, but they themselves stand shivering in the winter of sorrow, and their hungry hearts find no bread to eat.

All our study about Christ will do us no good if we do not take Him as our own personal Savior and learn to call Him "my Jesus." But when we can say of Him, "He is my Savior," all life is bright and full of joy for us. He is ready to be ours, to give Himself to us with all His blessed life, and all the privileges of being heirs in the Father's family, the moment we accept Him.

January 15

LOWLY SERVICE

For he hath regarded the low estate of his handmaiden.
Luke 1:48

What an appropriate name to call oneself! A handmaid is one who devotes herself to the service of another. A young girl is the handmaid of the Lord when she gives herself to Him, and then lives all her life just to please and serve Him. This does not always mean that she must give up her home and the comforts of life in her own country and go away to a heathen land, although it may sometimes. It has meant that for hundreds of young Christian women through the years. But for most people it means to serve Christ and live for Him in the ordinary life of each day.

There are a great many ways of serving Him. One is by always doing right. We are serving Him whenever we are listening for His voice and promptly following Him. He says, "If ye love me, keep my commandments" (John 14:15). Another way is by doing everything we can to make friends for Him, by getting other people to love and serve Him. Young girls are handmaids of Christ when they try to get others to come to Sunday school. Another way is by doing every kindness we can for others in His name. When Jesus was on the earth as a man, some women left their homes and went with Him, ministering to Him. It is probable that they made garments for Him, prepared food for His meals, and performed personal acts of service for Him. It is a sweet privilege to serve our Savior. No doubt if He were here now many young women would do the same. He is not here in human form; but He has told us that if we do these same kindnesses even to the least and lowliest of His friends who are in need, it is the same as if we did them to Himself. So it is not hard to be a handmaid of Christ.

January 16

◇

"HE CARETH FOR YOU"

◇

He that is mighty hath done to me great things.
Luke 1:49

Is it not wonderful that the mighty God, so great, so holy, should think of a poor, lowly sinner on this earth? But does He really? It scarcely seems possible. Only consider how many million people there are in this world. Can it be that the glorious God ever gives a separate, special thought to any one person among so many? He may give personal thought to a few great people—to kings and rulers, and to certain very good men and women; but surely He does not think of anyone so small and obscure as I am. Yes! He does.

A child was once dying of thirst in a desert, and God heard his cries amid all the noise of the world, and sent an angel to point out a spring of water to his mother and thus save his life. And you've heard the story of the baby that the mother could no longer shelter, and which she put into a little ark and laid among the banks beside the river. God cared for that helpless infant and provided for him in a wonderful way.

Jesus said our heavenly Father cares even for a sparrow and feeds it, and that He even clothes each little flower in the field. If there is not a bird or a flower that He does not think of and care for, surely He gives thought and care for us. We are more important than a sparrow, better than a flower. We have immortal souls; we are God's own children; and was there ever a true father who did not think of, and love and care for, his children? He calls each one of us by name. He hears our prayers. He knows when anything is going wrong with us, or when we are in any trouble. He watches over us, and sends blessings to us every day. What a wonderful thought, that God thinks of each one of us and does great things for us!

---◇---

SPIRITUAL HUNGER

---◇---

He hath filled the hungry with good things;
and the rich he hath sent empty away.
Luke 1:53

A great many people attend church and Sunday school, where the blessings of grace abound, and yet are "sent empty away." They are not fed. They do not carry anything with them from all the fullness of the gospel preached to them. They are no better, no stronger, no happier for the privileges they have enjoyed. Is it the minister's fault or the teacher's fault? No, the fault is often their own. They were not really hungry, or they would have been filled.

A lady was ill with a lung disease. She was advised to go to Florida to spend the winter. She wrote home glowing letters about the balmy climate, the wonderful foliage, the luscious fruits. While it was mid-winter at her old home in the North, it was summer where she was. She spoke of the table, how it was covered with all manner of tempting fruits. But in every letter she wrote there was one sad lament: "I have no appetite. If I only had an appetite, I am sure I should soon grow well amid such luxuries." Then in a little while word came that she was dead—dead, in the midst of abounding plenty, not for want of food, but for want of appetite.

So it is with many souls. They live amidst abundance of spiritual provision. God spreads full tables before them continually. They sit down beside them, and then are sent away empty; not because there is nothing there for them, but because they have no hunger for such things. Others sit close by them, at the same tables, with the same provisions before them, and are richly fed, and go away rejoicing in strength and hope, and refreshed in all their being—but these people came with spiritual appetites. Our constant prayer should be that God would make us hungry for Himself. The beatitude is, "Blessed are they which do hunger and thirst after righteousness: for they shall be filled" (Matthew 5:6).

January 18

THE DIVINE VISITOR

He hath visited and redeemed his people.
Luke 1:68

What a beautiful thought it is that God pays visits to His people in this world! We remember a number of visits He made in ancient times—to Adam and Eve, to Abraham, to Jacob, to Moses, to Joshua, and to others. But the most wonderful visit He ever made was when Christ came and stayed so long, and did so much to bless the world. After a while He went away; yet we must not think that He went away to stay, and that He never pays visits to this world anymore. Every time any of His children are in trouble He comes to help them. They do not always know it; for He comes unseen, and often so softly and silently that people do not know they have such a glorious visitor within their doors. He visits those who are not saved to try to persuade them to accept salvation. When we are in great danger, He visits us to deliver us. When we are sick or suffering, He visits us to give us grace to bear our suffering. Then oftentimes He comes and knocks at our doors, wanting to visit us and give us some rich blessing, and we will not open the door.

An old Scotch woman could not pay her rent, and the landlord said he would seize her goods. A good friend heard of it and went to her house to give her money to save her property. He knocked but could not get in. The next day he met her and told her of his visit. "Was that you?" she said with amazement. "I thought it was the officer coming to take my goods, and I had all the doors and windows barred, and would not let him in." So Christ comes and knocks. He knows of our need, and wants to bless and help us; and we bar our doors and keep Him out, not knowing who He is or why He comes. We must remember that when Christ comes it is always to do us good, and that we shall rob ourselves if we ever keep Him out or refuse His visit.

January 19

◈

THE DOOR OF MERCY

◈

The tender mercy of our God.
Luke 1:78

What would we ever have done if God had not been merciful? There could never have been a soul saved in this world. There is a story of a man who dreams that he is out in an open field in a fierce, driving storm. He is wildly seeking a refuge. He sees one gate, over which *Holiness* is written. There seems to be shelter inside, and he knocks. The door is opened by one in white garments; but none except the holy can be admitted, and he is not holy. So he hurries on to seek shelter elsewhere. He sees another gate, and tries that; but *Truth* is inscribed above it, and he is not fit to enter. He hastens to a third, which is the palace of *Justice*; but armed sentinels bar the door, and only the righteous can be received. At last, when he is almost in despair, he sees a light shining some distance away and hastens toward it. The door stands wide open, and beautiful angels meet him with welcomes of joy. It is the house of *Mercy*. He is taken in and finds refuge from the storm, and is hospitably entertained.

Not one of us can ever find a refuge at any door except the door of Mercy. But here the vilest sinner can find eternal shelter; and not mere cold shelter only, for God's mercy is "tender." We flee for refuge and find it. Strong walls shut out all pursuing enemies and cover us from all storms. Then, as we begin to rejoice in our security, we learn that we are inside a sweet home, and not merely a secure shelter. Our refuge is in the very heart of God, and no mother's bosom was ever so warm a nest for her own child as is the divine mercy for all who find refuge in it.

He that dwelleth in the secret place of the most High
shall abide under the shadow of the Almighty . . .
He shall cover thee with his feathers,
And under his wings shalt thou trust.

Psalm 91:1, 4

◇

THE LIGHT OF THE WORLD

◇

To give light to them that sit in darkness
and in the shadow of death.
Luke 1:79

Suppose the sun were never to rise again, and the light of every star were put out—what a gloomy world this would be! This is the picture of the world, in a moral and spiritual sense, without Christ, as it is painted in these words, "darkness and the shadow of death!"—no light to guide, to cheer, to produce joy and beauty. A world without Christ would be utter blackness, unillumined by a single ray of sun, or even by a single burning faraway star. Christ is light.

Only think what light does for us! It makes our days very bright; it shows us all the beautiful things that are around us. But it does far more. It nurtures all life on the earth, and then nourishes us. There would not be a bud or a root or a leaf were it not for the sun. Nor would there be any beauty, for the sun illumines every lovely thing in nature. Think of Christ, then, as light. His love brooding over us causes us to live and nourishes in us every spiritual grace. Every beam of hope is a ray of light. What the coming of light is to a prisoner in a darkened dungeon, that is the bursting of mercy over the guilty soul. Light gives cheer, and what cheer the gospel gives to the mourner, to the poor, to the troubled! Is it not strange that many refuse to receive this light?

If anyone would persist in living in a dark cave, far away from the light of the sun, with only dim candles of his own making to pour a few feeble, flickering beams upon the gloom, we should consider him insane. What shall we say of those who persist in living in the darkness of sin, with no light but the candles of earth's false hopes to shine upon their souls? There are many such, too. They turn to every "will-o'-the-wisp" that flashes a little beam—anywhere rather than to Christ. It is like preferring a candle to the sun.

PATHS OF PEACE

To guide our feet into the way of peace.
Luke 1:79

First, Jesus made the way of peace for us. Sin had destroyed the road to heaven, leaving only a rough and thorny way for human feet to go upon. There never would have been a path of peace had not Jesus Himself made it. All ways in life except that one which He has opened for us are full of pain and trouble, and lead only to sorrow, despair, and death. But Christ prepared a highway that is beautiful and blessed, and that leads to eternal joy and glory. It was not easy work building this road. In the construction of some of this world's great roads, thousands of human lives were sacrificed. We forget sometimes, as we move on in the highway of redemption, amid peaceful scenes, with soft music in our ears, and rich comforts in our hearts, and heavenly hopes to woo us forward, what it cost our blessed Lord; what toil and tears and blood, to prepare the way for us, to bridge over the chasms and level down the mountains. But now the way is open, and from beginning to end, it is a way of peace.

A great many people think that the Christian life is hard and unpleasant, that it is a rough and steep road; but truly it is a way of pleasantness and peace. The only really happy people in this world are those who are following Christ along the way of redemption. They have their share of troubles, disappointments, sorrows; but all the time in the midst of these they have a secret peace of which the world knows nothing. There are paths in the low valleys among the great mountains which are true symbols of the Christian's path of peace. High up among the peaks and crags, the storms sweep in wild fury, but on these valley-paths no breath of storm blows. Flowers bloom and springs of water gurgle along the wayside, and trees cast their grateful shadows, and birdsong fills the air. Such is Christ's "way of peace" in this world.

BLESSED NIGHT-WATCH
◆

There were . . . shepherds abiding in the field,
keeping watch over their flock by night.
And, lo, the angel of the Lord came upon them.
Luke 2:8–9

We should notice that it was while these shepherds were at their common, humble work that they had this wonderful vision. The best place to have the angels come to us is always at our post of duty, no matter how lowly it is. They never show themselves to one who is ashamed of his calling, or too lazy to be faithful at his proper work.

It did not seem a very pleasant way to live—to be poor, and to have to stay out all night in the field, and keep awake and watch the sheep. No doubt the people who lived in the great houses thought the poor shepherds had a hard time of it, and perhaps they even despised them for their lowly work and their poverty. It may be that the shepherds themselves sometimes envied people who had fine houses and lived in luxury, people who never needed to work hard or stay up nights. At least, a good many people in these modern days who have to work hard are disposed to be envious of the rich. But it is quite certain that these shepherds were never sorry after that night that they were poor shepherds, and that they were at their post at that time. If they had thought themselves too good or too fine to do such work, and had given up their position for something more elegant or more respectable, they would have missed the angelic visit that night, and would have lost the honor of being the first to hear the announcement of the Savior's birth.

We never know what we lose by being away from our place of duty. Celestial visions do not come to those who despise God's allotments in life. The angel honored poverty and faithfulness when he came to the shepherds rather than to the door of some lordly palace to proclaim his glorious tidings. The best place to be in is always the place of duty.

GOOD NEWS

Behold, I bring you good tidings of great joy.
Luke 2:10

Every word of the gospel is a joy-bell. Eastern poetry tells of a wondrous tree on which grew golden apples and silver bells. Every time the breeze went by and tossed the fragrant branches, a shower of golden apples fell, and the bells chimed and tinkled forth their sweet and airy music. Similar to this tree of fable is the gospel-tree, ever dropping rich and mellow fruits, and ringing joy-bells whose music thrills our hearts with its celestial sweetness.

The gospel is always good news. Who was ever made sad by it? It brings good news to the guilty sinner when it comes to tell him of forgiveness. It brings good news to the struggling soul in the strife of temptation, when it comes to offer him help to overcome. It brings good news to the man or the woman who has failed and is in despair over a ruined life and hopes dashed to the dust, when it says, "You may rise yet to a glorious life." It brings good news to the mourner when it breathes comfort, the assurance of divine sympathy and love, and a promise that good shall come out of sorrow.

Wherever the gospel goes, it tells good news, never bad. Think what joys it has begun in this world, what sadness it has chased away, what ruin it has restored to beauty. Think of the hymns of joy that have been sung along past Christian centuries, and are yet echoing in countless human hearts. Think of the heavenly songs in which millions will unite eternally. Then remember that all this song and gladness will be but the prolonged echo of that joy which the angel proclaimed. We must be sure that we let this good news into our hearts, or else we can never share this great gladness. Then we should in turn become joy-bearers, by ourselves repeating the good news, and likewise by letting all around us see in us what deep victorious joy the gospel of Christ can give.

January 24

---◆---

THE CHRIST-CHILD

---◆---

Unto you is born this day in the city of
David a Saviour, which is Christ the Lord.
Luke 2:11

How wonderful this was! We must remember who it was that was born. The birth of another child in this world was nothing strange, for thousands of children are born every day. But this was the Lord of glory. This was not the beginning of His life. He had lived from all eternity in heaven. His hands made the universe. All glory was His. The crowns of ultimate power shone upon His brow. Mighty angels called Him Lord. We must remember this if we would understand how great was His humiliation.

Schoolchildren have read that Peter the Great left his throne and, in lowly disguise, apprenticed himself at Zaandam and Amsterdam as a shipwright. Among the common laborers he worked, dressed in their working garb, living in a hut, preparing his own food, making his own bed. Yet in doing so he never for a moment ceased to be the king of Russia. His royal splendor was laid aside for a time; his regal power and majesty were temporarily veiled beneath the disguise he wore; but there was never an hour when he was not an emperor.

So Christ's glory was folded away under robes of human flesh. He never ceased to be the Son of God, and yet He assumed all the conditions of humanity. He veiled His power and became a helpless infant, unable to walk or speak, lying feeble and dependent in His mother's arms. He veiled His knowledge and learned as other children do. He laid aside His sovereignty, His majesty. What humility! And it was all for our sake, that He might lift us up to glory. It was as a Savior that He came into this world. He became Son of Man that He might make us sons of God. He came down to earth and lived among men, entering into their experiences of humiliation, that He might lift them up to glory to share His exaltation.

January 25

STRANGE INSIGNIA

*This shall be a sign unto you; Ye shall find the babe
wrapped in swaddling clothes, lying in a manger.*
Luke 2:12

What a strange sign this is by which to recognize the King of glory! The shepherds would not find Him robed in purple garments like the child of a prince, but wrapped in swaddling clothes. They would not find Him in a palace, but in a stable, with a manger for His cradle. Is it not strange that the very marks and authentications of Messiah's character and mission, by which these shepherds recognized Him when they found Him, were these tokens of poverty and humiliation? This tells us what empty things are the world's marks of greatness. No one would ever expect to recognize earthly royalty by any such signs as these. When Christ came, He despised all the badges of rank by which men indicate greatness and wore the garb of earthly poverty and meekness. Yet was He less great because He bore the world's stamp of lowliness?

True greatness is in the character, never in the circumstances. Do not worry about wearing a crown; make sure that you have a head worthy of wearing a crown. No matter about the purple; make sure that you have a heart worthy of the royal colors. No matter about a throne to sit on; make sure that your life is regal in its own intrinsic character—that men will recognize the king in you though you toil in the field or factory or serve in the lowliest place.

These humble tokens tell us also of Christ's sympathy with the lowliest aspects of life, with the plainest and poorest of the people. No one can say that Christ never came to him. If He had been born in a palace amid splendors, the common people would never have felt that He was their Savior. Christ went down and lived life at its lowest point that there might be none to whom His mission of love and grace should not reach.

GOD IS LOVE

Good will toward men.
Luke 2:14

Yes! That is the meaning of it all. It tells of the good will of God toward all men. There is a strange medieval legend which illustrates this truth. A rebel knight, in the heat of his mad, heaven-defying infidelity, determined to test, by the method to which as a knight he was accustomed, the reality and power of the God whose existence he denied. So, going out into the field armed as if for combat, he cast his glove down upon the ground in the way of the ancient challengers, and cried out to the heavens: "God!—if there be a God—I defy You here and now to mortal combat! If You indeed are, put forth Your might, of which Your pretended priests make such boasts." As he spoke, his eye caught a piece of parchment fluttering in the air just above his head. It fell at his feet. He stooped and picked it up, and found inscribed upon it these words, "God is love!" Overcome by this unexpected response, he broke his sword in token of his surrender, and kneeling upon the fragments, consecrated his life henceforth to the service of that God whom he had just before defied.

Thus to all men's defiance, to the rebellion of individuals, the answer that heaven has always let fall has been, "God is love!" This was the message that wafted down that night on the silent air in this sweet note of the angels' song. This was the meaning of the coming of Christ. Cold was the world; shut were men's hearts against God; defiant was the attitude of nations. Yet to this coldness, this defiance, this revolt, the answer was not swift judgment, but the gift of the Son of God as the Savior—"On earth peace, good will toward men." Wherever the gospel goes today, it breathes the same loving message. God does not hate us; He loves us with a love tender and everlasting.

DAILY DUTY

The shepherds returned.
Luke 2:20

They might have been so enraptured with the sight of the Christ-child that they would not have cared to go away again to their own dull work in the fields. Some people in their pleasure feel reluctant to devote themselves longer to the ordinary tasks of their common workday love. Peter wanted to stay on the Transfiguration Mount; earthly life, with its toils and struggles, would be too tame, he thought, after such ecstatic visions. And surely no human eyes ever gazed on a more glorious vision than these shepherds beheld that night. Yet they went back to their lowly toil, and no doubt they were just as faithful shepherds after that as they had been before.

We need to learn a lesson here. All our spiritual enjoyments ought to make us all the more diligent and faithful in the duties of our ordinary callings. It is not a true devotional experience which draws us away from our daily duty. The nearer we get to Christ, the better our work should become. Our love for communion with God and with His people should never make us negligent in the doing of the tasks that the common days bring to us. After our most heavenly experiences on the Sabbath or in private prayer, we should return to our work with ever fresh earnestness and zest.

God gives us our spiritual raptures, our glimpses of His face and His glory, our foretastes of celestial joy, our fragments of heavenly vision, for duty. It will be sad indeed, then, if they make us less fit for life here with its burdens and cares. We should seek to bring the heavenly visions down to earth, and give them reality in our lives, that others may see the beauty too, and be cheered by it. Our hours of communion with Christ should leave some gleams of brightness on our faces as we come to walk again in life's dusty ways.

---◇---

UPRIGHT DEVOTION

---◇---

The same man was just and devout.
Luke 2:25

Simeon was just in all his dealings with men, and devout in His feelings toward God. It takes both these elements to make true religion. Some people are just and not devout. They are scrupulously honest in all their dealings, yet they never think of God or of their duties to Him. They do not bow to Him in prayer; they never lift their hearts to Him in praise. They do not love Him. They confess no obligations to Him. Their whole religious duty is simply honesty toward their fellowmen, while they utterly ignore God, their Creator and Redeemer, in whom they live, from whose grace every hope in their lives flows, and upon whom they are dependent every moment for breath, for protection, and for all the blessings of life. It is readily seen that such religion is no religion at all. While we are just and honest in our transactions with men, it is to God that we owe the first and highest duties. We are His creatures; we are saved, if at all, by His grace; we owe to Him obedience, faith, love, honor, service. So we must be devout as well as just. On the other hand, there are some people who profess to be devout who are not just. They attend services, they sing and pray, and then they go out into the weekday world and are hard, unjust, greedy, and oppressive. It is very evident that this kind of religion does not please God. He wants our praise and honor, but He wants us to honor Him by our lives and actions as well as by our lips.

There are two tables of commandments, and the second table commandments are as binding as the first. We are to love God with all our heart, but we are also to love our neighbor as ourselves. While we are devout toward God, we are to be honest, true, and unselfish toward men. The two things must go together, and must never be torn asunder.

ARE WE READY?
◇

He should not see death, before he had seen the Lord's Christ.
Luke 2:26

It is a fearful thing for anyone to see death before seeing Christ. Death is terrible. It is a vale of shadows. It ushers us into the presence of God to be judged. What if we have never seen Christ? No matter how many great men we have seen during our life; no matter what we may have done in the way of good or great deeds. We may have seen the wonders of every land; we may have achieved honor and fame. But if we have not seen Christ, we are not ready to die. Even wicked men want to see Him before death, although all through their lives they have rejected Him. They want to live without Him, but without Him they dare not die.

There is a story of an unbeliever whose wife was a lovely Christian. The couple's beautiful young daughter was dying. Her father had always ridiculed Christ in her presence. When she was near death, she asked him whether he wanted her to die in his or in her mother's faith—as an unbeliever or as a Christian. With great emotion he said, "Mary, I would rather you would die in your mother's faith—die as a Christian." He was not content for his child to meet death as an unbeliever; all his skepticism vanished in the presence of this gruesome mystery.

Death tests all creeds. A belief that is not good to die in, which a man wants to give up and throw away as he enters the portals of eternity, surely cannot be worthy of acceptance by an immortal being. No one, as he entered the valley of shadows, was ever heard regretting that he had trusted his soul in Christ's hands. When we have truly seen Christ, we are ready for death any moment. We have already passed from death to life and have nothing to dread in the experience of dying. Departure will only be translation from darkness into light.

—◇—

"ASLEEP IN JESUS"

—◇—

Lord, now lettest thou thy servant depart in peace.
Luke 2:29

No one is ready to die in peace until he has seen Christ; but when he has seen Him, he needs no further preparation for dying. He may never have looked upon any of the wonders of this world; but it is not necessary that he should have done so, if he has also the Lamb of God. He may not have carried out one of his own ambitions in life, nor have achieved anything great or beautiful; but no matter—the one essential achievement in life is to see Jesus. When we have truly seen Him, dying has no more terrors, for He has robbed death of its sting and the grave of its victory.

The Christian has a soft pillow of peace to rest upon when he comes to die. Christ has lifted the curse from his soul and made death merely the way to glory. He Himself tasted death for His people; but now there is no death for any of them. He said to Martha, by her brother's grave, "I am the resurrection, and the life. . . . Whosoever liveth and believeth in me shall never die" (John 11:25–26). That means that those who are saved through Christ find no terror, no darkness, nothing to harm them in dying, but pass through the experience as through a beautiful gate into life everlasting.

The word *lettest* here means "set free"—"Set thy servant free to depart"—implying that what we call life is like the imprisoning of the eagle; and what we call death, after one has seen Christ, is blessed and glorious emancipation. What a beautiful thought concerning death. On the gravestone of a little child are the words: "Out of the darkness into the marvelous light!" All we need, then, is truly to see Christ before we die. When He has lifted the curse of sin and put His own holy life into our souls, we are already in the portal of heaven while in this world; dying will be only entering in, to behold Christ face-to-face forever.

◇

LOOKING UNTO JESUS

◇

Mine eyes have seen thy salvation.
Luke 2:30

Travelers come home from abroad and tell of the wonderful sights they have seen. They have stood among the mighty Alps and have been awed by their grandeur. They have walked on the streets of famous cities. They have visited the old cathedrals. They have stood enraptured before the pictures of the old masters. And they speak with pride of what they have seen. Yet it is a far greater thing to be able to say, "I have seen Jesus." The sight of beautiful and wonderful spectacles may have a refining and inspiring influence upon one's mind, may add to one's knowledge and broaden one's experience. But seeing Jesus changes one's whole life and destiny. It makes one an heir of heaven and glory; it transforms one into the likeness of Christ Himself. He that sees Jesus is saved.

One writer says: "Never lose an opportunity to look on beauty, for it will leave a touch of new beauty in your own soul." We may say, "Lose not the opportunity to look upon Jesus, for it will print glory in your soul." St. Paul tells us that by beholding the glory of Christ as it lies in the mirror of the Scriptures, we are changed into the same image.

The old monks had a superstitious notion that if they would gaze continuously and intensely on the fixture of the Christ on His cross which hung upon their cell wall, the marks of the wounds would appear in them—the print of the nails in their hands and their feet, and the scar of the spear-gash in their side. This is but a vague representation of the spiritual truth which lies behind it—that beholding Christ produces the real "marks of the Lord Jesus" in our souls. Looking upon Him with a steady, loving gaze, the glorious vision that our eyes behold prints itself deep in our hearts, and the "beauty of the Lord" shines out in our dull faces.

February 1

HOMAGE

When Jesus was born in Bethlehem of Judea . . .
there came wise men from the east to Jerusalem.
Matthew 2:1

What was the most wonderful birth that ever occurred in this world? It is not strange there were so many remarkable events accompanying it—that angels came down to announce it and to sing their song of rejoicing, and that wise men came from afar to pay their homage. It was the Son of God incarnate who slept His first sleep in the manger of Bethlehem.

This is so great a mystery that we cannot understand it; yet we know that the same one who then became flesh had been from all eternity with God, that He was God, that He made all things, that in Him was the fountain of all life and blessedness. That a child should be born was not a strange event; a child is born in this world with each of our heartbeats. That a child should be born in a stable was not a remarkable occurrence in that country. But when we remember who it was that was made flesh that night, we find ourselves in the presence of the most stupendous wonder of all ages.

We should certainly come with the shepherds and the Magi to pay our homage at the cradle of this same glorious child-King. The Magi came hundreds of miles to find Christ. The journey was difficult and perilous, and very costly. We ought to count no toil or sacrifice too great to find Christ. We ought to be ready to go thousands of miles, if need be, to find Him. He is the pearl of great price, and we shall be well repaid for our quest, though it cost us the loss and sacrifice of all things, and though we even have to lay down our lives to gain Him.

We notice also that it is not always those who are nearest to Christ who first see His glory. He was born right among the Jews, but nobody went out from Jerusalem to worship Him. Shall it be the same with us? Shall we miss the blessing of seeing the Savior who is so near?

THE KING OF KINGS

*Where is he that is born King of the Jews? For we have
seen his star in the east, and are come to worship him.*

Matthew 2:2

Surely it was strange that the Jews did not know of the birth of
their own King. Usually when future kings are born the
whole realm rings with joy. But when the Messiah was born
there was no rejoicing on earth. A few humble shepherds came to
look with wonder on the newborn babe which lay in the young
mother's arms; but that was all. The Jews had been looking for
their Messiah, but did not recognize Him when He came.

For one thing, we learn how quiet His advent was. There
was no blare of trumpets. Noise and show are not necessary
accompaniments of power. The mightiest events in this world are
oftentimes the quietest. The grace of God always comes quietly.
Angels minister noiselessly and often unseen. The most useful
Christians are not those who make the most ado in their work,
but those who in humility, unconscious of any splendor shining
in their faces, go daily about their work for Christ.

Another thought here is that we do not always know when
Christ comes to us. "He was in the world, and the world was
made by him, and the world knew him not. He came unto his
own, and his own received him not" (John 1:10–11). Yet why
should we complain of the Jews' response? Are we any better?
Our King is in our midst; do we recognize Him? Do we worship
and honor Him? These wise men had only a dim star to guide
them; yet they followed it with loving trust and unfaltering steps,
and it led them to the feet of the King of glory.

Even the faintest glimmerings of light should be welcomed
and their guidance accepted. We should not wait to know all
about Christ and to see Him in all His glory before we set out to
seek Him. We should follow the first faint gleams, and as we go
on the light will brighten, until we see Him in all His blessed
beauty, face-to-face.

February 3

◇

OFFERING GIFTS

◇

They saw the young child with Mary his mother, and fell down,
and worshipped him: and when they had opened their treasures,
they presented unto him gifts; gold, and frankincense, and myrrh.

Matthew 2:11

Those who follow the light will surely be led at last to the Christ. There is always joy in the heart when one has found the Savior. The first act is to adore and worship Him. These men saw only the little babe lying in the young mother's arms. There was no crown on His head. No glory gleamed from His face. His surroundings were most unkingly, without pomp or pageant. The child did nothing in their presence to show His royalty—spoke no word, performed no kingly act of power. Yet the Magi believed and worshipped Him.

Think how much more we know about the Christ than they did. We see Him in all the glory of His life, death, resurrection, and ascension; we see Him sitting at the right hand of God, King of kings, wearing many crowns. It is not hard for us to see the regal marks in Him. Shall we be less than the Magi in our adoration? They were not content merely to worship the King, showing Him homage in word and posture; but they also laid their gifts at His feet. It is not enough for us to sing our songs of praise to Christ, to look up adoringly into His face, to bow before Him in reverent worship, and to speak our heart's homage in words. We should bring our gifts as well to lay at His feet.

There is a great deal of mere sentiment in the consecration of our lives to God; when there is call for gifts of sacrifice, or for real service, it instantly vanishes. People sing missionary hymns with great warmth, and when the collection box comes to them they have no gifts to offer. These men not only brought presents, but they brought those that were costly. We should bring our best, our gold and frankincense and myrrh, the alabaster box of our heart's deepest love, and the best of all our life and service.

GUARDIAN ANGELS

When they were departed, behold, the angel
of the Lord appeareth to Joseph in a dream.
Matthew 2:13

We have a glimpse here of the closeness of heaven's watch over this imperiled Babe. A wicked king was plotting for the life of the child, and His earthly friends could not protect Him. But in the hour of human weakness heaven came quickly to shelter and save Him. The destinies of the human race were in that Child's life, and all God's power would have been used to deliver Him. It is a precious truth, too, that over every child heaven keeps a similar close and sure watch. A poet has said: "Heaven lies about us in our infancy"; and it is very true of every child. Speaking of the children, Jesus Himself said, "Their angels do always behold the face of my Father which is in heaven" (Matthew 18:10). This means that heaven's strongest, holiest, and most favored angels are sent to guard children in this world.

Fathers and mothers should never forget that their children are very dear to God and are under His unsleeping protection. This should give them great comfort and confidence as their little ones go out into the midst of the world's dangers. No human eye can be always upon them. No human hand can ward off evils that lurk in every shadow. But unseen guardians never leave them for a moment. Heaven is interested in the keeping of every tender child-life in this world. Christian parents may commit their little ones to God with implicit confidence. If they are only faithful as parents, God will not disappoint their hopes.

Children also should know that they are being cared for by celestial guardians whom they cannot see. Angels may not appear to men in these days, but they are continually around us, encamping about our homes and watching over us by day and by night. Though their bright faces are not seen by our dull eyes, their loving ministry never ceases.

HEAVENLY GUIDANCE

Be thou there until I bring thee word.
Matthew 2:13

All our movements should be under the direction of God. In very old times God guided His people by a pillar of fire and cloud, which lifted and moved when they were to move, showing them the way, and which rested and settled down when they were to halt. In these days of much fuller revelation, there is no need for any such visible token of guidance, yet the guidance is no less real and no less unmistakable.

It was an angel that brought to Joseph the call to flee into Egypt. Angels do not now appear to our eyes; but who will say that they do not whisper in our ears many suggestions which we think to come from our own hearts? At least we know that in some way God will always tell us what to do; and if only we have ears to hear, we shall never fail to receive guidance. We should always wait for God's bidding before taking any step. Especially in times of danger, when we are moving under His guidance, we should wait and not move until He brings us word.

It ought to give us great comfort and a wonderful sense of safety to know that God is caring for us so faithfully. Some people laugh at the simple faith of childlike believers in God and say that it is all fancy—that there is no one in heaven taking care of us. But we need not be worried by such skeptical ones. There is a God in heaven, and He is our Father. He never sleeps. He has charge of all the affairs of this universe, and He is always "at the helm." This should give us all confidence. Our entire duty is to be ready always to obey. Whenever the voice comes calling us to arise and depart, there is some reason for it, and we should not hesitate to obey. Wherever we are sent we should quietly stay till again God sends to call us away. The place of duty is always the place of safety, and we should never move until God brings us word.

February 6

◇

THE NAZARETH HOME

◇

He [Joseph] came and dwelt in a city called Nazareth.
Matthew 2:23

In that little village, until ready for His public ministry, Jesus made His home. It is a sweet thought that the Son of God dwelt for so many years in a home on earth. His pure and sinless life opened up there as a bud opens into a lovely rose, pouring fragrance over all the humble home.

The study of the childhood and the youth of Jesus, even from the few fragmentary glimpses of those years given us in the gospel, ought to prove an inspiration to every child and young person. No doubt we wish that we could know more of that sweet and blessed home-life; but the little we are told about it is enough, or God's Spirit would have given us more of the story.

We know there was no sin in Jesus, and we can think of His gentleness, His obedience, His love, His unselfishness, and of all His other graces and virtues of character. He was a natural child, glad, joyous, interested in beautiful things, studious, earnest without being morbidly religious. He was the type of boy that God loves, and as God would have every other boy strive to become. We have one glimpse of Him at twelve, when He began to think of His relation to the heavenly Father; yet we must note the fact that He went back to Nazareth and resumed His place of duty to parents, staying there for eighteen years longer. The Father's business on which He entered at twelve was not preaching and working miracles and going about doing good in a public manner, but for the time remaining at home, an obedient child, a glad, helpful youth, and an industrious developing young man.

THE MOTHER OF CHRIST

*And the child grew, and waxed strong
in spirit, filled with wisdom.*
Luke 2:40

One of the chief influences in molding Christ's life was His mother. When God wants to prepare a man for a great mission, He first prepares a virtuous mother, and puts the child into her care to be trained. The Jews had a saying, "God could not be everywhere, and therefore He made mothers." Nearly all the truly great men of the world have received the inspiration and stamp of their lives from their mothers. When Moses was to be trained for his work, the Lord put the little babe back in the hands of its mother as his first teacher. There is no doubt that in preparing Mary to be the mother of the Savior, the rarest and loveliest graces of womanhood were created by God into her nature. She was not sinless, but surely we may believe that no more perfect woman ever lived.

> *Woman! Above all women glorified;*
> *Our tainted nature's solitary boast;*
> *Purer than foam on central ocean tossed;*
> *Brighter than eastern skies at daybreak strewn*
> *With fancied roses.*
> *In whom did blend*
> *All that was mixed and reconciled in thee*
> *Of mother's love with maiden purity.*

Such a mother would exert a wonderful influence over the child Jesus. She was His first teacher. Her love wrapped Him around in its warm folds in His earliest infancy and through all His youth and young manhood. Her sweet life was the atmosphere that hung over His tenderest years. Her prayers kept heaven lying very close to Him. Her hands guided His feet and shaped His character. What a blessed mission is that of a mother, any mother! What woman in whose arms God has laid an immortal life will despise her glorious calling? What woman so honored will not die rather than prove unfaithful to her holy trust?

THE ROCK OF SALVATION

Jesus Christ, the Son of God.
Mark 1:1

Mark does not intend that there shall be room for mistake concerning the person of our Lord. Each of the names he uses here represents one particular phase of His character.

Jesus means Savior. "Thou shalt call his name Jesus: for he shall save his people from their sins" (Matthew 1:21). None of His names can be sweeter than this. It is enshrined in every Christian heart. This is the name that brings hope into our souls. The first thing we all need is to be saved, and He is the only Savior.

Christ means the "Anointed One." He is the one whom the Father has anointed to be prophet, priest, and king. He is our prophet, our teacher; He is our priest interceding for us, having already made Himself an offering for our sins; He is our king, and we ought to obey Him.

Son of God tells of His divine nature and His eternal sonship. This is the name that gives security to all our hopes and trusts. If He were only a man, he might be very tender, loving, and kind, but could he do for us everything we need? Could a man make atonement for our sins? Could a man put his own life into our dead souls? Could a man fight our battles for us, and rescue us out of the hands of Satan? Could a man be with us in all the ways of toil, sorrow, need, and struggle? Could a man save us in death and carry us through its dark mystery to glory? Could a man stand for us in the judgment? The divinity of Christ is the rock of our hope and our salvation. Our Savior and anointed King is the Son of God. We can lean upon His breast and know that we are covered with His divinity, that our refuge is the eternal God and that the arms which are clasped about us are everlasting. In all danger we may rest secure, for any power that would take us out from our resting place must be mightier than God's.

---◇---

REPENTANCE

---◇---

Repent ye: for the kingdom of heaven is at hand.
Matthew 3:2

This was John's gospel. At first it seems very unlike the story of love which Jesus preached, and yet it is part of the same story. Perhaps we need to be reminded of repentance in these days. We are in danger of making salvation too easy a matter and of being altogether too tolerant with ourselves. We forget, some of us, that sin is such a terrible thing, and we are too careless about getting rid of our sins. We misunderstand God's forgiveness if we think of it merely as an easy forgetting that we have done the wrong thing. Jesus did not come to save us merely from sin's penalties; He came to save us from the sins themselves, by leading us to forsake them forever. Unless we repent of our sins we never can have forgiveness.

We must make sure, too, that we do thorough work in our repenting. Repentance is not merely a little twinge of remorse at the recollection of some wickedness. It is not mere shame at being found out in some evil work or uncleanness or dishonesty. It involves drastic change of the whole of life. Sins wept over must be forsaken forever. Repentance is a change of heart, a turning of the heart completely the other way. It is well for us to make a diligent quest to be sure that we always abandon the wrongdoing which we deplore, that we leave the evil course which we regret, in order that we turn away from the sin which we confess.

A good many people get only half the gospel. They talk a great deal about believing, but very little about repenting. We need to remember that a faith which does not lead to genuine repentance is not a faith that saves. He who bewails a sin and confesses it, secretly intending to return to it again, has no good ground to hope that he is forgiven.

THE COMING OF THE LORD

Prepare ye the way of the Lord, make his paths straight.
Matthew 3:3

The Lord is always coming to us, or is always ready to come to us, if the way is open for Him. Yet no doubt we may continually lose His heavenly visits because the road is blocked. If we would receive these visits we must always keep the way open. Sins unconfessed, unrepented of, unforsaken, block the path, and Christ cannot come to us until we get them out of the way.

There is also another sense in which we need to prepare the way of the Lord. He may come any moment in death to call us away from our busy work. Is there no preparation needed now in our hearts for this coming of the Lord? Are we ready for Him at any moment? Are our lamps trimmed and burning? Are our loins girded, and have we our shoes on our feet and our swords in our hands? If He came this hour, how would He find us? Peter gives us good counsel when, speaking of Christ's coming again, he says, "Be diligent that ye may be found of him in peace, without spot, and blameless"(2 Peter 3:14). Would He find us in this state if He came today? Are we in a state of peace with God, peace with ourselves, peace with all the world? Would He find us without spot? Have we kept our hands clean, our hearts pure, and ourselves unspotted from the world? Would He find us living blameless lives, so sincere, so true, so without blemish that the world can find no cause of reproach in us, and that He Himself will approve of us?

It will be well for us to think of these things, and if the way for His coming is not prepared, to hasten to have it ready, for He may come any moment. The Jews were taught to prepare a way for the coming of the Lord by repenting of their sins and turning their hearts to God. That is just what everyone must do who desires Christ to come to him with blessing—every sin must be swept away.

February 11

◆

THE WRATH TO COME

◆

Who hath warned you to flee from the wrath to come?
Luke 3:7

There are a good many people who want to flee from God's wrath but are not willing to give up that which draws down the wrath upon them. When a godless man becomes sick, and it seems as though he may die, immediately he begins to look about for some way of flight from the wrath that he feels hangs over him. He sends for a minister or for some godly man. He has his long-neglected Bible brought from his parlor table and laid beside his bed. He will find refuge from his peril, if he can. He wants to have the Bible read to him; perhaps there is some virtue in that which will shield him. He wants the minister to pray for him; he has heard that a good man's prayers will save a soul. He wants to be baptized and to receive the Lord's Supper; he hopes that these holy ordinances may somehow shelter him from the wrath. All the while he has not really thought of trying to unload the burden which is crushing him. He is carrying his sins unconfessed and unforgiven. He has no true sense of sinfulness, no realization of God's holiness or of his own debt to Him; he is simply terrified and is trying to flee from the impending wrath. If he gets well again, he will very likely return to his old life and live on in sin as before, proving the insincerity and worthlessness of his repentance. If he were asked, "Who warned you to flee?" his answer could not be "love for Christ," or "a sense of my guilt," but "fear—the terrors of death and eternity."

It was a very proper question, therefore, which John asked the multitudes who came to him desiring to be baptized. The only flight that saves is away from sin to Christ. No man is saved who carries his sins with him in his flight. The door of the refuge is wide enough to admit the worst penitent sinner, but not wide enough to admit any cherished sin.

February 12

EVIDENCE OF REPENTANCE

Bring forth therefore fruits meet for repentance.
Matthew 3:8

There is only one way to prove that we have truly repented. It will not be enough to tell people that we have; they will wait to see the evidence of our lives. Suppose a wicked man joins the church and then goes back on Monday morning to his old, wicked ways. Will anybody credit his Sunday's profession? He must go on Monday morning to a new life if his repentance is to count for anything. Everybody knows what is right in such a case. No one is quicker to cry out against the insincerity and unreality of the man's profession than wicked people themselves, when they see him continue in his old evil ways. Even bad men know what it is to be good; thus they pay high compliment to Christianity. Repentance amounts to nothing whatsoever if it produces only a few tears, a spasm of regret, a little fright as a flash from eternity reveals to a man his guilt and danger, and then a return tomorrow to the same old wicked ways. What are the works that are an indication of repentance?

A grocer went home from the meeting one night where he had heard a sermon about false weights and measures, and he burned the scales he had been using to cheat his customers. A father who had been living carelessly in his home, when awakened to the truth, took down the old family Bible and confessed to his household his neglect, and re-established the family altar. These are illustrations of works demonstrating repentance. In short, we must leave the sins we repent of and do them no more, and we must walk in the new pure ways of holiness. The heart is the important matter in all spiritual life, and the heart reveals the inner life. If the life still be evil the heart can be no better, whatever external profession of improvement it may have made. The way to prove to men that we have really repented is really to repent, and the fact will soon speak for itself.

February 13

◇

THE DIVINE PATIENCE

◇

The axe is laid unto the root of the trees.
Matthew 3:10

The picture is very suggestive. The axe lying at the tree's root, or raised in the woodman's hand to strike, shows that judgment impends, hangs ready to fall. Any moment the tree may be cut down. The unused axe lying at the tree's root tells of patience in the husbandman; he is waiting to see if the fruitless tree will yet bear fruit. The axe leaning quietly against the tree is very suggestive. The meaning is very plain.

God waits long for repentant sinners to come to Him; He is slow to punish or to cut off the day of opportunity; He desires all to repent and be saved. Yet we must not trifle with His divine patience and forbearance. We must remember that while the axe is not lifted to strike, there is still not a moment when it is not lying close, ready to be used; when the summons may not come, "Hasten to judgment." The axe of death really lies all the while at the root of every life. There is not a moment when it is not true that there is but a step between us and death.

The chopping of the axe at the root suggests that its use is not pruning but cutting down. God has two axes. One He uses in pruning His trees, removing the fruitless branches and cleansing the fruitful branches that they may bring forth more fruit. The work of this axe is not judgment or destruction, but mercy and blessing. It is the good and fruitful tree that feels its keen edge. Then God has another axe which He uses only in judgment, cutting down those trees which after all His pruning bring forth no fruit. All life is critical to God. There is not a moment in any day in which the destinies of eternity do not play a role. It is an infinitely perilous thing for an immortal soul to rest an hour with the axe of judgment waiting to strike the blow that will end forever the day of mercy. Only the most supreme folly can be blind to the right action in such a moment.

February 14

◇

OUR EVERYDAY LIFE

◇

He answereth and saith unto them.
Luke 3:11

In John the Baptist's several answers to the different inquiries made of him, we see that religion is not something entirely apart from our everyday lives. He did not tell these men to fast for a week, or to enter upon a long course of devotions. Nothing of the kind. They were to begin at once to live according to God's commandments in their own particular calling—to do their everyday work diligently. The "people" were to begin practicing the law of love, thus giving up their greed and selfishness. The "publicans" were to cease practicing extortion, and to begin dealing honestly and justly with all men. The "soldiers" were to refrain from all acts of violence. He did not tell them to give up their calling, but to do their duty as good and true men in their callings—to carry the principles of true religion into all their actions.

It is well for us to observe this lesson. A good many people think that being a Christian is to pray a few moments morning and evening, to read a daily chapter or two in the Bible, and to attend church on Sunday. These duties are important as means of grace, but they are not religion. Religion is living out the principles of Christianity in one's ordinary weekday life. It is getting the Bible and the prayers and the services into *thought and act and character*. We must not cut our lives in two and call one part secular, governing it by one set of principles, while regarding the other part as sacred, to be controlled by another set of rules. All life is to be made religious in the sense that everything is to be done in such a way as to please God, under the direction of His counsel. We have just as much religion as we get into our weekday life, and not a whit more. Whatever we do, even to eating and drinking, we should do in the name of the Lord Jesus.

February 15

◇

SELF-RENUNCIATION

◇

John answered . . . one mightier than I cometh.
Luke 3:16

There is something very admirable in John's behavior on this occasion. The people were expecting Christ, and when John rose up in such strength, they were ready to accept him as the Messiah. So intense was the excitement, so wild was the enthusiasm, that almost the whole nation flocked to the Jordan to see and hear John. One word from him claiming to be the Messiah would have kindled a feeling among the people which would have crowned him as king. But the picture which we see is this great man rejecting the honors which lay within his grasp, and saying, "Nay, they are not mine to wear; put them on the head of Him who is coming after me."

Many of us are ready to accept honors for ourselves when we are doing Christ's work. We like to have people praise us and commend us. Sometimes we are in danger of striving to get honor for ourselves rather than to put honor upon Christ. How much more beautiful was John's self-renunciation! It is pleasant when we have helped people to have them come to us with their grateful tributes, to have them show their love to us and bestow honor upon us. Let us beware, however, lest we take that which belongs to Christ, and also lest our friends see only us and not Christ. Let us keep ourselves out of the way, that they may behold Him. Let us remember always that there is One coming after us, yea, standing unseen beside us while we do our work, who is far mightier than we, and that we should strive only and always to put the honor upon Him, utterly forgetting ourselves. He will look after us and honor us if we will only seek always His honor and never our own. But if we rob Him here of the praise that is His, to wreathe crowns for our own brow, we shall find ourselves stripped of honor and crown in the day of Christ's return.

BAPTISM

I indeed baptize you with water; . . . he
shall baptize you with the Holy Ghost.
Luke 3:16

Baptism with water is right. It is one of God's appointments, and He would require nothing that is useless. Some people think that there is no necessity for being baptized; but they make themselves wiser than Christ in saying this of that which He commanded to be done. Baptism has a meaning, and must never be despised. It teaches by symbol, showing us first that we are unclean and need washing, and then depicting the deep work of grace by which the heart is cleansed.

We should not lightly esteem a rite which has such solemn divine sanction. But while baptism with water is proper and should not be omitted, it cannot wash away sin or save our souls. We must not think that because we have been baptized we are necessarily Christians. There must be a change within us. We must be converted, born again. And no amount of washing with water will produce this change. Christ must baptize us with the Holy Ghost. There is danger that many are satisfied with the baptismal water and do not look for the regenerating grace. It is the peril of all forms of service that people trust in them and do not realize their need of Christ. A few drops of water on the brow make no change in one's life, and it is only when the baptism symbolized by the water is received by faith that real blessing comes upon the one who is baptized. When Jesus was being baptized He prayed, and the heavens were opened and the Holy Spirit descended and rested upon Him. A similar blessing descends from heaven upon everyone receiving the symbol who also by prayer seeks the heavenly baptism. The same is true of the Lord's Supper. When the ordinance is received in faith and with prayer, God gives the grace of which the symbol is only an image.

◇
WHEAT OR CHAFF?
◇

He will thoroughly purge his floor, and gather his
wheat into the garner; but he will burn up the chaff.
Matthew 3:12

The illustration which the preacher of the desert here uses is very striking. The wheat sheaves were gathered on the threshing floor and trodden over by oxen to free the grains from the chaff. Then came the process of winnowing, when the chaff was blown away and the wheat left on the floor ready for use. After that, the wheat was carried to the barn and the chaff was swept up and burned. God's penitent, believing ones are wheat, and the finally unrepentant and unbelieving are the chaff. Christ's gospel has a stern side. The same breath that cleanses the wheat drives away the chaff. Which are we—wheat or chaff? Very definitely our eternal destiny will depend on which type we are, and we ought to be very sure of it ourselves.

There is a great difference between wheat and chaff. Wheat has life in it; wheat grains dropped into the earth grow and yield a harvest. Wheat is food; it makes bread and satisfies hunger. Wheat is precious; it is highly prized in the market. Chaff has no life in it; it does not grow and only rots in the ground. It is not food; it satisfies no hunger. It is not of any value, and it is good only to throw away or to burn. Which of these descriptions best fits our lives?

What sadder thing is there in this world than a human life, made to be golden wheat to feed men's hunger, yet proving only worthless chaff? Apart from the doom facing those who do not repent, who, with an immortal soul and almost infinite possibilities of usefulness and blessedness, should be content to be worthless chaff? Made to be children of God and heirs of glory, and to live in blessedness in heaven forever, shall we tear ourselves away from our high destiny and, by our own unbelief and folly, doom ourselves to be swept by the divine wrath into unquenchable fire?

February 18

---◇---

EXTERNAL RITES

---◇---

*Then cometh Jesus from Galilee to Jordan
unto John, to be baptized of him.*
Matthew 3:13

We may look at the baptism of Jesus in several ways. For one thing, it tells us that He honored the external rites of religion. Some people cannot see why it is necessary to make a public confession and to observe the ordinances of the church. These are only forms, they argue, and do no good. What benefit is it, they ask, to a man or woman to be plunged into water? What blessing can come to one's soul from eating a little piece of bread and drinking a sip of wine as a religious ceremony? Or what good does it do to one to "join the church"?

There are many reasons that might be given why we should observe the ordinances which God has appointed, but none ought to have more weight than Christ's own example. He thought external rituals to be of sufficient importance to be observed by Him. He came all the way from Galilee to the Jordan to be baptized, and then insisted on receiving the cleansing. He was publicly baptized, thus showing all men where He stood, enrolling Himself under the banner of righteousness.

Shall we say, then, that there is no necessity for public confession of Christ, for declaring ourselves on His side, for uniting with His church? The disciple is not above his Lord. Surely Christ would not have ordained baptism if baptism is a mere empty and valueless form. He would not have commanded us to observe the Lord's Supper if the Lord's Supper is nothing more than a common meal. It is the same with every means of grace. The fact that the wise and holy Christ ordained them ought to make them sacred to every loyal Christian heart. And the fact that Christ thought these necessary for Himself ought to silence men's shallow talk that they do not need to observe these "forms."

THE BAPTISM OF JESUS

Jesus came from Nazareth of Galilee, and was baptized of John.
                                                      Mark 1:9

One meaning of Christ's baptism was that it was His consecration to His public ministry. For thirty years He had dwelt in the quiet home at Nazareth, doing no miracles, wearing no "halo," manifesting no divine glory. But He had been sent into this world on a definite mission, and now the time had come for Him to enter upon the work of that mission. So, obeying the heavenly bidding, He left His home and came to the Jordan to be baptized, and became consecrated to the ministry of redemption. He knew what was involved in His work. From the edge of the Jordan, He saw through to the end. The shadow of the cross fell on the green banks and on the flowing river, fell also across the gentle and holy soul of Jesus as He stood there. He knew what that baptism meant, to what it introduced Him, what its end would be. Yet, knowing all, He voluntarily came to be baptized, thus accepting the mission of redemption.

It was a solemn hour to Jesus when He stood before John waiting for the ordinance that would set Him apart to His work. It was a literal laying of Himself on the altar, not for service only, but for death. It is always a solemn hour when anyone stands before God and men to make a public confession of Christ and to enter His service. The act is nothing less than the consecration of a human soul to a service for life or for death. On the seal of an old missionary society an ox stands between an altar and a plow, and below is the motto, "Ready for either"—ready for service or for sacrifice. This should be the heart-motto in every public confession; it should be a solemn devotion to Christ—an entire surrender of the whole life to Christ and His service. Such consecration all have made who have publicly given themselves to Christ.

---◇---

THE SHADOW OF THE CROSS

---◇---

*Suffer it to be so now: for thus it becometh us
to fulfil all righteousness.*
Matthew 3:15

One meaning of Christ's words here is that, as man in the place of sinful people, He must take upon Him all the conditions of humanity. He had no sins of His own to confess, and yet He came to John as other men came. He did this because He was in the place of sinners. A little later John pointed to Him and said, "Behold the Lamb of God, which taketh away the sin of the world" (John 1:29). So we see Jesus coming to be baptized, because "all we like sheep have gone astray . . . and the Lord hath laid on him the iniquity of us all" (Isaiah 53:6). This baptism with water, however, was but the mere shadow of what the bearing of our sins cost Him.

In Holman Hunt's picture "The Shadow of the Cross," Jesus is represented at age thirteen, standing in the carpenter's shop at the close of the day. He stretches out His arms, and the setting sun casts His shadow in the form of a cross on the opposite wall. The artist's purpose is that across the soul of the gentle youth there fell early indeed the shadow of the cross. No doubt the thought is true. Especially here, as Jesus entered His public ministry, this shadow fell upon Him. This baptism was but the symbol of the other harder baptism. This was only with water and was symbolical. He had another baptism to be baptized with—the baptism of sorrow, of death, and of curse, when He "redeemed us from the curse of the law, being made a curse for us" (Galatians 3:13). Here we see Him entering the beginning of His difficult baptism, from which He finally comes on the morning of His resurrection. We ought never to forget, as we enjoy the blessings of redemption, what it cost our Lord to procure them for us. He endured His nameless baptism of sorrow, pain, and death that we might receive the blessings of peace and joy. He tasted death for us that we might have deathless life.

THE SPIRIT LIKE A DOVE

◇

He saw . . . the Spirit like a dove descending upon him.
Mark 1:10

Even Christ with all His divine power needed the anointing of the Holy Spirit to set Him apart and make Him ready for His life-work. How much more do we, His disciples, need the same anointing before we are truly set apart for work and qualified for it.

There is rich suggestion also in the form in which the Spirit descended. A great many tender associations cluster around the dove. It was the dove that the very poor were permitted to bring to the altar as an offering substituting for a more costly animal. The appearance of the dove was one of the harbingers or prophecies of coming spring. The dove was always remembered by the Jews in connection with the receding of the waters of the deluge, when it returned to the ark bearing the olive leaf. Along with the olive branch, the dove has become an emblem of peace among all Christian nations. The dove was also referred to by Christ as a symbol of gentleness and harmlessness. All these associations made the dove a most fitting symbolic form for the Holy Ghost to assume when descending upon Jesus, for Jesus came to be a sacrifice for all, even the poorest. He came as the spring comes, bringing life to a dead world. He came bringing a message of peace from heaven to everyone who will open up to Him. And He is like the dove in gentleness and meekness.

It is this same holy dove that must descend upon us if the kingdom of heaven is truly to begin in our hearts. Until the Holy Spirit has been given to us and received by us there is no life in our souls and no power in us for work. But this divine anointing is promised to all who truly consecrate themselves to Christ and believe on Him. No vision of separated heavens and descending dove appears to human eyes, but above every scene of holy devotion to Christ this blessed reality hangs.

◇

ENDURING TEMPTATION

◇

*Then was Jesus led up of the spirit into the
wilderness to be tempted of the devil.*
Matthew 4:1

The time of this event is to be noted. It was just after the wonderful scene of our Lord's baptism. The heavens were opened, the Spirit descended and rested upon Him, and the Father's voice was heard from heaven in approval and witness; then immediately came the terrible experience here described. Spiritual privileges do not save us from fiery trials. Indeed there is no time when Satan is so sure to come with his subtle arts as just when we have passed through some season of special blessing. When we go from our private prayer after a time of tender communion he meets us at the door with some evil suggestion. It is after we have been nearest to God that we are sure to find the devil most active. He is not half so anxious to tempt worldly Christians as those who are glowing with spiritual zeal.

An old writer says: "All the while our Savior lay in His father's shop and meddled only with carpenter's chips, the devil did trouble Him not; now that He is to enter more publicly upon His mediatorship the tempter pierces His tender soul with many sorrows by invitation to sin." It is the same with us. So long as we move on quietly in our ordinary lives he does not bother to harm us; but when we arise to new consecration and new activity in God's service, he pounces upon us and tries to destroy us. It is, therefore, in our times of greatest spiritual exaltation that we need to be most watchful. We learn here also that we may expect to endure temptation in this world. New power came to Jesus through His conflicts. His life was developed and made perfect through sufferings. Then He was designed for sympathy with us in our temptations by Himself being tempted in all points as we are. Temptations resisted always bring new strength. Victorious struggle prepares us for helping others in their temptations.

◇

OUR TRUE LIFE

◇

*Man shall not live by bread alone, but by every
word that proceedeth out of the mouth of God.*
Matthew 4:4

There are other needs of life besides those which bread supplies. Sometimes we hear it said as a pretext for doing wrong or deceitful things—"Well, I must live,"—as if hunger excused stealing or fraud or other sinning in order to get bread. But it is not true that we must live, or that living is in itself the best thing for us. It certainly is not true that we must live if we cannot live without sinning. We have a higher life than our physical, and this, our true life, is nourished by communion with God.

It is never right for us to starve our spiritual nature to get bread for our bodies. It is our first duty to keep God's commandments, and in obedience is the highest good that we can attain in this world. Sometimes the best thing that one can do for one's life is to lose it; we had better any day starve to death than commit the smallest sin to get bread. Jesus said, "Seek ye first the kingdom of God, and his righteousness; and all these things shall be added unto you" (Matthew 6:33).

Getting bread should not be our first object in living, and is really not our business at all. Life's true object is to obey every word of God and seek His righteousness. So let us settle it once and for all that we are never to do any wrong thing to get bread; that we are to be true to God always and everywhere, and then leave to Him the care of our bodies. He promises that He will do this if we seek first and only His kingdom and righteousness. If He wants us to suffer, it will be because in some way suffering will be best. At least we should leave that to Him. Then if we are to go hungry for a time, He will give us strength to endure the pangs until He sees fit to send relief. Even if we are to die for want of bread, our soul, our true being, shall live, and shall pass unstained into God's eternal blessedness.

—◇—

SCRIPTURE WITH SCRIPTURE

—◇—

Jesus said unto him, It is written again.
Matthew 4:7

C hrist is our example in all things. Here we see how He met the tempter in order to conquer him. We see just what weapons He used in His victorious conflicts. He used Scripture as a quiver, and He drew from it the sharp arrows which He hurled so successfully against His opponent. We notice, too, that He did not have to get down His Bible and search through it to find texts to use in His battle. He drew them from memory. This shows that He had made the Scriptures a study in the quiet days at Nazareth, and had His heart filled with the precious words, so that when He needed them they were ready. The lesson for us is very apparent. If we would be ready to meet the assaults of the tempter, we must have our quiver filled with the polished shafts of Scripture. We must have the words of the holy Book laid away in reserve in our hearts, so that at any sudden call we may use them.

There is another thought here. Jesus said, "It is written again." We must compare Scripture with Scripture, so as to be sure of the will of God. A single text taken by itself may not give us the whole mind of the Spirit on any subject; it may be necessary to take other passages, presenting other aspects of the truth, in order to get the whole truth.

Here the case is very plain and very instructive. The devil had quoted a sublime promise but had distorted it, omitting the qualifying or contextual words in it. It is very true that God gives His angels charge over us, but it is true also that to get this heavenly care and protection we must walk in the ways of obedience and duty; the moment we turn away unbidden into other paths and go where God has not sent us, we forfeit this protection. So we must remember always, when we are tempted to expect God's care or blessing in any sinful or willful course of our own, that it is written again, "Thou shalt not tempt the Lord thy God" (v. 7).

THE LAMB OF GOD

And looking upon Jesus as he walked,
he saith, Behold the Lamb of God!
John 1:36

This was the <u>first gospel sermon</u>, and it is a model for all preachers and teachers. The preacher pointed his own followers away from himself to Christ. This same model of unselfishness appears in all John's ministry. He was only a voice, announcing the coming of a King. He was not that Light, but only one bearing witness of that Light. With throngs following him, the moment Jesus came John asked the crowds to leave him and follow Jesus. His whole ministry was simply a pointing of men to another.

This is what all Christian workers should do: they should preach and teach Christ, not themselves. They should not seek to win attention to themselves, but to get all to see Christ and to love Him. Like John, they should be willing to decrease that Christ might increase; they should be satisfied to fade away like the morning star in the brightness of the sun's rising.

This name by which John drew attention to Jesus is important. He called Him "the Lamb of God." This meant that Christ had come into the world not only to be a teacher, but chiefly to be a sacrifice for the sin of the world, to die in the place of sinners. He was called a lamb, no doubt, because of His gentleness and meekness; but the principal reason was because He was to save us from our sins by bearing them Himself.

Just the day before this, John said of Jesus, "Behold the Lamb of God, which taketh away the sin of the world" (John 1:29). Not only did He take our sin upon Himself; He cast it away into eternal forgetfulness, to be remembered no more forever. Now all who come to Him are safe forever from condemnation. Long ago their sins were laid on the atoning Lamb, and they will never have to be carried a second time. "There is therefore now no condemnation to them which are in Christ Jesus" (Romans 8:1).

◇

WHAT SEEK YE?

◇

*They followed Jesus. Then Jesus turned, and saw them
following, and saith unto them, What seek ye?*
John 1:37–38

Here we see how easy Christ makes it for those who set out to find Him. When we start to seek Him, ever so timidly and fearfully, He does not leave us to seek Him without success, but quickly turns to meet, cheer, and help us. Then He does not stand apart on some lofty mountaintop far away, or hide Himself out of sight, compelling us to seek alone and struggle through great difficulties to get to His feet. He sees us when we take our first steps toward Him and notes the very beginnings of our hearts' longings for Him.

In the parable, the father was watching and saw the prodigal as he came painfully and wearily homeward; and when he saw him he ran to meet him. Christ does just this when He sees a penitent sinner turn his face toward Him.

Notice His question also, "What seek ye?" This is Christ's question to all who begin to go after Him. He wants us to know ourselves just what it is that we are seeking for. Once, when two blind men cried after Him, He turned and asked, "What will ye that I shall do unto you?" (Matthew 20:32).

It is good for us to get our desires into definite requests. Many people are unhappy and know that they need something, but do not know what it is. They are unsatisfied with themselves; they are conscious of imperfection, of sin, of unrest; they bend their hearts toward Christ and begin to pray to Him, but their prayers are vague and indefinite. Then Jesus turns and asks, "What do you seek?" If we will settle definitely what we want, He will be ready to answer. The form of this question also veils a promise: "Tell me what ye seek, and I will give it to you." The question is nothing less than a key to Christ's treasure house. We need to be only sure that we seek sincerely, but we must remember that seeking is a very strong task.

BEGIN AT HOME
◇

He first findeth his own brother Simon . . .
and he brought him to Jesus.
John 1:41–42

Nobody told Andrew to go after his brother; it was the impulse of his own heart that sent him so quickly away on his love-errand after he had found Christ himself. The lesson lies on the surface. "Even a dog," as the saying goes, "that has had its leg mended will bring other limping dogs to the man that was kind to it." One who has been cured of some disease will bring all his afflicted friends to the physician who cured him.

You have had your soul saved. All about you are those whose souls are lost, as yours was a little while ago. How many have you brought to Jesus? Do you think you can hold up clean hands, free from the blood of souls, unless you try very earnestly to bring some others to Christ?

Notice that it was his own brother that Andrew brought, and the words indicate that the other man—John—brought his brother too, only Andrew was quicker. Home, then, is the place where we ought to begin. Yet, strange to say, it is the last place many of us speak about Christ. The old proverb has it, "The shoemaker's wife is always the worst shod." Often it is the preacher's or the teacher's own home that gets the least benefit and blessing from his messages of love, or from his Christian life and influence. Surely the dearest in the world to you are home's precious ones; go first to them, therefore, if any of them are unsaved, and try to bring them to your Savior, that they may find what you have found.

Of course you will not stop with your home. Let the circle widen until your influence reaches as widely as possible, but do not overlook those nearest and dearest to you while you stretch out your hands toward the heathen in China or in Africa, or even reach over the fence to save a neighbor next door. That is a mistake some people make.

February 28
◇
FINDING CHRIST
◇

We have found the Messias.
John 1:41

We must notice the kind of argument Andrew used with his brother. He just went to him with a great joy in his heart—the joy of discovery and satisfaction—and told him about it.

An English preacher gave the following illustration in a sermon showing how much more convincing power there is in a little bit of true Christian living than there is in a large amount of apologetics.

> A minister in his pulpit delivered a very fine course of lectures in refutation of some form of infidelity. He delivered the course chiefly for the benefit of one man who attended his place of worship. The man was skeptical, and the preacher hoped to remove his doubts. Shortly after the close of the lectures, this man came and declared himself a Christian. The minister was very glad, and said to him, "Which of my talks was it that removed your doubts?" The answer was, "Oh, it was not any of your sermons that influenced me. The thing that set me to thinking was a poor woman that came out of the chapel beside me one night and stumbled on the steps. I reached out my hand to help her, and she said, 'Thank you'; then she said, 'Do you love Jesus Christ, my blessed Savior?' I did not, and I went home and thought about it; and now I can say, I love Jesus." An ounce of a heart's giving is worth more than a ton of head knowledge in winning souls.

When we have really found Christ ourselves, the best way to bring others is just to tell them what Christ is to us. One word of genuine and heartfelt confession of Christ by a person whose soul is full of the newfound joy is worth more than the most eloquent sermons to lead others to believe in Christ. Let us be sure that people know from us that we have really found Christ; then they cannot but be impressed. It will surely be a pity if we should so live that they will not suspect that we are Christians.

February 29

◇

THE WEDDING FEAST

◇

*There was a marriage in Cana . . . And both Jesus
was called, and his disciples, to the marriage.*

John 2:1–2

Jesus approved, sanctified, and supported marriage by attending this wedding feast. The Bible from the beginning to the end puts high honor upon marriage. God Himself ordained it in Eden. It is not without peculiar significance that Christ made this His first public appearance, and performed His first miracle, at a marriage, thus showing His approval and putting His sanction upon this relationship.

There is no subject on which young people in these days need to receive more careful instruction than marriage. The many ill-advised and unhappy marriages, the alarming frequency of separation, and the ease with which for the slightest reason divorces are obtained, show that the ordinance is losing its sanctity in the public mind. Jesus should be invited to every wedding, as He was to this one at Cana. No marriage relationship should ever be entered into when His presence would not be welcome and on which His blessing cannot be sought and obtained.

It should be noted further here that it was a wedding feast which Jesus attended. His ministry opened amid scenes of human happiness. We need to learn that Christ is not merely a friend for our sorrowful hours but also for our times of joy. We do not ponder enough on this. We regard religion too much "as a lamp burning dimly in a death place" and not as a sun shining amid the brightness and the radiance of the fairest day. No doubt it is when trouble comes that Christ seems most precious to us; but He is a Friend for our gladness as well. We should not lose this lesson from the Cana wedding. Our Lord does not frown upon pure innocent pleasures. Joy is a duty in its place as is prayer. We need not to be afraid to invite Christ to our social events; indeed, if we cannot invite Him, something must be wrong with the pleasures themselves.

March 1

◆

UNFAILING JOYS

◆

They have no wine.
John 2:3

This incident is a very fitting illustration of the failure of all the world's ways. The wine gave out at a wedding feast. There was not enough of it to last through to the end of the feast. It is the same with all earth's pleasure. It comes in cups, not in fountains, and the supply is limited and soon exhausted. It is so especially with sin's pleasures. The prodigal son runs through his abundance and begins to be in want. A poet compared the pleasures of sin to a snowflake on the river: "a moment white, then gone forever." But it is true in a sense also of pure pleasures.

Even the sweetness of human love is but a cupful which will not last forever. The joy which so fills us today, tomorrow is changed to sorrow. Amid the gladness of the marriage altar there is the knell of the end in the words, "till death us do part." One of every two friends must hold the other's hand in farewell at the edge of the valley—must stand by the other's grave and walk alone part of the way.

The best wine of life and of love will fail. If there were nothing better in this world, how sad it would be! But it is here that we see the glory of Christ's gospel. Jesus comes when earth's wine fails and gives heaven's wine to supply the lack. How profound and how true is the picture here—the failing wine, and then Jesus coming with power and supplying the want! That is what He is doing continually. He takes lives which have drained their last drop of earthly gladness, and He satisfies them with spiritual good and blessing, so that they want nothing more. When human joy fails, if we have Jesus with us, He gives new joy, better than the world's, and in unfailing abundance. How sad it is for those who have not taken Christ into their lives, and who have nothing but the empty cup when earth's wine gives out!

March 2

THE LORD'S TIME

Mine hour is not yet come.
John 2:4

Christ meant that His time for beginning to work miracles had not yet come. With all divine power slumbering in His hands, He would do nothing at any bidding but His Father's. Even His human mother's request He could not regard in this matter.

One thought here is our Lord's perfect devotion to His Father's will. We find the same all through His life. He did nothing of Himself. He took His work moment by moment from His Father's hand. He waited always for His "hour." He had no plans of His own, but followed the divine purpose in all His acts. All those early years at Nazareth, with omnipotence in His grasp, he performed no miracle. Even now, though appealed to by His mother whom He so deeply loved, He would not do anything even one minute before His time came.

The practical lesson for us here is devotion to God's will. We should always wait for God. Too many of us run before we are sent. In our zeal for God's cause and kingdom we do not wait for divine direction. We speak words out of season which, despite their earnestness and sincerity, do harm rather than good. We try to feed others with unripe fruits. We address people before they are prepared to hear, and oftentimes in words that drive them beyond our reach. We hurry out to preach when we ought ourselves to be sitting quietly at our Master's feet as learners. The most common fault among Christians is that we are too slow in doing Christ's work and in heeding His calls; but it is a fault also to go too fast for God, to go before He sends us. With warm love for Christ we must learn to wait for Him till our hour is come. He must prepare us for the work before we are ready to do it, and then He must prepare the work for our mission. In Christian work we need patience and self-restraint as well as zeal and earnestness.

Whatsoever he saith unto you, do it.
John 2:5

That is the word for all Christ's servants. That is the motto of true consecration at all times and in all places. Every word in this sentence is emphatic and rich in its meaning. "Whatsoever he saith." There is no other one who has a right to command us. We belong to Christ because He has redeemed us. He is our only Lord and Master. "Whatsoever he saith." We may not choose some of His commands for obedience and some for neglect, inattention, or rejection. We are not to do the pleasant things He bids us to do, and leave undone the things that are not according to our own taste and feeling. We are to do even the things that cost pain and personal sacrifice. It was in this way that Jesus Himself did the will of His Father. That will took Him to His cross; but He did not shrink from accepting it when He saw the way growing dark before Him, or when He felt the thorns under His feet and the burdens increasing into crushing weight upon His shoulders. If we would walk in His steps, our obedience must be complete.

"Whatsoever he saith." But how can we know what He says? We cannot hear His voice as the servants at the wedding heard it. He speaks now in His Word, and the reverent heart may always hear what He says, as the sacred pages are prayerfully pondered. He speaks in the conscience that is kept tender by loyal obedience; He speaks in the providence that brings duty to our hand. There never is any real uncertainty as to what He says, if we are truly intent on knowing His will. "Whatsoever he saith unto you, do it!" It is the doing that is important. We should never ask questions or make suggestions when Jesus has spoken; the one thing for us is obedience. We should never ask what the consequences may be, what it may cost us; we are simply to obey. Christ knows why He wants us to do that thing, and that should be reason enough for us.

March 4

CO-WORKERS WITH CHRIST

*Fill the waterpots with water. And they filled them up
to the brim. And he saith unto them, Draw out now.*
John 2:7–8

The servants' part in this miracle was important; they had to carry the water and fill the vessels, and then draw out and bear the wine to the guests. They became co-workers with Christ in His miracle. So our Lord always calls His people to be His helpers in blessing the world. We cannot do much. The best we can bring is a little of the common water of earth; but if we bring that to Him, He can change it into the rich wine of heaven, which will bless weary and fainting ones. If we take simply what we have and use it as He commands, it will do good. Moses had only a rod in his hand, but with this he accomplished great wonders. The disciples had only five barley loaves, but these, touched by Christ's hand, made a feast for thousands. So the common water carried by these servants, under the Master's blessing, became wine for the wedding.

Christ passes the gifts of His love and grace through human hands to others. The redemption is divine, completed by Christ alone, but the priesthood that mediates is human; human hands must distribute the blessings. Gifts of mercy can get to the lost only through those who have been saved. Then how striking is the other side of this truth: the servants carried only common water from the spring, but with Christ's blessing the water became good wine. So it always is when we do what Christ bids us to do—our most mundane work produces heavenly results.

No labor is in vain which is completed in the Lord. Our most common work amid life's trivialities, in business, or in the household, which seems only like carrying water to be emptied out again, is transformed into radiant service, like angelic ministry, and leaves glorious results behind. The simplest things we do at Christ's bidding may become immortal blessings to other souls or to our own!

March 5

◇ SILENT CHANGE ◇

The ruler of the feast . . . knew not whence it was.
John 2:9

Christ performed this miracle without noise or show. He said nothing to call attention to what He was going to do. The people about Him did not know of the wonderful work He had accomplished. He works today in the same way. He is not in the storm, the earthquake, the whirlwind, but in the "still small voice." His kingdom comes into men's hearts, not with observation and show, but silently, without parade. The bad life is changed by His word into moral purity, and yet no one saw the change made or the hand that brought it about. Silently help comes in the hours of need, silently prayer's answers come down, silently the angels come and go.

It is significant also that the "servants which drew the water knew." Those who work with Christ are admitted into the inner chamber where omnipotence is unveiled. The lesson is very simple and beautiful. Christ takes into His confidence those who serve Him—calls them no more servants but friends. Those who do Christ's will know of His doctrine and see His ways of working. If we would see Christ's power and glory, we must enter heartily into His service.

Oftentimes it is in the lowliest ways, and in the paths of humble, self-denying service, that much of His glory appears. The ruler did not know from where the wine came; is it not often the same with us? People do not know from where the blessings come which steal so softly into their hearts. Many a troubled Christian kneels in prayer in great fear, oppressed by a sense of need, and rises with new rich joy in his heart, yet knowing not from where the strange sweet blessing came. We drink the cups which God fills for us with heavenly sweetness, we receive the gifts which are brought down to us from the very throne, and yet oftentimes we do not know from where these things come, nor recognize the divine presence that works so closely beside us.

"MORE AND MORE" OF BLESSING

*Every man at the beginning doth set forth good wine;
and when men have well drunk, then that which
is worse: but thou hast kept the good wine until now.*

John 2:10

The world gives its best first and the worst comes afterward. It is so in all sinful pleasures—first exhilaration and then bitter remorse. It is so in the chase for wealth, power, fame—gratification first, and then painful disappointment. At first money brings gladness, a sort of satisfaction; but as time rolls on and wealth increases, cares multiply, anxieties thicken, burdens grow heavier, and at last the rich man finds that in all his riches he has less comfort than he had in the days when he was a poor boy. It is so in all mere worldly ambitions. The first cups of fame are sweet, but soon they pall upon the taste. This truth holds especially in the sinful life.

We need not deny that at the beginning sin is sweet, but bitterness is found at the bottom of the cup. In grace, however, this is reversed; the good wine is kept to the last. Christ Himself had humiliation, darkness, and the shame of the cross, then exaltation, power, glory.

In Christian life the same law holds. First there comes bitterness, but out of the bitterness sweetness flows. There is the deep sorrow of penitence, but this gives way to the blessed joy of forgiveness. First there are self-denial and cross-bearing, but out of these experiences comes a holy peace that fills all the heart. Sorrows are to be endured, but the good wine of comfort is poured into the emptied cup. There is also a constant progression in the blessings of the divine life. We never get to the end of them; indeed we never get to the best. There is always something better yet to come. Then Christ keeps the really best wine to the very last, in heaven. Sweet as is earth's peace to the Christian, he will never know the fullness of the love of God until he gets home to the Father's house.

THE FIRST MIRACLE

This beginning of miracles did Jesus in Cana
of Galilee, and manifested forth his glory.
John 2:11

The glory was there before; it had been slumbering in His lowly, human life all along those quiet years of toil and service at Nazareth; but it was now revealed for the first time. This was the first shining forth before men of the divine splendor. We should notice also that it was in a simple act of thoughtful kindness to a perplexed household that this glory was first seen. Christ did not wait for some great occasion, but threw the earliest gleams of His divine glory upon this homely scene. It should be further noticed that it was in the midst of gladness and festivity that these first beams shone forth.

Thus we see that the glory of Christ was the radiance of love. We follow on and we find the same glory burning out more and more brightly, until at last He goes to His cross, revealing in one great act the amazing splendor of the love of God for the world. No wonder His disciples believed on Him when they saw this miracle at Cana. It was a gleam of divinity which flashed forth from His lowly form and accomplished the marvelous sign.

We should note, too, before leaving the story of this first miracle, that this transformation of water into wine was a fitting symbol of the complete work of Christ in this world. We have but to look about us and back along the Christian centuries to see the same glory blazing everywhere, the same transformation perpetually going on. Wherever the gospel goes forth, wonderful change is brought about. The desert is made to blossom like a garden. The worst lives are touched and transfigured into spiritual beauty.

Who that looks upon the perpetual miracle of Christianity in the world can refuse to believe on Christ? No mere empty creed could produce such results. There is a life in Christ which quickens and transforms whatever it touches.

SECRET DISCIPLESHIP

The same came to Jesus by night.
John 3:2

I t was better to come by night than not to come at all, though we usually think that it showed timidity on the part of Nicodemus. We must remember, however, that Jesus did not rebuke him, nor did He refuse to accept even his secret discipleship. He seems to have received him with loving welcome and to have taught him in the quiet way Nicodemus chose to come. We must remember, too, that the times then were not as they are now. Christ had not yet died, nor had the Christian church been established. Certainly, secret discipleship is not justifiable now, whatever excuse Nicodemus may have had for it in his time.

We know, too, that it was not satisfactory even in his case. We know that the time came when he could no longer remain a secret friend. When Jesus was dead on His cross, and when His body, as that of a crucified criminal, was about to be buried in dishonor among other criminals, it is remarkable that the two men who came forward and rescued it from such shame and gave it honorable burial had both until that day been secret disciples. The death of Christ so touched their hearts and aroused their timid, hesitating love, that they could no longer continue to be secret disciples. The true love of their hearts could not be repressed, and they came forward and risked and dared all for Him whom they had never before had courage openly to confess.

Secret discipleship is not satisfactory. It does not get the hearty approval of one's own conscience. It does not bring full, rich peace to the heart. It allows only a crippled and hampered Christian life at best. If we love Christ, we should come out boldly and confess Him at a time when our confession will honor Him and bring blessing to ourselves. We have a glorious promise that those who confess Him here, He will confess at the day of judgment before angels and men.

March 9

THE GOSPEL

For God so loved the world, that he gave his
only begotten Son, that whosoever believeth
in him should not perish, but have everlasting life.
John 3:16

This verse is a little Bible in itself, for it contains the whole gospel. It shows us the source of man's redemption—God's love. It shows us the fullness of this divine love—God gave His only begotten Son. It shows us how the redemption was accomplished—by the sacrifice of Christ. It tells us how to be saved—by believing on the Son of God. It tells us who will be saved—whosoever believes on Christ. It shows us what salvation is—deliverance from perishing, and the gift of eternal life.

Anyone who truly believes that God loves him is saved; the consciousness of this blessed truth is life in the soul.

A story is told of a child in Luther's time who thought of God only with dread, as of a terrible Judge. In her stern home God had been held before her only in this way, to terrify her. She had never heard a word about God's gentleness or affection. But one day in her father's printing office, she picked up a scrap of paper and found on it just the first part of this verse, "God so loved the world that He gave—" The remaining words were torn off, but even this mere fragment was a revelation to her. God loved—loved the world—loved it well enough to give something. What He gave she did not know, but it was enough for her to know that God loved at all, and that He loved the world enough to give anything to it. The new thought changed all her conceptions of God. She learned from this time to think of Him as one who loved her, and this thought brought sweet comfort to her. We have the whole verse, and we know that God is love; we know just what His love gave— the most costly and most valuable gift in all the universe. This revelation should fill us with unutterable joy.

HE SAT ON THE WELL

*Jesus therefore, being wearied with
his journey, sat thus on the well.*
John 4:6

In all the gospel story there are few more tenderly suggestive pictures of Jesus than that which we have in these words. He has been traveling all day in the hot sun, and coming to this resting place He sits down on a well-ledge. He is weary and way-worn with His long journey. He is both hungry and thirsty. This is the image of Jesus for tired people. In other places we have pictures for the tempted, for the bereft and sorrowing, for the penitent, for mothers and children, and for the blind, the deaf, the lame, and the persecuted. Here, however, is the symbol for the weary. As we look at it we see the human side of Christ's life.

Here is one of His experiences which we can understand. As we see Him healing, teaching, raising the dead, transfigured, He is far above us, and we cannot enter into His feelings. But in His bodily weariness, after His long journey in the heat and dust, He is down among us, and we can tell just how He felt. The chief comfort comes from the fact that He is able now to sympathize with us when we are tired, because that day, so long ago, He was tired.

Do we get all the blessing we might get from the truth of our Lord's actual human experiences? When we have been working hard all day and are weary and faint, let us remember this picture—Jesus, footsore and dust-covered, sinking down in sheer exhaustion on the stone ledge. He has not forgotten even in His glory how He felt that day, and as He sees us in our weariness, His heart feels tenderly for us. He looks down upon us in compassion and sends to us a blessing of strength and cheer. Let all the people whose work is hard, and who oftentimes are very tired, frame this picture in their memory and keep it always hanging up on the walls of their hearts.

GIVE ME TO DRINK

There cometh a woman of Samaria to draw water:
Jesus saith unto her, Give me to drink.

John 4:7

This illustrates to us how full of Christ are the world's common endeavors. This woman went out from her home on a very ordinary and commonplace errand, to draw a little water from the public well, and before she returned she had met the Messiah and He had revealed Himself to her soul as her Savior. She was not seeking for Christ except as the unsatisfied yearning of her heart was a faint cry for Him whom she did not know. We never know when we are to meet Christ. He waits for us in all the paths of life. She was in the way of simple duty when He met her.

The way of duty is always the surest place to come upon Christ. Too many times we expect to find Him in the path of disobedience. This woman was unaware of the glory of the presence beside her. Jesus met her in the form of a weary and way-worn man and won His way to her conscience and heart before He revealed to her the glory of His personality. Christ continually comes in unrecognized ways, getting near to us and drawing out our love and trust before we know that it is Christ we are loving and trusting; then He drops the veil and shows us His blessed face.

There is another lesson here: Jesus began His ministry of blessing to this woman by asking a simple favor of her. "Give me to drink," He said. He continually stands before us in a form of disguise, asking some service. He Himself has told us that in the least of His little ones who appeal to us for bread in their hunger, or relief in their distress, He Himself comes, and that what we do for these we do for Him. So we never know when it is Christ who stands before us, in some suffering or needy one, with a timid request for help. We should be careful how we treat the lowliest, lest some day we deny a cup of water to the blessed glorious Christ.

March 12

EARTHLY JOYS

Whosoever drinketh of this water shall thirst again.
John 4:13

That is just as true of all earth's springs of joy as it was of Jacob's well. Men and women drink of them today and find a measure of satisfaction for a little time, but soon they are as thirsty as ever. The human soul cannot be satisfied with any of the earth's good things. This is not the fault of the things of earth—they are good and beautiful in their way and in their place. But the soul is spiritual and immortal and cannot be filled with any good that is not also spiritual and immortal. Money and fame and power can never be food for a soul made in the divine image; nothing less than God Himself can answer its cravings. We could not make the angels happy by giving them gold and diamonds, building them fine marble palaces to live in, and putting crowns and fine clothes on them. No more can we satisfy our own souls with such things. Men try to do so, but their thirst is only momentarily quenched, and soon they must drink again. Gratification only intensifies desire.

There is said to be a plant in South America which finds a moist place and sends its roots down and becomes green for a little while. When the place becomes dry, it draws itself out and rolls up and is blown along by the wind until it comes to another moist place, where it repeats the same process. On and on the plant goes, stopping wherever it finds a little water until the spot is dry; then in the end, after all its wanderings, it is nothing but a bundle of dry roots and leaves. It is the same with those who drink only of this world's springs. They drink and thirst again, and go on from spring to spring, blown by the winds of passion and desire, and at last their souls are nothing but bundles of unsatisfied desires and burning thirsts. We must find something better than this, or perish forever.

◇

A LIVING SPRING

◇

Whosoever drinketh of the water that I shall give him shall never thirst; but the water that I shall give him shall be in him a well of water springing up into everlasting life.

John 4:14

The soul was made for God, and when it returns to God it finds peace and satisfaction. It is not meant here, of course, that the Christian has no more desires; for longing is the very condition of more blessedness. "Blessed are they that hunger and thirst after righteousness: for they shall be filled" (Matthew 5:6). If there is no thirst, there really is no life. The dove that flew away from the ark went on weary wing everywhere, but found only a wide waste of desolate waters, with no place to alight. Then she flew back to the ark, and was gently drawn inside, where she found warmth, safety, and rest.

The story of the dove illustrates the history of the soul that wanders everywhere seeking rest, at last returning to God. How much better if men believed the truth of universal experience and went at once to God! An immortal soul, from its very nature, cannot find what it needs anywhere except in God Himself.

This word of Christ tells us also what true religion is. It begins in the heart. It is not something outside—a mere set of rules or laws to be obeyed, a guide to be followed, an example to be copied. It is new spiritual life in the soul. It is Christ Himself coming into the heart and dwelling there. It is a fountain of life— not a mere well, but a living spring open and ever flowing. It is fed from heaven, and no matter then how dry this world may be, this living fountain in the heart shall never be exhausted, for its connection is with the river of life, which flows out from under God's throne. Wherever we go we have our faith with us, in us, if we are true Christians. We are not dependent upon circumstances. Trouble does not destroy a Christian, because the fountain of his joy is within. This new fountain of life when opened in the soul is the beginning of eternal life.

March 14

◇

TRUE WORSHIP

◇

*God is a Spirit: and they that worship him
must worship him in spirit and in truth.*
John 4:24

God loves to be worshiped—to have the praise, the adoration, and the homage of His children. In the old days burning incense was the symbol of worship; its odors rose up toward heaven, and God smelled a sweet savor. What the fragrance of flowers coming up from dew-anointed fields and gardens is to us, the breath of true worship as it ascends from earth's believing hearts is to God. God is well pleased with it. He is not satisfied with bare, cold obedience. What parent would be content with mere dutifulness, such as a slave might render to a master, without affection, confidence, regard? God cannot be pleased with the most scrupulous external obedience if there is no heart in it. We must obey Him because we love Him.

This word tells us also how we may worship God if our worship is to be acceptable. It must be spiritual worship that we render to Him. Stately forms do not please Him in themselves. The music of splendid choirs and the repeating of creeds and prayers do not make worship. Worship is heart adoration, and the only true homage that rises from an assembly or from private prayer where one bows alone is simply the love and praise and prayer and devotion of hearts ascending in the words of human lips.

No mere forms of worship are acceptable; the form must be breathed full of love and life. No offerings or gifts avail in worship unless they are the expression of holy affections. The teaching here is not that we are not to use forms of worship; we cannot worship well without forms. The most basic ritual and the simplest ceremony will be pleasing to God if heart's love fills them; but the most magnificent ritual will be empty of real worship, and will be an abomination to God, if there is no true worship of the spirit in it. All depends upon what we put into the forms.

BREAD FROM HEAVEN

I have meat to eat that ye know not of.
John 4:32

The disciples had left Jesus hungry when they went away to buy bread; they came back to find His hunger had left, and in these words we have the reason He gave for it. He was intently engaged in His Father's work, doing His will, and in this He found perfect satisfaction. He had found spiritual refreshment, and His bodily weariness and hunger had vanished. His joy in saving a poor lost soul was so great that it made Him forget His hunger. But the joy was not the only food which Christ had: while doing His Father's work, special divine grace was imparted to Him from heaven, which nourished and strengthened Him. He literally fed on bread from heaven—spiritual bread.

We have other examples of the same. When He had gone through His sore temptation and was hungry, we are told that angels came and ministered to Him. In Gethsemane also, after His bitter agony, we read that there appeared an angel from heaven strengthening Him. May we not suppose that always when He had any special service, costing Him a reserve of strength, spiritual refreshment was imparted to Him in some secret way by His Father? Certainly we have the promise of this in our lives.

When Paul asked that his trouble, his "thorn in the flesh," might be removed, the answer was no: "My grace is sufficient for thee; for my strength is made perfect in weakness." When we are united to Christ, our weakness to His strength, our emptiness to His fullness, all our need there is satisfied from His supply adequate to our want. We see constant illustrations of this in our homes, where frail servants called to nurse the sick are sustained in a wonderful way through long, wearisome days and sleepless nights of vigil, as if nourished with supernatural food. They have meat to eat that others know not of. There flows from Christ's fullness a strength for their need.

March 16

---◇---

DOING THE FATHER'S WILL

---◇---

My meat is to do the will of him that sent me.
John 4:34

Jesus explained to His disciples how He had been nourished during their absence. He had been laboring in His Father's work, and this labor had revived Him. There is for all Christ's people a wonderful secret of hidden blessedness in these words. There is a life higher than mere bodily existence. As our Lord elsewhere said, "Man shall not live by bread alone, but by every word that proceedeth out of the mouth of God "(Matthew 4:4). It is only the lower life that can be nourished by bread, and this may be well fed while the true life is starving. The higher existence is sustained by communion with God, and this communion is maintained by doing God's will.

Obedience secures the divine presence and companionship. It was this communion with the Father that sustained Christ in all His sufferings. At one time He said, "He that sent me is with me: the Father hath not left me alone; for I do always those things that please him "(John 8:29). The simple joy of doing the Father's will was another element in the "meat" on which Christ fed here. There was also the joy of saving a lost soul. We do not begin to realize the joy that it gives Christ to see penitents coming home. It was this same "meat" that sustained Him in all the sorrows of the cross—"who for the joy set before him endured the cross, despising the shame" (Hebrews 12:2).

These are only a few of the many deep and rich suggestions of truth which lie in this one divine sentence. We should learn the lesson for ourselves, for it is true for us as it was for Jesus that doing the will of God nourishes our souls. Complete and loving submission to the divine will in time of suffering lifts the spirit above fleshly pain. Complete devotion to God's work brings a Christian into such living communion with his Lord that he even rejoices in toil and sacrifice. To do God's will brings us into living communion with Him, and that is life.

FRUIT UNTO LIFE ETERNAL

*He that reapeth receiveth wages, and
gathereth fruit unto life eternal.*
John 4:36

Those who work for this world often fail of reward; but those who do God's work are sure of good wages and of a glorious harvest. "The wages of sin is death," and the wages of much of earth's toil is disappointment; but the wages of doing good is life, and the joy is sure and eternal. It is often hard work which the Christian has to do. The sowing is oftentimes in tears, but the reaping is always in joy. Christ Himself found the sowing hard and sorrowful, but He has never been sorry in heaven for what it cost Him here. The old prophet, having spoken of the sorrows and sufferings of Christ's life, said, "He shall see of the travail of his soul, and shall be satisfied"(Isaiah 53:11). As He sits now on His throne and sees the millions of the redeemed coming home to glory, all saved through His sufferings, He never regrets that He gave such a price for their redemption, but rejoices and is satisfied with the wages which He receives. It will be the same with all His followers who are permitted to suffer in any way in bringing lost ones home. The wages will a thousand times compensate for all the sacrifice and cost.

No true work for Christ has ever been in vain. On earth many a seed is dropped which dies in the soil; but no seed of heavenly truth which is sown in faith and watered with tears ever fails to spring up somewhere and some time into a plant of righteousness. It may not always grow as the sower hoped, nor always just where he hoped, nor when; yet no living word of God can ever die. We should notice the kind of wages God gives His reapers. He does not pay them in gold and silver, but in life—life eternal. Those who work in God's harvest-fields may not grow rich in men's eyes, but they themselves grow into richer, riper, holier spiritual blessedness.

SOWING AND REAPING

One soweth, and another reapeth.
John 4:37

This word of Christ is oftentimes illustrated in its literal sense. Many a man sows a field of wheat, and before the harvest he lies in his grave. Many a man plants a tree and does not live to taste its fruits; others coming after him enjoy the benefit of his labor. Then still more frequently is this word illustrated in its spiritual sense. Oftentimes the sower does not reap any harvest in this world. Many people work hard and faithfully for Christ all their lives and see no results. Then, eventually others come and with almost no toil gather from the same fields abundant harvests. One pastor preaches and prays for many years and sees but a few souls brought to Christ. He dies, or goes away, and a new man comes. Almost immediately a revival begins and many souls are brought into the kingdom. One sowed, another reaps. But who will say that the sower's work was not just as important as the reaper's? If the first pastor had not labored so faithfully and so long, could the second have gathered such a harvest? We are sure that in heaven they will both rejoice together. There is no danger that there will be any jealousy there as to whose is the just reward of honor.

Many a mother teaches her children the story of the love of Christ and presses upon them the acceptance of the Savior. With prayer and faith she awaits the result, hoping to see them confess Christ. But at length her eyes are closed upon earth and her children are still unsaved. At last, however, there comes a gentle reaper, and they are gathered into the barn. So it is with many a faithful teacher or other Christian worker. We do not need to then concern ourselves about the reaping. Let us sow everywhere the good seed, and whether we reap the harvest, or some other hand gather it, it will make no difference; sower and reaper shall rejoice together.

—◇—

TRIALS LEADING US TO CHRIST

—◇—

When he heard that Jesus was come . . . he
went unto him, and besought him that he
would come down, and heal his son.
John 4:47

The trouble in his home sent this man to Christ. Perhaps he never would have gone at all had it not been for his son's sickness. Many of those who went to Christ in the old days were driven by their anxiety of heart. They tried everything else first and then at the last moment they hurried to Jesus. The same is true in these days. Many persons who have never prayed before have gotten down upon their knees by the bedside of their sick and dying children and cried to God on their behalf. Many persons have first been sent to God by their own troubles. It was not until the prodigal was in dire want, and every other resource had been exhausted, that he said he would arise and go to his father. Many sinners never think of Christ until they are in despair under the sense of guilt. Not until they see the storm of God's wrath gathering do they seek the shelter of the cross. But what a comfort it is that even going so late to the Savior He does not reject or cast away those who come!

We ought to always remember that when any trouble comes to us, whatever other purpose it may have it is certainly intended to send us again to Christ. Perhaps we have drifted away from Him, or grown careless, or lost our first love. The trouble that touches us is the merciful hand of God laid on us to lead us back to our place of safety and blessedness at His side.

A man was traveling and was hungry, but did not know where to go to find food. There came a sudden and violent storm, compelling him to seek shelter. Fleeing under a tree for refuge, he found not shelter only, but food, for the storm had brought down fruits from the tree's branches for his hunger. Those whom trouble drives to Christ also find both shelter from the storm and food to meet their necessities.

◇

DEATH, THE GATE OF LIFE

◇

He was at the point of death.
John 4:47

He was just on the edge of death, just at its door. The point of death is a point to which all of us some time must come. We pass through this world by many different roads. Our ways run in diverse directions, crossing each other at every possible angle. No two of us go in precisely the same path. If we could see a map of the world, with all human paths marked out on it, it would be a strange network that we should behold. But however diverse our courses, every one of us comes at last to the "point of death." This is a point no one can ever evade. There is no road in life which goes around it. It is a final point. Here our life suddenly passes out of sight, passes from earth, and enters on a new existence in the eternal world.

What preparation have we made for this "point of death"? Are we ready for it, so that our sudden coming to it at any moment shall not terrify us? What preparation is necessary? Only this—that we be saved in Christ, and have our work for Him well and faithfully done up to the last moment. Christ changed this "point of death" to a "point of life." He tasted death for every man, and absorbed all death's blackness and curses. *Now if we are true believers in Christ, dying is but leaving darkness and sin and danger to pass into light and holiness and safety.*

A poet represents one coming up to a gate on a mountainside, over which were written the words, "The Gate of Death"; but when he touched the gate, it opened, and he found himself amid great brightness and beauty; then turning about, he saw above the gate he had entered the words, "The Gate of Life." If we are in Christ, death is abolished, and the point which earth calls the point of death is really the point of life. We need then to make sure of only one thing—that we are truly Christ's by living faith and loving obedience.

THE RETURN TO NAZARETH

He came to Nazareth, where he had been brought up.
Luke 4:16

It was a hard place for Him to visit and to preach in. He had lived there from infancy. The young people knew Him as a schoolmate and playfellow, and as the village carpenter. One day He went away from home, and soon there began to come back strange reports about Him. Up in Jerusalem and in other places, it was said, He was performing miracles and preaching with wonderful power, and the people everywhere were thronging to hear Him and bringing out their sick to be healed by Him. It requires no deep insight into human nature to know how His neighbors would regard all this. In their envy they would sneer at the reports about Him. He was only a carpenter! Then one day He came home again and went to the village church and preached. But they could not endure to hear His words, and they were filled with anger. They rose up and cast Him out of the town and tried to hurl Him over a cliff to kill Him.

There are some lessons which we ought to gather from this visit of Jesus to His old home. One is that we ought to seek the salvation of our neighbors and friends, not turning our back upon our old home, though we may have grown great and famous elsewhere. Another is that as young people we ought to live so carefully that when we grow up we may be able to stand up in the midst of those who have always known us and bear testimony for Christ. There are some good men now whose preaching would have little effect where they were brought up because of the way they lived when they were at home in youth. But Jesus' life had been so pure and blameless that He had no need to be embarrassed when He looked His old neighbors in the face and began to preach to them. Every young person should live in a way that he or she will never be ashamed to hear bad reports of anything he or she is said to have ever done.

◈

CHURCH ATTENDANCE
◈

*As his custom was, he went into the
synagogue on the sabbath day.*
Luke 4:16

There is much evidence that Jesus had strong religious habits. Here we have an example of His attending the synagogue worship on the Sabbath. This had been His custom from childhood, and although He was the Son of God, Lord of earth and heaven, and had been revealed as the Messiah, He still continued to observe the custom.

Some people are careless about church attendance. They find fault perhaps with the minister—he does not feed them, they say. They often mean that he does not entertain them. Now no doubt Jesus heard a great many dull talks and sermons, but He did not for that reason stay away from the synagogue. He went there to worship God, not to enjoy intellectual enrichment. Others stay away from church, as they say, because there are so many inconsistent Christians who attend, because the church is so imperfect. We know that it was just the same when Jesus was on the earth. There were a great many church members in Nazareth and elsewhere who were very imperfect. Our Lord knew all about men's true character, and He saw the worst there was in them. What He saw in some very prominent church people we may learn from some of His own bitter words against the prominent religious leaders of His day. Yet this did not keep Him from the services. If He could worship God in a congregation of fallen people, we should be able to do it too.

Another thought is that if He, with all the resources of His own divine nature to draw upon, still needed the means of grace, surely we need them far more. Still another point to be remembered is the importance of forming religious habits, especially the habit of going to church. Here the lesson particularly touches children and young people. Jesus brought this custom from His youth, and He never violated it in His manhood.

"Now Is The Accepted Time"

He hath anointed me . . . to preach
the acceptable year of the Lord.
Luke 4:18–19

I f there is an "acceptable year," then there must be a year or a time which is not the "acceptable year." We know that this "acceptable year" was the time Jesus ministered in Judea, when He offered the Jewish nation the kingdom. When they nailed their Messiah to the cross, this "acceptable year" was over. For a number of years things went on as before. There was a degree of prosperity. Their city stood in its splendor, and the people dwelt in their homes in a certain amount of peace. But the day of their merciful visitation ended when they rejected Christ. When Jesus stood on Olivet and looked down upon the city and wept over it, and said, "If thou hadst known, even thou, at least in this thy day, the things which belong unto thy peace! but now they are hid from thine eyes"(Luke 19:42)—when He spoke these words amid a flood of tears, the "acceptable year" closed. After that the doom hung over the beautiful city that in a few years burst upon it in all its woe and terribleness.

This is history, but there is another way to look at this event. There is an "acceptable year" for each soul. It begins when Christ first comes to us and offers salvation. It continues while He still stands at our door and knocks. It closes when we drive Him away from our door by utter and final rejection, or when death comes and hurries us away forever from the world of mercy. This "acceptable year" to each one is NOW. Has the reader of these words closed with the mercy and love of Christ? If he or she has, he knows the preciousness of the "acceptable year of the Lord." If he or she has not, let him or her remember that the "accepted time" will soon close. In another place it is called a day—"the day of salvation." A day is short, and when the time of its setting draws to a close, no power in the universe can prolong it one moment. It would be a fearful thing were the accepted time to end and leave us not saved.

CHRIST THE GREAT HEALER

This day is this scripture fulfilled in your ears.
Luke 4:21

The words had been written *seven hundred years before*. Now Jesus reads them and says, "I am the One to whom these precious sentences refer. This scripture is being fulfilled before your eyes. I am the Anointed One, and this is the mission on which I came to this world."

The entire Old Testament was full of Christ. There were a thousand fingers along its pages, every one pointing to Him. All its types and prophecies and promises were fulfilled when He came, and lived, and died, and was raised up and glorified. It is very interesting to take up Christ's whole public life and ministry, and show how perfectly He lived out the supreme mission which the prophet here outlined for Him centuries before He came. He preached the gospel to the poor; He was the friend of the poor. He healed the brokenhearted. Wherever He went, broken and troubled people came flocking around Him. As a magnet draws steel filings to itself from a heap of rubbish, so there was something in Him that drew the needy to Him.

There are always two classes of the brokenhearted. There are those whose hearts are broken because of sin. There are those who are crushed by suffering. Both these classes came to Christ. Sinners came and found in Him not a stern, cruel Judge, but a tender, compassionate Savior. The afflicted came and found true comfort. He loved all and sympathized with them, and was able to help them. Then He also brought deliverance to sin's captives, setting them free, breaking their chains. He opened blind eyes—not only the natural eyes to see the beautiful things of this world, but the spiritual eyes as well, to behold the things of heaven and everlasting life. Then He lifted the yoke of the crushed and oppressed, inviting all the weary to Himself to find rest for their souls. Thus His whole life was simply the fulfilling of all these Old Testament truths.

March 25

◇

THE FIRST DISCIPLES

◇

Jesus, walking by the sea of Galilee, saw two brethren . . .
casting a net into the sea: for they were fishers.

Matthew 4:18

When Christ needs men for important positions, He never looks for them among idlers. He always seeks in the ranks of busy people, among those who are at their posts and are faithfully doing their duty. When the Lord wanted a man to be the deliverer of His people, He found Moses tending sheep in the wilderness. When He sought for a man to be king over Israel, He found a shepherd boy watching over his flocks. When He wanted a man for a prophet, He found Elisha at his plow. When Jesus needed men to become apostles, to lay the foundation of the Christian church, He walked by the sea and looked for them among those who were busiest. No doubt there were many idlers strolling along the shore that day, lounging among the boats and watching those who were at work; but Jesus did not call any of these to be His apostles. He did not want for His apostles lazy men; so He passed by all the loungers and kept His eye on the men who were at work. He must have men of activity, men of energy and earnestness, and He knew where to look for them.

We should not forget this lesson. If we want Christ to call us to important places, we must be busy and active, that when He comes seeking for persons to do His work He will see that we are competent and worthy. We should notice also that Christ often calls those who are engaged in lowly pursuits. If we think our occupation unworthy of us, the way to rise to a better one is to be faithful and diligent where we are, until we are called to a nobler and worthier pursuit. It is to him who is faithful in little things that the charge of greater things is promised. He who does not fill well the lower place is wanted neither by God nor by others for the higher place.

March 26

◇

FISHERS OF MEN

◇

Come ye after me, and I will make you to become fishers of men.
                                                          Mark 1:17

Personal attachment to Jesus is the very beginning of all
Christian life. Believing a creed does not make one a Christian. We may believe every word we find in the Bible about
Christ, and every word of His that we have in the Gospels, and
yet not be His disciples. A Christian is one who has joined Christ's
church in this world and attached himself to Christ as a personal
follower. All the invitations Jesus gave implied this. He said,
"Come unto me"; "Come after me"; "Believe on me"; "Follow
me." He always wanted men to come out from the world and
personally identify themselves to Him. Then after they have
joined themselves to Him, and He has put His own Spirit into
them, He begins to use them. He cannot use them in the saving of
souls until they really belong to Him.

We cannot become "fishers of men" in the same way we
became carpenters, or merchants, or physicians. It is not one of
the trades or professions to be taken up and learned as trades and
professions are. Colleges and theological seminaries cannot make
people "fishers of men." They may teach them how to think, how
to write, how to speak; they can furnish them with knowledge of
many kinds, can teach them systems of theology, and make them
exegetes, logicians, rhetoricians, or orators. But these things do
not make men "fishers of men." These acquirements may be
helpful to them in their spiritual work if they are consecrated to
Christ. But the point to be remembered is that Christ alone can
make anyone truly a "fisher of men." Teachers in Sunday school
should remember this. With all that they can learn in classes
about how to teach, and all they can get in teachers' meetings or
from lesson helps regarding the lesson, they still need to go to
Christ to learn to win the souls of their scholars.

◇

AT THE CALL OF CHRIST

◇

They straightway left their nets, and followed him.
Matthew 4:20

Their nets were probably all they had. It was with these that they earned their living. Yet at the call of Christ they gave up all, cut themselves off from their means of support, and in simple obedience and faith went with Him. That is just what we all should do when Christ calls us. We should obey instantly and without questioning. No matter how much the sacrifice involves, we should make it cheerfully for His sake. Though to obey cuts us off from our ordinary means of livelihood, and leaves us without provision even for tomorrow, we should not hesitate. Christ takes care of His servants when they are faithfully doing His will. He asks for absolute surrender to Him. He wants us to trust Him while we obey Him unquestioningly.

The faith in Christ which the gospel requires is the utter, unreserved devotion of one's whole life to Him, and the unreasoning committal to Him for time and for eternity of every interest and hope. The question of what He will do with us or for us, how He will provide for us, should not for an instant be raised. There must be no conditions in following Him and being consecrated to Him. We may not bargain with Him for an easy time, for "ways of pleasantness," but should simply give ourselves to Him absolutely and forever, to follow where and to whatsoever He may lead us.

The "straightway" is also important. Many people are forever postponing duties. But every call of Christ should be answered immediately. Let us get this ringing gospel "straightway" into our lives. Many people obey so weakly, so reluctantly, and so long after they are called, that half the value of their obedience is lost. Christ wants His followers always obeying instantly. There is no tomorrow with Him. Tomorrow He may not need us, or we may not be here to do the duty He now asks of us.

"SHE MINISTERED UNTO THEM"

He came and took her by the hand, and lifted her up; and immediately the fever left her, and she ministered unto them.

Mark 1:31

That is just what Jesus is doing all the time to people sick in body, to those sick in soul, and to those who are fallen in any way and unable to rise. He does not stand far off when He would help people and call them to come to Him, but He comes to them with a brother's warm heart and ready hand. That is the way we should learn to help each other, by extending a strong, uplifting hand to those who are falling.

Many fall and perish who would be saved for life and glory if someone would come in Christ's name and help them up. The example of this woman must not be overlooked. Christ had given her back her life, and what should she now do with it but consecrate it to the service of Him who restored her? This she did, not in mere words of thankfulness, not in warm and tender emotions of praise only, but in service; she arose and ministered to her Healer and His friends. Her ministry, too, was of the most practical and helpful kind. She did not request some opportunity to do a great service for Jesus; she simply embraced the service that came first to her hand and set out to render the commonplace duties of a housewife server.

There is a whole cluster of lessons here. Every sick person who is restored, whether in an ordinary or extraordinary way, should hasten to consecrate to the service of God the life that is given back. Surely it was spared for a purpose, and we shall be disloyal to God if we do not devote it to Him. A great many persons are always seeking opportunities to minister to Christ, imagining some fine and splendid service which they would like to render. In the meantime they let slip through their hands the very things in which Christ wants them to serve Him. True ministry to Christ is doing first one's daily duties well.

COMMUNION WITH GOD

*In the morning, rising up a great while before day, he went
out, and departed into a solitary place, and there prayed.*
Mark 1:35

Jesus would always find time for prayer, or make time for it. If
His days were full of excitement and toil, He would take time
out of His nights for communing with God. He never allowed
Himself to be robbed of His hours of devotion. There are some
Christians who think they are excused from prayer and medita-
tion in secret because they are so busy. Their work presses them
so much in the morning that they cannot possibly get time to
pray. Their cares occupy them so much all day that they do not
find one quiet moment to go apart with God. In the evening
there are so many social or other engagements—meetings, societies, parties—or they are so tired, that prayer is crowded out.
The example of Christ speaks its solemn rebuke of all such excuses. We must find time for communion with God, or God will not
find time to bless us.

There are some people, also, who claim that they can pray
and commune with God just as well in one place as in another.
They do their praying while they walk around and while they
work. They see no use in going apart to pray. Surely if anyone
could pray well in a crowd or while engaged in work, Jesus could.
No doubt He did hold communion with His Father even in His
busiest hours, but this did not meet all the needs and longings of
His soul. He left the crowd, left even His own disciples, and
retired into places where no eye but God's could see Him, where
no human presence or voice could interrupt the quiet of His soul,
and where He would be absolutely alone. Surely if He required
such conditions in praying, we do too. We need to find a place for
prayer in which nothing can intrude to break the continuity of
thought or devotion. "Enter into thy closet, and when thou hast
shut thy door, pray" (Matthew 6:6).

March 30

"HE WENT ABOUT DOING GOOD"

He said unto them, Let us go into the next towns,
that I may preach there also; for therefore came I forth.

Mark 1:38

Jesus went about doing good. He did not confine his blessings to single localities. He sought to reach as many souls as possible. He did not wait for people to come to Him but carried the news to their own doors. He taught us by example that His gospel is for all people and not for any particular place or people. He taught us also that we should make the most of our lives and opportunities, scatter the blessings of grace as widely as we can, and tell as many persons as possible the good tidings of God's love. He wants His church to keep on preaching the gospel to the "next towns" till there is not a town left in which it has not been heard.

Jesus shows us a pattern of a true life. We should especially study His life as the highest example of consecrated ministry. Here we have a glimpse of the way He sought to do good. He went about, carrying into every place He could reach the blessings of His grace and love. There is something intensely inspiring in the picture which this verse gives us. He seems in eager haste to get to as many places as possible. He has the appearance and the movement of a man who knows He has not long to stay, and that He has a great deal to do before He goes away. He wants to miss no town, to leave no person unvisited.

There surely is much in this stirring picture which we ought to imitate. We are here on an errand of blessing to men. We have something to give to the world, a message from the Father to deliver to His children, blessings to scatter upon needy lives. Somewhere not very far before us waits the end of our lives. What we do we must do quickly. We should hasten on from one task to another with the gifts of love, help, and comfort which our Master has given us to scatter.

HEALING SICKNESS

*Jesus went about all Galilee . . . preaching the gospel
of the kingdom, and healing all manner of sickness.*
Matthew 4:23

It is sometimes said that religion is only for people's souls, that it gives no aid to their bodies. But the charge is without foundation. The most casual glance over the gospel story shows that Jesus Himself was deeply moved by the people's sufferings and was continually putting forth His power to heal them. Nearly all His great works were miracles of healing. Then it should be remembered that the whole system of institutions for the relief of suffering and for the care of sufferers—hospitals, institutions for all classes of unfortunate people, and homes for the orphaned and the aged and the mentally ill—is the fruit of Christianity. Wherever angels of mercy go among the sick, the wounded, the suffering, ministering in any way to their comfort, there Jesus goes about with sympathy and healing. He cares not alone for men's souls, but for their bodies as well. Any trouble of ours whatsoever, whether of body, mind, or soul, moves Him with compassion.

It is a great comfort to know that while we may not expect miraculous healing of our bodily illnesses, we are sure at least that our Lord is not indifferent to these distresses; that He plans to use them for our spiritual benefit; that He is ready to give us the grace we need to endure them patiently and submissively; and that He is ready to heal us when His wise purpose in these afflictions has been accomplished. We may always be sure of the sympathy, love, and help of Christ in all our sickness. He sits constantly in every Christian sickroom, and where faith is strong and clear He gives great comfort and peace. When He was on earth He did not go very often to the places of festivity, but whenever there was anyone sick in a home, He was sure to go there. Sickness and pain draw Him to us, and whenever He comes He brings blessings.

April 1

"MAKE ME CLEAN"

Lord, if thou wilt, thou canst make me clean.
Luke 5:12

This prayer shows a magnificent faith. The leper had no doubt whatever of Christ's ability to heal him. The only question in his mind was whether He would be willing to do it. There might be some reason that the Lord would not wish to answer his request. It would be an unutterable blessing to have this loathsome, terrible leprosy taken away. Jesus could do it if He wished, and He would do it if it were best that it should be removed. So we find in his brief prayer willingness as well as humility.

This was a prayer not for spiritual but for physical blessing, and in such things we never can know what really is best for us. A mother may bend over a dying child and plead with affectionate yearning for its life. God will never blame her for the agonizing persistence of her plea; yet she dare not pray willfully. She must end her most intense pleading with the submissive refrain, learned from Gethsemane, "Nevertheless, not my will, but thine be done" (Matthew 26:39). It may not be the best blessing to her or to her home to have her child spared.

Or a man may be threatened with loss of property. He turns to Christ for help. "If You will, You can save me from this sore loss." Yes, He can—there is no doubt about that; but will He? He will if it is best, for He never chastens but for His people's good. But will it be a blessing to have this calamity averted? The man cannot tell. Perhaps it may be necessary for him to suffer this misfortune in his temporal estate, that he may not lose his inheritance in heaven. Paul's "thorn in the flesh" is an illustration. He wanted it removed; but it was necessary to keep him from spiritual pride, from being highly exalted. Prayer should be resigned as well as earnest. We do not know what we should pray for, nor if what we desire would really bless us.

April 2

◇

THE MASTER TOUCHED HIM

◇

He put forth his hand, and touched him.
Luke 5:13

None of the Jews would have done this. They kept the leper far away. To touch him would defile them. But Jesus was not afraid of defilement. He could as easily have stood far off and cured the leper by a word, for He sometimes cured others from miles away. But the man needed a touch from a warm hand to assure him of love and sympathy. The touch left no taint of disease on the Master, but it left the leprous body clean as a child's.

There are some who want to help others, if at all, at a convenient distance. They work through committees or agents. It is a great deal better to come close to those to whom we would do good. There is a wondrous power in a human touch. A gift to the poor may do good in whatever way it comes; but if you give it yourself and express personal interest and sympathy, its value will be largely increased. You put something of yourself into your gift. The gospel may save the fallen, though coming through the cold air from a lofty pulpit; but it will be far more likely to save if the sinner feels the touch of a hand of love and catches the message warm from quivering lips.

There is no danger of receiving defilement even from touching the worst outcasts if you go to them with the love of God in your heart, wishing to do them good. Do not stand far off and toss the bread of life to them, as men throw gifts into leper hospitals. Do not slip your tract under the door and hurry away as if you were ashamed of what you had done. Go to the homes of the worst people. Give them your hand; it will not soil it to hold theirs, and you never can know what a thrill of new life it may start in hearts long unused to tenderness, yet yearning for sympathy. Put heart and inspiration into all you do. You never can know what a thrill of inspiration and life you may give to weary and disheartened ones.

◇

"HE COULD NOT BE HID"

◇

It was noised that he was in the house.
Mark 2:1

I t never can be kept quiet long when Jesus gets into any house. He cannot be hid. The neighbors will soon find out that He is there. The people cannot keep the secret. They will let it out in a number of ways. They will show it in their faces. Those who have Christ in their homes do not look like other people. There is a radiance or glow about them when they come out that tells of an unworldly source of joy. There is something about their speech, too, that lets out the secret; they cannot help talking about their Guest. So, in spite of themselves, the family in whose house Jesus is will disclose the secret.

Fragrant flowers cannot be concealed, and there is a fragrance about Jesus that always reveals His presence. Light cannot be hidden, and there is so much light in Him that it shines out at every window and through every chink and crevice of the house where He abides. Love itself is invisible, but wherever it dwells it produces such effects that its presence soon becomes known. It makes people gentle, kind, thoughtful, and unselfish, and it fills them with new desires to do good and to serve and bless others. And wherever Christ is, love is, in all its pervasive, transforming influence.

Some people like to gather beautiful things into their homes—paintings, sculptures, rare things from foreign lands, objects of interest and attractiveness. Some pride themselves on the elegance of their furniture and the fineness of the decorations in their houses. But in no other way can the Christian bring into his home so much beauty, so much joy and comfort, so much true peace, as by making Christ his abiding guest. No matter how quietly Jesus enters, the neighbors will soon know it, and they will also get the benefit and blessing of it; for from a home where Christ abides there always goes forth a fragrant influence and a loving, helpful ministry.

DIVINE POWER

The power of the Lord was present to heal them.
Luke 5:17

It was not always so. Once we read that Jesus could not do any mighty works at a certain place. It is not said that He would not, but that He could not. It seems strange that "could not" should ever be written of the omnipotent Christ. Did He then have His weak hours? Were there times when the power fled from His arm? But we read on and find that the reason He could not do any mighty works at that time and place was because of the unbelief of the people. Their hearts were shut against Him. He came with rich blessings in His hand to bestow upon them and, finding no reception, had to carry them away again with a sad heart. So no doubt the reason the power of the Lord was so graciously present to heal at this time was because the people's hearts were open to take what He had to give. They met His compassion and love with faith, and the divine power in Him was unrestrained.

We should not miss this lesson. There is never any lack of power in Christ to bless us, and yet we may be near Him and still receive no blessing from Him. He may have come to us eager to impart the rich gifts of strength, comfort, joy, help, wisdom; and yet He may be unable to bestow them. We ourselves must be in condition to receive what He has to give, or the blessing cannot be bestowed. We can shut up our hearts so close as to keep the mighty Christ outside. Weak as we are, even the divine omnipotence cannot force any blessing into our lives. There must be willingness on our part to receive. It is because of our unbelief that the power of God is not always present to heal and to bless. Then whenever we have faith and are willing to receive what Christ will give, His power will be present to pour all sorts of rich blessings into our hearts and lives. He will never force us to accept His gifts.

April 5

◇

BEARING ONE ANOTHER'S BURDENS

◇

*They come unto him, bringing one sick of
the palsy, which was borne of four.*
Mark 2:3

T hat was a very touching sight, those four strong men carrying their helpless friend to the Healer. That is the kind of
help we ought always to be willing to give to one another. There
are all around us many persons who need to be helped. There are
lame people to be assisted over rough places, and blind people to
be led along the way they cannot see themselves, and even paralytics who have to be carried in strong hands. The Christian law
of love requires that we shall be ready always to lend a hand to
those who need the aid we can give. We never can tell how soon
it may be our turn to require for ourselves just such friendly aid
as our neighbor requires from us today. If we expect to have people turn aside from their work to help us in our time of need, we
must be willing to do as much for others who now require help.

There are many ways of doing the neighborly duty to others.
These four men carried their friend to Jesus. They could not heal
him themselves, but they could carry him to the One who could
heal him. All about us are neighbors and friends who are spiritual
paralytics. We cannot cure them, but perhaps we can take them
to One who can do for them what we cannot do.

We should notice, too, that there were four of these men
who carried their friend to Jesus. One of them could not have
done it; two of them could not have carried him with ease; even
for three the trembling burden would have been hard to bear.
But when all four of these brawny men united their strength,
they carried the man along without difficulty. So it is in helping
sinners to Christ. There is strength in the union of hearts and
hands. When one alone cannot take his friend to the Savior, let
him call others to his aid, and let them unite in their efforts on his
behalf.

April 6

FAITH SEEN IN OUR WORKS

When he saw their faith.
Luke 5:20

So far as we know no one had spoken a word to Jesus about the sick man, but there really was no need for words. The pains to which the friends had gone to get this poor sufferer into the presence of Christ told of a very strong faith. *The best evidence of faith is the effort we make to obtain faith's prize.* Abraham proved his faith first of all when he promptly obeyed God's call and left his own home and country to go out he knew not where, simply following where God might lead. He proved his faith again when he was asked to offer his only son as a burnt offering, and without a question or retort he obeyed. It was after this that God said, "Now I know that thou fearest God, seeing thou hast not withheld thy son, thine only son, from me" (Genesis 22:12). There is no need of words or objections of faith when there are such acts of faith to attest it.

God can see faith. He can see it in the heart where it is exercised, even before there has been any expression of it in word or act; but here the emphasis lies on the fact that He sees it in action. *He is pleased when we show our faith by our works.* There are many prayers without words; God sees them when He does not hear them.

There is in the Bible at least one instance of God forbidding spoken prayer and commanding action instead. At the edge of the Red Sea He said to Moses, "Wherefore criest thou unto me? speak unto the children of Israel, that they go forward" (Exodus 14:15). So we should learn to put our faith into instant action. There are times when we should stop praying, get up from our knees, and hurry out to duty. *Praying for a friend in trouble is well, but it is a cheap and selfish way of showing our love if he has needs that we can supply.* Praying for missions is right, but it is no acceptable substitute for giving if we are holding the Lord's money in our hands. God wants to see our faith.

STRENGTH BESTOWED

I say unto thee, Arise, and take up thy bed, and go thy way.
Mark 2:11

That was surely a very strange command to give a paralyzed man. He could not rise up. He could not lift up his bed. He could not walk a step. He was as helpless as a corpse. Why did Jesus require of him such an impossible task? But as we look on the helpless form we see that it at once arises. The limbs move; the man gets up, takes up his bed, and walks away in the presence of all the people. As we watch him going his way, we learn that when Christ gives any command which seems impossible, He always gives strength to perform it. As the man's will began to obey Christ's bidding, power came back into his long-paralyzed body, and he was able to rise up and walk.

It is the same in spiritual life. We have no power in ourselves to do Christ's will, but as we begin to obey, the needed grace is given. Young people often say that they are afraid to enter upon a Christian life because they cannot do what will be required. In their own strength they cannot. It would be as easy for them to climb to the stars as to live a holy and lovely Christian life unaided. Human strength in itself is inadequate to life's greatest needs. But the young Christian who sets out in obedience to Christ, depending upon Him to disclose the path of duty, will never fail of strong help at the moment of need.

Older Christians also often shrink from duties because they do not have the ability to perform them; but for them, and for all who attempt any work or service in obedience to Christ, it is true that the effort to obey will always bring with it the strength to obey. We should notice too that the strength will not come until we try to obey. If we will not attempt to do our duty, we shall remain forever poor paralytics; but as we put forth the effort the life will flow into our souls, and we shall be strong.

April 8

BLESSED BY SICKNESS

A certain man was there, which had
an infirmity thirty and eight years.
John 5:5

That period was a long time to be sick. It is very hard to be an invalid year after year. This day's reading may come to some who have been afflicted like this, and we may well stop a minute to think about their case. Christian invalids have many comforts, if they will only take them to their hearts. God makes no mistakes in dealing with His children. He knows in what school they will learn the best lessons, and in what experiences they will grow best. Richard Baxter has a strange note on this passage: "How great a mercy it was to live thirty-eight years under God's wholesome discipline! O my God, I thank thee for the like discipline of fifty-eight years; how safe a life is this in comparison with full prosperity and pleasure!"

The furnace fires of sickness burn off many a bond of sin and worldliness. Many now in heaven will thank God forever for their invalid status in this life which kept them from sin. We may be sure that God never calls any of His children apart into sickness without the purpose of blessing them. There is some lesson He wants to teach them, some new glimpse of His love He wants to show them, some beauty in them He wants to bring out. Sickrooms should always be to us sacred places, as we remember that God has summoned us there for some special work upon our souls.

We need to be very careful lest we miss the good He wants us to receive. It is only those who trust Christ and lie upon His bosom that are blessed by sickness. Too many invalids grow discontented, unhappy, sour, and fretful. Sickness oftentimes fails to do good to those who suffer. There are few experiences in which we so much need to be watchful over ourselves and prayerful toward God. Be sure to keep the sickness out of your heart, and keep Christ there with His love and peace.

April 9

"EVEN SO SEND I YOU"

*I have no man, when the water is
troubled, to put me into the pool.*
John 5:7

A re there not many unsaved people in every community who
might also say, "I have no one to bring me to Christ"? There
are many lost souls for whom no one is caring. It may be said that
the gospel is offered to all, that all could come if they would. Yet
Christians must not forget that the unsaved can receive grace
only through the saved; that those who are forgiven must carry
the news of mercy to the unforgiven. The redemption is divine—
none but Jesus can save; but the priesthood is human. God's ordinary way of finding sinners and bringing them to the Savior is
through the love and pleading of other saved ones. Christ's commission ran: "As my Father hath sent me, even so send I you"
(John 20:21). We are to do for the unsaved just what Christ did
when He was here, what He would do now if He were living just
where we live, among them—go to them and ask them if they
will be made whole.

Are there not lost ones about us who can say at God's judg-
ment-bar, "The Christians about me would not lead me to the
fountain, never even ask me to come to it for cleansing"? This
man waiting at the fountain's edge is a symbol of many about
us—close to the healing waters, with hungry, unsatisfied hearts,
needing only the help of a human hand to lead them to the Savior, yet never getting that help or that sympathy, and sitting there
year after year unsaved. Surely we should not allow any unsaved
ones about us to perish without trying in every way to lead them
to the cleansing, healing waters. What evidence have we that we
are saved ourselves if we are not interested in the salvation of
other lost ones? Let us look about us and see if any of our neighbors could say what this poor man at Bethesda said. Then let us
go quickly and lead them to the Savior.

"IMMEDIATELY MADE WHOLE"

Jesus saith unto him, Rise, take up thy bed, and walk.
And immediately the man was made whole.

John 5:8–9

The man might have said, "I cannot rise. That is the very thing which I have not been able to do for thirty-eight years. Take up my bed! I could not lift a feather; and as for walking, I could as easily fly. I cannot do these things until I am healed." We have all heard people talk this way about starting in the Christian life. They plead their helplessness as reason for their delay. There is a fine lesson for such in this man's obedience. The moment he heard the command he made the effort to rise, and as he made the effort the strength was given. New life came with his simple obedience. Christ never commands an impossibility. When He bids us rise out of our sin and helplessness and begin the Christian walk, He intends to give grace and strength to enable us to do it.

The same is true of all that Christ requires of us in His service. People think it is "humility" to be timid about duty and about accepting responsibility at Christ's call; but it is not humility at all; it is unbelief and sin. We lie on our poor rugs and say, "I have no strength for this, no wisdom for that," while if we simply arose to obey every call of Christ, He would use us for noble service. This man showed his faith by immediately exerting himself to do what Christ had called him to do. Had he not done this, he would not have been healed. Many lie spiritually paralyzed, year after year, just because they are waiting to be healed before they try to rise and walk. There are many who never do any worthy service for Christ and lie in a condition of uselessness through the years, because they think themselves unable to do the duties to which they are called. It is time we learned to step forward instantly, to do whatever Christ bids us to do. When we begin to do this, we shall find ourselves strong.

April 11

THE SABBATH

The sabbath was made for man, and not man for the sabbath.
Mark 2:27

The Sabbath was not made for man merely as an arbitrary law which he must observe. It is as much a law of his nature, or in harmony with his nature, as is the night which bids him cease his toil and seek rest and sleep. It was made for man's physical nature. It has been proved many times that the body needs the Sabbath.

Then it was made for man's spiritual good, to give opportunity, not alone for physical rest, but for communion with God, when the noise of business and of toil has ceased. It was made for man to promote his welfare in every regard. All history proves that the Sabbath is a blessing wherever it is observed, and that its violation always brings loss and suffering.

Our Lord clearly showed by His example and teaching that the Sabbath is never meant to be a burden or to work oppressively. Though secular work is forbidden on the Sabbath, it is not a violation of the sacredness of the day for us to prepare food sufficient to meet the hunger of our bodies, or to lift out of a pit a beast that has fallen into it, or to heal a man who is sick.

There is no great need in these days to say much on this side of the question. Not many people are now disposed to make the Sabbath a burden or a cruel yoke. The tendency is the other way. At the same time it is well to understand just what our Lord taught on this subject. He never sought to make the Sabbath oppressive or a burden. Works of necessity are allowed, even though they may seem to violate the letter of the law. So also are works of mercy, works of benevolence. It will be hard, however, to get out of this great saying of our Lord any excuse for the hundredth part of the secular goings-on that men want to bring in under the shield of Christ's teaching.

April 12

THE GREAT PHYSICIAN

He had healed many; insomuch that they
pressed upon him for to touch him.
Mark 3:10

Though the plots of His enemies drove Jesus out of the city, they did not stop His doing good. Though some rejected His love, His heart was not closed. Capernaum lost much when He went out to its gates, but on the throngs that followed Him the gracious blessings fell.

That is oftentimes the way. The gifts of love that Christ bears in His hands are rejected by those to whom they are first offered, but they are then carried to others, who receive them with gladness. Persecution generally scatters the seed which it means to destroy. When the first Christians were driven from Jerusalem, it was eventually to carry the word into all the countries into which they fled. They "went everywhere preaching" (Acts 8:4). Opposition should never silence the lips that carry the words of life. If one rejects and scorns us, we must bear our message to another.

The picture of the people thronging here about Christ, pressing upon Him, each one eagerly struggling to touch Him, is graphic and vivid. A touch was enough. All who touched Him were made whole. Life and health flowed into the diseased bodies when the trembling fingers came in contact with the Healer, even with His garments. So a touch is enough always. Anyone who really touches Christ is healed. But we must be sure to touch Him. It is not enough to be in the crowd that gathers about Him. Only those are healed whose faith brings them in contact with Him. It is not enough to be in the congregation that worships. One praying or worshiping next to us may receive a great blessing while we receive none at all. It is because he reaches out his hand of faith and touches Christ, while we, as close to Christ as he is, do not put out our hand to touch Him, and therefore do not receive a blessing.

◇

THEY CAME UNTO HIM

◇

He . . . calleth unto him whom he
would: and they came unto him.
Mark 3:13

That is what Jesus is doing continually—standing and calling men to come to Him. And here we see the way everyone who hears His voice should answer—leave the world's company, step boldly out, cross over the line, and take his place by the side of Jesus.

There are several things to be said about the way these men responded to Christ's call. They did it freely. Although He had chosen them out of a whole nation and called them, there was no compulsion to go with Him. They could have refused if they had chosen. Christ never makes disciples by force. We must be willing, and we must choose to come to Him. Then they responded promptly. There was no hesitation. They said nothing about considering the matter for a while. They did not talk about being unfit or unworthy. They did not tell Jesus they were afraid they could not continue to be faithful. They did not say, "Tomorrow we will go." The moment they heard their names called they answered.

Then their answer was given in a way that could be understood. Whenever they heard the call they stepped out with firm resolve and, crossing over the space between the crowd and the Master, they joined with Him. It was not done secretly. They did not wait until they were alone with Him and then tell Him quietly that they had resolved to accept His invitation. They did not propose to become His disciples and yet stay among their old friends and keep working at their old businesses. They immediately separated themselves from the people about them and went over to Him, putting themselves trustingly into His hands, to be His and to do His bidding so long as they lived. This is the way these men began, and this is the way everyone should start whom Jesus calls to be His disciples.

TRANSFORMING POWER
◇

Simon he surnamed Peter.
Mark 3:16

I n a gallery in Europe are shown, side by side, the first and the last works of a great artist. The first is very rude and most faulty; the last is a masterpiece. The contrast shows the results of long culture and practice. These two names are like those two pictures. "Simon" shows us the rude fisherman of Galilee, with all his rashness, his ignorance, his imperfection. "Peter" shows us the apostle of Acts and the Epistles, the rock firm and secure, the man of great power before whose Spirit-filled eloquence thousands of proud hearts bow, swayed like the trees of the forest before the tempest; the gentle, tender soul whose words fall like a blessing, the noble martyr witnessing to the death for his Lord. Study the two pictures together to see what grace can do for a believer.

It is not hard to take roses, lilies, and all the rarest flowers, and with them make forms of exquisite beauty; but to take weeds, dead grasses, dried leaves trampled and torn, and faded flowers and make lovely things out of such materials is the severest test of skill. It would not be hard to take an angel and make him into a glorious messenger; but to take such a man as Simon, or as Saul, or as John Newton, or as John Bunyan, and make out of him a holy saint or a mighty apostle—that is the test of power. Yet that is what Christ did and has been doing ever since. He takes the poorest stuff—despised and worthless, outcast of men and women oftentimes—and when He has finished His gracious work we behold a saint whiter than snow.

The sculptor beheld an angel in the rough, blackened stone, rejected and thrown away; and when men saw the stone again there was the angel cut from the block. Christ can take us, rough and unpolished as we are, and in His hands our lives shall grow into purity and loveliness, until He presents them at last before the throne, faultless and perfect.

◇

BEATITUDES

◇

Blessed . . . Blessed . . . Blessed . . .
Matthew 5:3–10

The "Blesseds" of the Scriptures shine all over the inspired pages, like stars in the midnight sky. The Bible is a book of beatitudes and blessings. God's mercy lies everywhere.

Wherever we see Christ He is imparting blessings as the sun imparts light and warmth. While He was here on the earth He was always reaching out His hand to give a blessing to some life that sorely needed it. It was on the children's heads, on the leper, on the blind eyes, on the sick, on the dead, that He laid those gracious hands, and always He left some rich gift of blessing. Then we remember one day when those gentle hands were drawn out by cruel enemies, and with iron nails fastened back on the cross; yet even then it was in blessing that they were extended, for it was for our sins they were transfixed thus on the wood. As we see them stretched out as wide as they could reach, the attitude suggests the wideness of the divine mercy. Thus the arms of God are open to the utmost to receive all who will come to seek refuge. There is room for the worst sinners.

Then it is a striking fact that the last glimpse we have of the Savior in this world shows Him in a gesture of blessing. He had been talking with His disciples as He led them out, and then He lifted up His hands and blessed them; and while He was blessing them He parted from them and was received up into heaven. Surely there could be no truer picture taken of Jesus at any point in His life than as He appeared in that last view of Him which this world enjoyed. In heaven now He is still a blessing Savior, holding up pierced hands before God in intercession and reaching down gracious hands full of blessings for our sad, sinful earth. If any life goes unblessed with such a Savior, it can be only because of unbelief and rejection.

HUMILITY

Blessed are the poor in spirit: for theirs is the kingdom of heaven.
Matthew 5:3

This beatitude is not given to the poor in their earthly condition; for one may be very poor and yet very proud, or one may be rich in worldly goods and yet be very lowly in spirit. Nor is it on the poor in mind; for mental poverty is not necessarily a state of blessedness, and ignorance is certainly not desirable. It is the poor in spirit, in disposition, on whom the beatitude is pronounced; that is, the lowly in heart, the humble, those who are conscious of unworthiness. Humility is not thinking poorly of oneself, holding one's gifts or abilities to be of no account. We are under obligation to recognize our talents and make the fullest possible use of them. We are also to recognize our place and our privileges as God's redeemed children—no longer condemned sinners and servile slaves.

What, then, is humility? It is a spirit that bows reverently before God, and then holds its divine gifts as not too good nor too fine to be used in Christ's name in the service of the lowliest of God's creatures. The Bible everywhere speaks its praises of humility. Christ refers only once in the gospel to His own heart, and then it is this picture that we see: "I am meek and lowly in heart" (Matthew 11:29). To be poor in spirit is to be rich toward God, while pride of heart is spiritual poverty.

Humility is the key that opens the gate of prayer, while to the loud knocking of pride there comes no answer. The proud Pharisee in his prayer found no blessing, but the lowly publican went away with heart and hand full of heaven's divine gifts. Pride is the cold mountain peak, sterile and bleak; humility is the quiet vale, fertile and abounding in life, where peace dwells. The kingdom of heaven belongs to those who are lowly. They may wear no earthly crown, but a crown of glory, unseen by men, rests here upon their heads.

April 17
◇
COMFORTED
◇

Blessed are they that mourn: for they shall be comforted.
Matthew 5:4

We do not usually regard sorrowing people as blessed. Here, however, is a special beatitude for mourners. Probably Jesus meant particularly repenting mourners. In all this world there is nothing so precious before God as tears of contrition; no diamonds or pearls shine with such brilliance in His sight. It was Jesus Himself who said there is joy in the presence of the angels of God over one sinner who repents. Truly blessed, therefore, are those who in true repentance grieve over their sins; a holy light shines from heaven upon all such mourners. They are comforted with God's pardon and peace.

But no doubt the beatitude refers also to those children of God who are in sorrow, from whatever cause. Blessing is always nearer to us when we are in affliction. If we do not get it, it is because we will not receive it.

Someday we shall see that we have gotten our best things from heaven, not in the days of our earthly joy and gladness, but in the times of trial and affliction. Tears are lenses through which our dim eyes see more deeply into heaven and look more fully upon God's face than in any other way. Sorrows cleanse our hearts of worldliness and strengthen our lives. The days of pain really do far more for us than the days of rejoicing. We grow best when clouds hang over us, because clouds bear rain, and rain refreshes. Then God's comfort is such a rich experience that it is well worthwhile to endure trial, just to enjoy the sweet and precious comfort which God gives in it. But to receive from our sorrows their possibilities of blessing, we must accept the affliction as a messenger from God and pray for true comfort—not the mere drying of our tears, *but grace to profit by our affliction*, and to get from it the peaceable fruit of righteousness.

MEEKNESS

Blessed are the meek: for they shall inherit the earth.
Matthew 5:5

Meekness is not a popular quality. The world calls it a cowardly spirit that leads a man to remain quiet when insulted, to endure a wrong without resentment, to be treated unkindly and then to give kindness in return.

Men of the world say that this disposition is unmanly—that it shows weakness, cowardice, a lack of nerve. It might be so if we went to *Plutarch's Lives* for our models of manliness. But we have a truer, a more divine example for our pattern of true character than any that this world has produced. Jesus Christ was the only perfect person who ever lived on the earth, and meekness was one of the noblest qualities of His character. He was gentle in disposition, not easily provoked, patient under wrong, silent under reproach. When He was reviled, He reviled not again; when He suffered, He threatened not. Possessing all power, He never lifted a finger to avenge a personal injury. He answered with tender love all man's wrath; and on His cross, when the blood was flowing, He prayed for His murderers.

Meekness is not a cowardly spirit, since in Christ Jesus it shone so luminously. It is divine to forgive those who have wronged us, to bear long with those who treat us poorly, to give the soft answer that turns away wrath, to bathe in the fragrance of love the hand that strikes us, to always give blessing for cursing, good for evil. The lesson is hard to learn, for it goes directly against nature; we can learn it only as our lives are transformed into the divine image, only as Christ enters into our hearts and dwells there. This beatitude shows, too, that meekness is not a weakening grace. The meek shall inherit the earth. Those who commit their lives to God, who judge righteously, and leave Him to deal with the inequalities of human treatment received by them, do not suffer in the end.

April 19

◇

SPIRITUAL HUNGER

◇

Blessed are they which do hunger and thirst
after righteousness: for they shall be filled.
Matthew 5:6

It strikes us somewhat strangely at first that there should be a beatitude for dissatisfaction. We know that peace is promised to the Christian, and peace is calm repose and satisfied restfulness. The words "hunger and thirst" appear to suggest experiences incompatible with rest and peace. But when we think a little more deeply, we see that spiritual hunger must form a part of all true Christian experience. Hunger is a mark of health. It is the same in physical life; the loss of appetite indicates disease. So a healthy mind is a hungry one; when one becomes satisfied with one's attainments, one ceases to grow. The same is true in spiritual life. If we become satisfied with our faith and love and obedience, and our communion with God, and our consecration to Christ, we have ceased to grow.

Invalids die often amid plenty—die of starvation; not because they can get no food, but because they have no appetite. There are many professing Christians who are starving their souls in the midst of an abundance of spiritual provision because they have no hunger. *There is nothing for which we should pray more earnestly and more incessantly than for spiritual longing and desire.* It is indeed the very soul of all true prayer. It is like the empty hand reaching out to receive new and richer gifts from heaven. It is the heart's cry which God hears with acceptance and always answers with more and abundant life. It is the ascending angel that climbs the radiant ladder to return on the same bright stairway with blessings from God's very hand. It is the key that unlocks new storehouses of divine goodness and enrichment. It is indeed nothing less than the very life of God in the human soul, struggling to grow up in us into the fullness of the stature of Christ. Such spiritual hunger never fails to secure a blessing.

April 20

◇

THE GOLDEN RULE

◇

Blessed are the merciful: for they shall obtain mercy.
Matthew 5:7

People receive back in this world just what they give to it. If we think the world is a hard place to live, the probability is that the hardness is in ourselves, and that it is the echo of our own words that we hear, the rebound of our own transgressions that we feel, the reflection of our own ugliness of disposition and temper that we see, the harvest of our own sowing that we gather into ourselves. If we are untrue to anyone, it is quite likely that someday somebody will be untrue to us. If we are unjust to another, there is little doubt that some time someone will deal unjustly with us. On the other hand, if the world seems to us full of love, it is quite likely that we give the world quite a lot of love. People generally treat us as we treat them. The generous man finds people generous. The sympathetic man finds sympathy. The merciful man obtains mercy. The selfish man always thinks this world very selfish.

Hence the Golden Rule rests on a deep principle in life. "Whatsoever ye would that men should do to you, do ye even so to them" (Matthew 7:12). What we do to others they will do to us. That is the principle. If we want mercy, we must be merciful; if we expect sympathy and help, we must give both sympathy and help. We have only to change places with people and then ask them what we would want them to do to us. As a rule people do not give warmth for coldness, courtesy for rudeness, kindness for unkindness. The principle applies even to the divine treatment of us. In God's judgment we receive according to our deeds. He who obtains forgiveness is he who forgives others. He who finds mercy is he who shows mercy to others. He whom Christ will confess before His Father is he who here before men confesses Christ. So for eternity we shall reap what we have sowed and gather what we have scattered.

April 21
◇
PURITY OF HEART
◇

Blessed are the pure in heart: for they shall see God.
Matthew 5:8

There is no beatitude in the Bible for anything unclean. We are told also that there is no room in heaven for anything that corrupts. Therefore, if we hope to enter heaven we must prepare for it here. To a child who expressed the wonder of how he could ever get up to heaven, it was so far away, a wise mother's reply was, "Heaven must first come down to you; heaven must first come into your heart." The words were very true. Heaven must really be in us, or we can never enter heaven. And just when we become pure in heart is when heaven is entering into us.

But what is purity of heart? It is not sinlessness, for none of us is sinless. A pure heart must be a penitent heart that has been forgiven by Christ and cleansed by His blood. We have a Bible promise that though our "sins be as scarlet, they shall be as white as snow" (Isaiah 1:18). The pure heart is one, then, that Christ has cleansed. It is one also that is kept pure by obedient living and close communion with God.

We are taught in the Scriptures that an important part of true religion is to keep oneself unspotted from the world. It is an evil world in which we live; but if we faithfully follow Christ, doing His will, keeping our hearts open to every influence of the divine Spirit, we shall be kept by divine power from the corruption that flows around us. As the lily remains pure and unstained amid the soiled waters of the bog in which it grows, so does the lowly, loving, patient heart of the Christian disciple remain pure in the midst of all this world's corruption. Over such a heart God's face beams in perpetual blessing. The vision on earth, of course, is never full and clear, but it grows brighter and brighter as the believer walks ever toward the morning, and at last it will be unclouded and full in the perfect day of heaven.

PEACEMAKERS

◇

Blessed are the peacemakers: for they
shall be called the children of God.
Matthew 5:9

This seems to often be an overlooked beatitude. There are many people who are really strifemakers rather than peacemakers. They do not seek to heal estrangements between others, to prevent quarrels and contentions, and to bring together those who have begun to drift apart. Indeed, their whole influence goes toward widening breaches, intensifying bitterness, and promoting anger and hatred. When they find in anyone a seed of suspicion or dislike of another, they stimulate the evil growth. Is it not time that we should get our Lord's beatitude down out of the skies and begin to work it into our lives? Is it not time that we should become peacemakers in a world whose beauty is marred by so much strife?

The peacemaking spirit is divine. No one in heaven finds delight in separating friends. Only so far as we take the peacemaking spirit into our lives do we bear the mark of God's image. To be peacemakers we must first of all strive to live peaceably with all men. "If it be possible, as much as lieth in you," says St. Paul, "live peaceably with all men" (Romans 12:18). But, further, we are also to strive to make and promote peace between others. Our ministry is not to be confined to the settlement of great quarrels, but may find even its most fruitful work in the healing of the petty disagreements which we discover all about us. Whenever we find one man angry with another, we should seek to remove the angry feeling. The little fits in others' friendships we should strive to heal. The unkind thoughts of others which we find in people's minds we should seek to change into kindly thoughts. We can do no more Christlike service than to seek always to promote peace between man and man, to keep people from drifting apart, and to get them to live together more lovingly.

April 23

◇

LET YOUR LIGHT SHINE

◇

Ye are the light of the world.
Matthew 5:14

Every true Christian is a candle shining in this dark world. The Bible speaks of the spirit of mankind as the candle of the Lord. In the natural state, before regeneration, we are unlighted candles. We are candles, however, capable of being lighted; for God made us in His own image, though sin has put out the flame or left it only a smoking, smoldering spark. But a thousand unlighted candles in a dark room would not make the room light; so when we receive Christ into our hearts, the Holy Spirit touches these candles with the divine flame, and they begin to shine. Thus every believer becomes truly a candle of the Lord.

We must remember that we never can shine of ourselves; we are light only as we are lighted by the life of Christ in us. We are to let our light shine—that is, we are to keep the wick trimmed, so that the flame shall be always bright; and we are to keep the windows of our life clean, so that the beams may pour out without hindrance. We should also always be sure to have reserves of oil to replenish our lamps when they burn low; that is, we must live in constant communion with Christ, abiding in Him, that we may draw always from His fullness.

Then, each one in his own place, we must give light to their lives, and make the one little spot in this world that is close about us brighter and happier with love and grace. The great lighthouse lamp pours beams far out to sea, but it does not lighten the space around its base. Some people send brightness far away, preaching to the heathens and doing deeds which benefit the world, while they fail to brighten their own homes and the lives close beside them. We ought not to be such lights as these; while we send our influence abroad as far as possible, we should live so that we shall be blessings to those who are nearest to us.

◇

THE OLD TESTAMENT AND THE NEW

◇

I am not come to destroy, but to fulfil.
Matthew 5:17

There are not two Bibles in one. The Old Testament and the New are not two distinct books, but parts of the same. The New Testament does not set aside the Old, but is simply the rich, ripe harvest of which the Old was the sowing and the early sprouting. The gospel which we have in the New Testament is not a different religion from what we have in the Old Testament, but the same faith more fully developed, more clearly taught. In the Old Testament, Christ was foretold at times in prophetic promises, sometimes in pictures and types; in the New these promises are fulfilled, these pictures and types find their realization, and we see the Son of God walking among men in the beauty and glory of His incarnation.

The blossoms are not destroyed when they fall off and the fruit grows in their place; the ripe fruit is but the fulfillment of the promise and prophecy of the blossom. The artist's outline sketch is not destroyed when the splendid picture covers the canvas, hiding the first light tracings; the finished work of art is merely the completion, the filling out of the original drawing until in every feature life glows. Christ destroyed nothing of past divine revelation when He came. He was the warm summer, wooing the slumbering buds and dry roots, and bringing prophecies of life into full, luxurious growth. He was the great Master, taking the dim sketches and shadows of the Old Testament and filling them out in His own blessed life and death. So we ought not to discard our Old Testament as an antiquated book, of no value to us since we have the gospel. The Old Testament is full of precious truths. One of the strongest proofs of Christianity is the wonderful fulfillment of Old Testament prophecies in the life, sufferings, and death of Jesus Christ. Let us love the whole Bible; not one word of it is obsolete.

April 25

◇

PROMISES AND PROPHECIES

◇

*One jot or one tittle shall in no wise pass
from the law, till all be fulfilled.*
Matthew 5:18

Christ referred here primarily to the promises and prophecies of the Old Testament. There are thousands of blossoms on the trees in the springtime that never become fruits; but there are no lost blossoms on the Old Testament tree. The exact fulfillment of prophecy is irrefutable evidence of the truth of Christianity. But the assurance of these words refers also to every promise of the Scripture. Not the smallest of these shall ever fail anyone who trusts them. "No word he hath spoken shall ever be broken." Every pledge God has made He will surely keep. Whenever we find a divine word we may take hold of it with perfect confidence and know that we are clinging to a rock that never can be shaken. "For the mountains shall depart, and the hills be removed; but my kindness shall not depart from thee, neither shall the covenant of my peace be removed, saith the Lord that hath mercy on thee" (Isaiah 54:10).

This is true also of the divine threatenings against sin. Not one of these shall fail to be accomplished upon those who reject God's words of grace and mercy. Christ said, "He that believeth on the Son hath everlasting life"; and that word will prove true to every one who receives it. But He said also in the same sentence, "He that believeth not the Son shall not see life; but the wrath of God abideth on him" (John 3:36); and this word shall just as surely be fulfilled as the other. In these days when so many people hold liberal views of God's Word, it is right that we know deeply in our minds that whatever God says in the Holy Scriptures He says with authority—that His promises are sure as eternity itself, and that every sentence of His is absolutely irrepealable. "Only words," we sometimes say, as if words were unreal and unsubstantial; but the words of God are more real and substantial than even earth's great mountains.

◆

LITTLE SINS

◆

*Whosoever therefore shall break one of these least
commandments, and shall teach men so, he shall
be called the least in the kingdom of heaven.*
Matthew 5:19

A great many people are careful about breaking large commandments and committing grave sins, while they continually and without scruple break smaller commands. They would
not tell a direct lie for the world, but their speech is full of little
falsehoods. They would not take money from the pocket or draw-
er of another, and yet they continually commit small thefts. For
example, the grocer by mistake gives them too much change, and
they do not think of returning it. Through the carelessness of an
official the postage stamp on a letter is left uncanceled, and they
take it off and use it a second time. They would not try to blacken
a neighbor's name or destroy his character, yet they repeat to others the evil gossip about him which they have heard, and thus
soil his reputation. They would not swear or curse in the coarse
way of the street, but they are continually using words that are
mild, timid substitutes for profane oaths. They would not do fla-
grant acts of wickedness to disgrace themselves, but their lives are
honeycombed with all manner of unkindness, impurities, selfishness, and bad tempers.

We need to remember that little disobediences bring one
down to an inferior place in the kingdom of heaven. Little sins
mar the beauty of the character, and they are sure to grow. Oftentimes, too, they are infinite in their consequences. The little rift in
the lute widens and by and by destroys all the music. The trick-
ling leak in the dike becomes a torrent deluging vast plains. We
ought never to indulge even the smallest faults or evil habits but
should aim always at perfection. We ought to be satisfied with
nothing less than perfection in character, and perfection is made
up of obedience in trifles.

April 27

◇

TRUE RIGHTEOUSNESS

◇

*Except your righteousness shall exceed the righteousness
of the scribes and Pharisees, ye shall in no
case enter into the kingdom of heaven.*

Matthew 5:20

In place of abolishing or destroying the law, Jesus put new meaning into it. As He expounded it, it went far more deeply into people's lives than the Pharisees of His time had understood it to go. They had taught that a rigid external obedience was required; but Jesus told them that if this were all that was required they could not enter the kingdom. Instead of lowering the requirements of the divine law, He elevated them and gave them a new meaning. He said the righteousness of His followers must be a great deal better than that of the average professors of religion in His day. They had a sound creed and were scrupulous in the observance of the ten thousand minor rules about ceremony, dress, attitude, and devout manners; but their lives were full of hardness, pride, selfishness, and hypocrisies.

Jesus said that unless His disciples had a better righteousness than these orthodox Jews had, they would never get into the family of God. We ought to apply this truth very carefully. Uniting with the church does not make one a Christian. The careful observance of all the ordinances and rules of the church is not being good. There must be faith, love, dutiful obedience, submission. Christ demands in His followers a high standard of morality. In place of mere external and formal obedience, the law is written on the heart of the true believer, and he obeys it from within. We should strive to make our obedience so deep and so loyal that our lives will reflect in every feature the radiancy of Christ.

◇

ANGRY WITHOUT CAUSE

◇

*Whosoever is angry with his brother without a
cause shall be in danger of the judgment.*
Matthew 5:22

We ought to learn to read the commandments within the light of our Lord's teachings. So long as the sixth commandment is interpreted to mean only actual murder, most people get along well with it; they are not troubled in their consciences about its violation. There are not many literal murderers loose in our Sunday schools and churches, or living in our homes. But when we hear our Lord's interpretation of this commandment, and learn that this literal sense does not exhaust the meaning of the commandment—that we break it, too, when we are angry with a brother—we cannot be quite so sure about our innocence. We have never killed anyone, but have we never been angry with another? Elsewhere we read, "Whosoever hateth his brother is a murderer" (1 John 3:15). This does not mean that hatred is as great a crime as murder, but that it grows from the same root and is of the same nature. *Murder is only anger full-grown.*

The Master's words here should be carefully considered. They condemn all self-centered anger against another, all expressions of scorn or contempt. The obedience of this commandment which our Lord requires is: love that thinks no evil, that cherishes no resentment, that is patient, gentle, thoughtful, reverent, unselfish. Yet are we not all too apt to allow the passion of anger to take possession of our breasts? Do we not too frequently permit envyings and jealousies and unkind and uncharitable thoughts to enter our hearts and nest there, like evil birds? If we but remembered that the spirit of murder is in all these emotions, we surely would not cherish them for an instant; none of us want the mark of murderer upon us. The way to keep such feelings away is to yield to every gentle and loving impulse of the Spirit—to "overcome evil with good."

ACCEPTABLE WORSHIP

*If thou bring thy gift to the altar, and there rememberest
that thy brother hath ought against thee; leave there thy
gift before the altar, and go thy way; first be reconciled
to thy brother, and then come and offer thy gift.*

Matthew 5:23–24

There is something to do before we kneel down to pray in privacy, or begin to worship in the sanctuary, or come to the Lord's table. There ought to be a look inward at our own hearts before the look upward at the face of God. Are we ready to pray? Are the obstructions out of the way? Is our heart ready for worship? *The worship that pleases God the best is love in the heart.* He has no pleasure in sacrifices and ceremonies and ordinances while the heart is full of bitterness. He cares nothing for our professions of love to Him so long as we hate our brother. "If a man say, I love God, and hateth his brother, he is a liar: for he that loveth not his brother whom he hath seen, how can he love God whom he hath not seen?" (1 John 4:20).

If, therefore, we want our worship to be acceptable to God, we must be sure to come into His presence with hearts cleansed of all bitterness, wrath, anger, envy, and all malice. Thus every approach to God in prayer requires self-examination; and if we can remember that we have wronged anyone, or that there is any jealousy or strife, we should seek reconciliation before we pray. At least we must see that our own spirits are thoroughly cleansed of all bitterness before we come to God's altar. This rule is made to keep our hearts always free from anger. Paul counsels that we should not let the sun go down upon our wrath. No day should be allowed to close with anger in our hearts. We may never see another day, and we should not lie down to sleep cherishing bitterness against any other. The evening prayer should cleanse our spirits of all feelings of anger, as we pray, "Forgive us our trespasses, as we forgive those who trespass against us."

April 30

TRUE CHARITY

*When thou doest alms, let not thy left hand
know what thy right hand doeth.*

Matthew 6:3

There are some people who want every good thing they do well advertised. If they give money to some good cause, they want to have it publicized. If they are kind to the poor or relieve some case of distress, they are particular that the matter should be broadcast. They take pains that their charities shall not fail to be credited to themselves. But this is not the kind of spirit our Lord taught to His disciples. He told them that seeking attention marred the beauty of their good deeds; that instead of announcing to all men what they had done, they should not even let their own left hand know that their right hand had been doing commendable deeds.

Of course Christ did not mean that we should not be good in front of people—that we should never give of our resources except where the act would be absolutely secret. It is the motive that Christ was concerned about. His disciples should never give for the sake of men's praise.

Religious acts instantly lose all their value when any motive but the honor of God and the desire for His approval is in our heart. We should not even ourselves think about our good deeds, but should forget them as the tree forgets the fruit it drops. We should train ourselves therefore to do our good deeds without seeking praises or recognition of men. We should not be so anxious to have our card tacked on every gift we send. We ought to be willing to do good and let Christ have all the glory, while we stay in the background unknown and unrecognized. Florence Nightingale, having gone like an angel of mercy among the hospitals during the Crimean War until her name was enshrined in every soldier's heart, asked to be excused from having her picture taken, that she might be forgotten, and that Christ alone might be remembered as the author of all the blessings which her hand had distributed.

May 1

SECRET PRAYER

When thou prayest, enter into thy closet, and when thou hast shut thy door, pray to thy Father which is in secret.
Matthew 6:6

One of the most important things we ever do in this world is praying. No business transacted anywhere so deeply touches the interests of our lives. We ought therefore to learn to pray correctly so as to be sure of an answer. We ought to be eager to get every small fragment of instruction about prayer.

Here we have one of our Lord's plainest and most significant instructions about the manner and the nature of prayer. He is speaking, not of public prayer, as when the minister leads the congregation, but of personal prayer, when the child of God wants to talk to his Father of his own affairs, and lay at His feet his own individual burdens. We should seek to be alone in all praying such as this. Other presences about us disturb our thoughts and restrict our freedom. We are to go into our closet and shut the door.

This shutting of the door is significant in several ways. It shuts the world out. It secures us against interruption. It ought to shut out worldly thoughts and cares and distractions, as well as worldly presences. Wandering in prayer is usually one of our chief troubles. Then it shuts us in, and this also is important and significant. It shuts us in alone with God. No eye but His sees us as we bow in secrecy. No ear but His hears us as we pour out our heart's needs and desires. Thus we are helped to realize that with God alone we are responsible, that He alone can help us. As we are shut up alone with God, so also are we shut up to God. There is precious comfort in the assurance that when we pray we are not talking into the air. There is an ear to hear, though we can see no presence, and it is the ear of our Father. This assures us of loving regard in heaven, also of prompt and gracious answers.

May 2

"OUR FATHER"

Our Father which art in heaven.
Matthew 6:9

This is the golden gate of the temple of prayer. When our Lord taught His disciples how to pray, it was in this way He said they should begin. They were not to come merely to infinite power, or to unknowable mystery, or to inaccessible light, but to fatherhood. This precious name at the gateway makes the approach easy.

The name assures us of love and care. Does a true parent care for a child? Much more does our Father in heaven care for His children on the earth. He cares even for the birds, seeing that they get their daily food. He cares for the flowers, weaving with threads of light the lovely robes they wear. He surely cares more for His children. So the precious name assures us that we shall never be neglected or overlooked in this great world.

It gives us assurance also of unhindered access to the divine presence. The children of a great king are not kept waiting at their father's door as strangers are. God's children have perfect liberty in His presence. They can never come at an untimely hour. He is never too busy to see them and to listen to their words of love and prayer. In the midst of the affairs of the vast universe He thinks of His humblest child in this great world and, amid all its confusion and noise, hears and recognizes the faintest cry that rises from the lips of the least and lowliest of His little ones.

This name interprets also for us the grace and mercy of our God. We are always conscious of sin. How, then, can we gain access to a holy God? He is our Father. We know that even an earthly father does not shut the door on his disobedient child. The candle is left burning in the window through the long dark nights that the wanderer, out in the blackness and longing to return, seeing the bright beams, may be assured of love and a waiting welcome. Infinitely more gracious is our Father in heaven.

GLORIFYING GOD

Hallowed be thy name.
Matthew 6:9

While the name "Father" over the gate of prayer assures us of loving welcome and of all tenderness, thoughtfulness, and care, the words "which art in heaven" remind us of the surpassing glory and majesty of God. We should not rush into His presence as we do into the presence of an earthly parent. We should remember His infinite greatness and holiness, and should come always with reverence. His is a name to be hallowed. "Holy and reverend is His name" (Psalm 111:9). This petition reminds us of this. It checks the flow of our thoughts and feelings, and bids us approach God with a suitable sense of our unworthiness and of His holiness. It calls us to be reverent though bold.

This is a prayer for the glorifying of God in this world. When we pray it we must be sure that we do our part in making His name hallowed. We can do this by our own reverent use of that holy name. Good Christian people sometimes grow very careless in speaking of God. They become so accustomed to using His name in prayer and speech that they utter it as lightly as if it were the name of some familiar friend. I have seen a miner with black, grimy hand pluck a pure flower from the stem, and it seemed profane. But what shall we say of our own taking on our sin-defiled lips the holy and awful name of God? We ought to learn to hallow that blessed name in our speech.

Then we should hallow it in our lives. We are God's children, and we bear His name. How may a child honor a parent's name? Only by a life worthy of that parent. We must take heed, therefore, that in every act of ours—in our behavior, in our whole character and influence—we live so that all who see us shall see in us something of the beauty of God. It would be a sad thing, indeed, if we gave people a wrong idea of God or of the religion of Jesus Christ.

May 4

◇

HEAVEN BROUGHT TO US

◇

Thy kingdom come.
Matthew 6:10

This is a very comprehensive prayer. It pleads for the extension of God's spiritual realm in this world—His power over men's hearts and lives, the subjugation of earth's kingdoms to His sway. It is a prayer that men may be better—that they may put away their sins and amend their lives; that they may take Christ as their king and yield every thought and desire to Him. It is not a longing to be lifted away to heaven, but a craving that heaven may be brought to us, into our hearts and lives.

We are in danger of thinking too much of other people and the coming of God's kingdom into other hearts and lives as we offer this prayer. *The little plots of earth for which we are first responsible are those which lie within our own hearts and lives.* While then we pray "Thy kingdom come," we should look within ourselves to see if we have submitted to the reign of Christ.

> *Thy kingdom here?*
> *Lord, can it be?*
> *Searching and seeking everywhere*
> *For many a year,*
> *"Thy kingdom come" has been my prayer;*
> *Was that dear kingdom all the while so near?*
>
> *Was I the bar*
> *Which shut me out*
> *From the full joyance which they taste*
> *Whose spirits are*
> *Within thy Paradise embraced—*
> *Thy blessed Paradise, which seemed so far?*
>
> *Let me not sit*
> *Another hour*
> *Idly waiting what is mine to win,*
> *Blinded in wit.*
> *Lord Jesus, rend these walls of self and sin;*
> *Beat down the gate, that I may enter in.*

May 5
◇
DOING THE WILL OF GOD
◇

Thy will be done in earth, as it is in heaven.
Matthew 6:10

Many people always quote this petition as if it meant only submission to some painful providence. They suppose it refers only to losing friends or money, or being sick or in trouble. But this is only a little part of its meaning. It is for the doing of God's will, not the suffering of it, that we here pray.

It is a good deal easier to say prayers like this for others than for ourselves. We all think other people ought to do God's will, and we do not find it a difficult prayer to make that they may do so. But what about ourselves? There is no other person in the world for whose life we are really and finally responsible but one-self. This prayer, then, if we offer it sincerely, is that we may do God's will as it is done in heaven. We can pray it, therefore, only when we are ready for implicit, unquestioning obedience to the divine will the moment we know what that will is.

Then sometimes it is a passive doing that is required. God asks of us something that costs pain or sacrifice or earthly loss; when this is true, our prayer may cut deeply into our own hearts. It may mean a giving up of some sweet joy, a losing of some precious friend, the sacrifice of some dear possession, walking in the way of thorns and tears. We should learn always to say the prayer, and then to hold our lives close to the line of the divine will, never rebelling nor murmuring, but sweetly doing whatever God gives us to do.

> *He always wins who sides with God,*
> *To him no chance is lost;*
> *God's will is sweetest to him when*
> *It triumphs at his cost.*
>
> *Ill that He blesses is our good,*
> *And unblest good is ill;*
> *And all is right that seems most wrong,*
> *If it be his sweet will.*

May 6

◇

DAY BY DAY

◇

Give us this day our daily bread.
Matthew 6:11

This seems a very small thing to ask—only bread for a day. Why are we not taught to pray for bread enough to last a week, or a month, or a year? For one thing, Jesus wanted to teach us a lesson of continual dependence. He taught us to come each morning with a request simply for the day's food, that we might never feel we can get along without our Father. Another lesson He wanted to teach us was that the true way to live is by the day. We are not to be anxious even about the supply of tomorrow's needs. When tomorrow comes it will be right for us to take up its cares. The same great lesson was taught in the way the manna was given—just a day's portion at a time.

> *Make a little fence of trust*
> *Around today;*
> *Fill the space with loving work,*
> *And therein stay.*
> *Look not through the sheltering bars*
> *Upon tomorrow;*
> *God will help thee bear what comes*
> *Of joy or sorrow.*

We should not overlook the word "us." It is plural and calls us to pray beyond our own individual needs and remember God's other children. This should always be a prayer for daily bread for our hungry neighbor as well as for ourself. Then while we enjoy our own plenty, we must share with those who have need.

> *This crust is My body broken for thee,*
> *This water His blood that died on the tree;*
> *The holy Supper is kept, indeed,*
> *In whatso we share with another's need—*
> *Not that which we give, but what we share—*
> *For the gift without the giver is bare:*
> *Who bestows himself with his alms feeds three—*
> *Himself, his hungering neighbor, and Me.*

May 7

A FORGIVING SPIRIT

Forgive us our debts, as we forgive our debtors.
Matthew 6:12

The first part of this petition is not so hard to say. Most people are willing to confess, at least in a general way, that they are debtors to God, that they have sinned. But the second part is harder to repeat. When someone has caused us an injury, and we are feeling bitter over it, it is not so easy to ask God to forgive us as we forgive. Perhaps we do not forgive at all but keep the bitter feeling in our heart against our brother. What is it, then, that we ask God to do for us when we pray, "Forgive us as we forgive"? God has linked blessing and duty together in this petition. If we will not forgive those who have wronged us, it is evident that we have not the spirit of repentance to which God grants remission of sins. If we would enjoy the sweet peace of God in our own breasts, we must keep our minds free from all bitterness and anger and all feelings of unforgiveness.

> *Forgive us, Lord, because we have forgiven,*
> *Not as we have forgiven, is our prayer—*
> *Earth is so lower far than highest heaven,*
> *Man is not even as the angels are,*
> *And thou to angels art as sun to star;*
> *Measure thy pity not in our poor scale,*
> *But in thine own which weighs eternities.*
> *We do our little part, we strive, we fail,*
> *Our wine of charity has bitter lees;*
> *Our best unselfishness seeks self to please;*
> *Our purest gold with base alloy is dim;*
> *Our fairest fruit hangs tainted on the tree;*
> *Our sweetest songs heard by the seraphim*
> *Would all discordant and unlovely be,*
> *Save for the charity they learn from thee.*
> *But thou canst pour forgiveness with a word,*
> *O'er countless worlds an all-embracing ray,*
> *Beyond our hopes, our best deserving, Lord,*
> *Forgive us, then, and we in our poor way*
> *Shall catch thy higher meaning as we pray.*

ENDURING TEMPTATION

Lead us not into temptation, but deliver us from evil.
Matthew 6:13

It is impossible to live in this world and escape temptation. In old times men fled from active life and from human companionship, hoping to evade enticement to evil. But they were not successful; for wherever they went they carried in their own hearts a fountain of corruption, and were often exposed to temptation. The only door of escape from all temptation is the door that leads into heaven. We grieve over our friends whom the Lord calls away—the little child in its sweet innocence, the mother in her growing saintliness, the young man in his pride of youth; but do we ever think that we have far more reason for anxiety, possibly for grief, over those who live and have to battle with sin in this world? Those who have come inside, in the victorious attainment of Christian faith, are forever secure; but those yet in the great battle are still in peril.

This petition is a prayer that we may never be called needlessly to meet temptation. Sometimes God wants us to be tried, because we can grow strong only through victory. We have a word of Scripture which says: "Blessed is the man that endureth temptation: for when he is tried, he shall receive the crown of life" (James 1:12). Yet we ought never ourselves to seek any way of life in which we shall have to be exposed to the peril of conflict with sin. Temptation is too terrible an experience, filled with too much danger, to be sought by us, or ever encountered save when God leads us in the path on which it lies. We must never rush unbidden or unsent into any spiritual danger. There are no promises for presumption. "It is written," said the Master, "Thou shalt not tempt the Lord thy God" (Matthew 4:7). When God sends us into danger, we are under His protection; when we go where He does not send us, we go unsheltered.

May 9

THE LOVE OF MONEY

Ye cannot serve God and mammon.
Matthew 6:24

We had better look very carefully into the meaning of these words, remembering that it was our blessed Lord who spoke them. Mammon means riches. To serve means to be the slave of. St. Paul loved to call himself the servant or slave of Christ. Now Jesus says here that we cannot be God's slave and mammon's slave too. We cannot belong to any two masters at the same time. If we are mammon's slave, that ends it—we are not God's. If we belong to God, mammon is not our master. Think, too, what a degrading thing it is for anyone bearing the image of God to be the slave of money. To use the word "serve" in its mildest English sense, no man should ever be the servant of money. Riches are meant to be a person's slave; now think how degrading it would be for any person to become servant or slave to his own slave. A person should be ashamed to call riches his master.

Money is meant to be a person's servant, and so long as he is its perfect master, it may be a blessing to him and an instrument with which he may do great good. But when he gets down on his knees to it, and crawls in the dust for its sake, and sells his soul to get it, it is only a curse to him. Thus it is easy to see why anyone who serves God cannot serve mammon. God must have all of your heart and must rule in all of your life. He will not share His throne with the god of gold. God's true servants may have money, and may even be very rich; but they must use their money as a means for honoring God and blessing the world in Christ's name. They must own the money; the money must not own them. They must carry it in their hands, not in their hearts. This is a very important thing for us to learn. Many Christian people are in danger of forsaking the sweet, blessed service of Christ for the slavish service of mammon.

ANXIOUS THOUGHT

Therefore I say unto you, Take no thought for your life.
Matthew 6:25

Of course we are to take thought in a true sense. Why were we made with brains if we are not to think with them? It would be as if God told us not to walk after He had given us feet, or not to talk after giving us tongues. We are to train our minds and to think with them, and think about the future too, laying plans with long foresight into the years before us. It is not fore-thought that is forbidden, but anxious thought, worry, fear.

We shall see as we go on just what we are to do instead of being anxious. At present let us get the simple lesson that we are never to be anxious. This is not a rule with exceptions. It is not a bit of creed that will not work in life. It is a lesson that we are to strive to carry out in all our days, however full they may be of things calculated to distract us.

But why are we to take no thought? The "therefore" helps us to the answer: "Ye cannot serve God and mammon. Therefore . . . take no thought." So, then, taking thought seems to be serving mammon. We say we are God's children, and yet when mammon seems in danger of failing us we get anxious. Practically, then, we trust mammon more than we trust our Father. We feel safer when mammon's abundance fills our hands than when mammon threatens to fail and we have only God. That is, we trust God and mammon. Anxiety about the supply of our needs is therefore distrust of our heavenly Father. If we serve God only, we should not worry, though we do not even have bread for tomorrow; we should believe in our Father's love. Money we may lose any day, for "riches . . . make themselves wings; they fly away as an eagle toward heaven" (Proverbs 23:5); but we never can lose God. Nothing can rob us of His love, nor rob Him of the abundance He possesses from which to meet our needs. So if we trust God we should never be anxious, though we have nothing else.

May 11

❖

A LESSON OF TRUST

❖

Behold the fowls of the air . . . your heavenly Father
feedeth them. Are ye not much better than they?
Matthew 6:26

Are we to draw the inference that since birds neither sow nor reap, we should put forth no exertions to provide for our own wants? No: if we did nothing to earn our own bread we should soon starve. God would not feed us as He feeds the birds. He has given us powers by which we can make provision for our own wants; He feeds us, not by bringing the bread to us, but by making us able to sow and reap and gather into barns. God nowhere encourages that "trust" which idly sits down and waits to be cared for. Little babies, and sick and feeble people, and any who are incapacitated for exertion, may live as the birds do, and may expect to be cared for. But hearty people, with active minds and strong hands, will fare very poorly if they try to live the birds' way.

The point of the illustration lies elsewhere. God's care extends even to birds. There are two reasons, then, why it will more certainly extend to His people. First, they are better than birds. Birds have no souls, do not bear the divine image, have no spiritual nature, cannot worship nor voluntarily serve God, have no future or immortal life. The God who cares for a little soulless bird will surely care much more thoughtfully for a thinking, immortal, godlike man.

Then the other reason is that God is our Father. He is the creator and provider for the birds, but not their Father. Surely a father will do more for his children than for his chickens; a mother will give more thought to her baby than to her canary. Will not our heavenly Father provide more certainly and more tenderly for His children than for His birds? So from the birds we get a lesson of trust. Every little bird sitting on its bough, or singing its sweet song, ought to lead us to renewed confidence in the care of our Father.

May 12

◇

USELESS ANXIETIES

◇

*Which of you by taking thought can
add one cubit unto his stature?*
Matthew 6:27

It is useless to worry. A short person cannot, by any amount of anxiety, make himself an inch taller. Why, therefore, should he waste his energy and fret his life away in wishing he were an inch taller? One worries because he is too short, another because he is too fat; one because he has a lame foot, another because he has a mole on his face. No amount of fretting will change any of these things. People worry, too, over their circumstances. They are poor and have to work hard. They have troubles, losses, and disappointments which come through causes entirely beyond their own control. They find difficulties in their environment which they cannot overcome. There are hard conditions in their lot which they cannot change.

Now why should they worry about these things? Will worrying make matters any better? Will discontentment cure the lame foot, or remove the ugly mole, or reduce obesity, or put flesh on a thin body? Will complaining make the hard work lighter, or the burdens easier, or the troubles fewer? Will anxiety keep the winter away, or the storm from rising, or put coal in the cellar, or bread in the pantry, or get clothes for the children? Even wise philosophy shows the uselessness of worrying, since worrying helps nothing, and it only wastes one's strength and unfits one for doing one's best. Then religion goes further, and says that even the hard things and the obstacles are blessings, if we meet them in the right spirit—stepping stones lifting our feet upward, disciplinary experiences in which we grow. So we learn that we should quietly and with faith accept life as it comes to us, fretting at nothing, changing hard conditions to easier if we can; if we cannot, then using them as means for growth and advancement.

◇

LESSONS FROM THE FLOWERS

◇

Why take ye thought for raiment? Consider the
lilies of the field. . . . Even Solomon . . .
was not arrayed like one of these.
Matthew 6:28–29

Without any toiling or spinning on their own part, God clothes the flowers in loveliness far surpassing any adornment which the most skillful human arts can provide. Flowers bloom but a day and fade. We are better than flowers. If our Father lavishes so much beauty on perishing plants, is there any danger that He will not provide clothing for His own?

Of course it is not implied that like the lilies we need neither toil nor spin. It is all right for lilies just to stand still and grow. That is their mission; that is the way God made them to grow. But He gave us hands, feet, brains, tongue, energy, and will; and if we would be cared for as are the flowers, we must exert our energies to produce the results of comfort. Yet Jesus tells us to consider the lilies, how they grow. We ought to study the beautiful things in nature and learn lessons from them. Here is a lesson of contentment we are to learn. Who ever heard a lily complaining about its circumstances? It accepts the conditions in which it finds itself and makes the best of them. It drinks in heaven's sweet light, air, dew, and rain, and unfolds its own loveliness in quietness and peace.

The lily grows from within. We should grow this way, having within us the divine life, to be developed in our character and spirit. The lily is an emblem of beauty; our spiritual life should unfold likewise in all lovely ways. It is a picture of perfect peace. Who ever saw wrinkles of anxiety in a lily's face? God wants us to grow into peace. The lily is fragrant; so should our lives be. The lily sometimes grows in the black bog, but it remains unspotted. So should we live in this world, keeping ourselves unspotted amid its evil. These are a few of the lessons from the lily.

◇

GOD WILL PROVIDE

◇

Seek ye first the kingdom of God, and his righteousness;
and all these things shall be added unto you.

Matthew 6:33

We are to take no thought for our own life, for food or clothing, because that is God's part, not ours. There is one thing, however, for which we are to take thought, not anxious but very earnest thought. We are to think about our duty, about doing God's will and filling our place in God's world.

We ought to get this very clearly in our mind. Too many people worry far more about their food and clothes, lest they shall be left to want, than they do about doing well their whole duty. That is, they are more anxious about God's part in their lives than they are about their own. They fear God may not take care of them, but they do not have any fear that they may fail in fidelity to Him. We ought to learn well that providing for our wants is God's business, not ours. We have nothing at all to do with it. But we have everything to do with our own duty, our appointed work, the doing of God's will. God will never do these things for us. If we do not do them, they must remain undone; if we do them with fidelity, God will care for us.

The noblest life possible in this world is simple consecration to Christ and to duty, with no anxiety about anything else. We may not always be fed luxuriously, nor be clothed in scarlet and fine linen; yet food convenient for us will always be provided, and clothing sufficient to keep us warm. But suppose we are near starving! Well, we must just go on doing our part and not worrying; in due time, somehow, God will provide. Here we have our Lord's own promise of this. The truth is, too many of us take a great deal more thought about our support than about our duty. Then of course we forfeit the promise and may suffer. How much better the other way—ours the doing, God's the providing.

May 15

ONE DAY AT A TIME

Take . . . no thought for the morrow: for the
morrow shall take thought for the things of itself.
Matthew 6:34

This last reason our Lord gives against anxiety for the future is that we have nothing to do with the future. God gives us life by days, little single days. Each day has its own duties, its own needs, its own trials and temptations, its own griefs and sorrows. God always gives us strength enough for the day as He gives it with all that He puts into it. But if we insist on pulling back tomorrow's cares and piling them on top of today's, the strength will not be enough for the load. God will not add strength just to humor our whims of anxiety and distrust.

So the lesson is that we should keep each day unique and attend strictly to what it brings us. Charles Kingsley says: "Do today's duty, fight today's temptation, and do not weaken and distract yourself by looking forward to things which you cannot see, and could not understand if you saw them." We really have nothing at all to do with the future, except to prepare for it by doing with fidelity the duties of today.

No one was ever crushed by the burdens of one day. We can always get along with our heaviest load till the sun goes down; that is all we ever have to do. Tomorrow? Oh, you may have no tomorrow; you may be in heaven. If you are here God will be here too, and you will receive new strength sufficient for the new day.

> One day at a time. A burden too great
> > To be borne for two can be borne for one;
> Who knows what will enter tomorrow's gate:
> > While yet we are speaking all may be done.
>
> One day at a time—but a single day,
> > Whatever its load, whatever its length;
> And there's a bit of precious Scripture to say
> > That according to each shall be our strength.

May 16

JUDGING OF OTHERS

Judge not, that ye be not judged.
Matthew 7:1

Few faults are more common than this judging of others. It would not be so bad if we were inclined to look at people charitably, but we are not. Our eyes are far keener for seeking flaws and blemishes than marks of beauty. Not many of us are forever finding new features of loveliness in others; not a few of us can find an indefinite number of faults. If we were ourselves up to the standard whereby we judge others, we should be very saintly people. If we were free from all the faults we so readily see when they appear in our neighbor, we would be nearly faultless.

This word of our Lord not only instructs us not to be critical of others and judgmental, but it presents the strongest kind of motive against such judging. It makes the appeal to our own interest. Others will return to us just what we gave to them in terms of judgment. None of us like other people to be critical and fault-finding toward us. We wince under unjust judgments. We resent unfair remarks. We demand that people shall judge us fairly. We ask for forbearance and charity in our failures in duty and for blemishes in our character. Can we expect other people to be any more lenient toward us than we are toward them?

If we wish to receive positive judgment from others, we must give the same to them. If we criticize another today in a harsh manner, we need not be surprised if we hear someone's harsh criticism of us tomorrow. But if, on the other hand, we speak kind, appreciative, and charitable words of someone today, very likely we shall hear tomorrow some pleasant word that another has said of us. So we make the music or the discord for our own hearts. We get back what we give. We gather the harvest of our own sowing. Then, even in the last judgment, we shall receive from the Judge what we have shown to others.

---◇---

FINDING FAULT WITH OTHERS

---◇---

Why beholdest thou the mote that is in thy brother's eye,
but considerest not the beam that is in thine own eye?
Matthew 7:3

It is strange how oblivious we can be of our own faults and blemishes, and how clearly we can see those of other people. A man can see a little speck of dust in his neighbor's eye while utterly unaware of the great beam in his own eye. He observes the most minute fault in his brother while unconscious of his own far greater fault.

We would say that a beam in a man's eye would so blind him that he could not see the mote in another's eye. As our Lord represents it, however, the man with the beam is the very one who sees the mote and thinks himself competent to pull it out. So it is in morals. No man is so sharp at seeing a fault in another as he who has the same or a similar fault of his own. A vain man is the first to detect the signs of vanity in another. A bad-tempered person is most apt to be judgmental toward a neighbor who displays bad temper. One with a sharp uncontrolled tongue has the least patience with another whose speech is full of poisoned arrows. A selfish woman discovers streaks of selfishness in others. Rude people are the very first to be hurt and offended by rudeness in a neighbor.

It is always this way. If we are quick to perceive blemishes and faults in others, the probability is that we have far greater blemishes and faults in ourselves. This truth ought to make us exceedingly careful in our judgments and exceedingly modest in our expressions of criticism, for we really are telling the world our own faults. It is wiser, as well as more in accordance with the spirit of Christ, for us to find lovely things in others and to be silent regarding their faults.

May 18

A Self-Righteous Spirit

Or how wilt thou say to thy brother, Let me pull out the mote out of thine eye; and, behold, a beam is in thine own eye?
Matthew 7:4

But is it not a kindness to a friend to take the mote out of his eye? If we met a neighbor with a cinder in his eye, would it not be a brotherly thing to stop and take it out for him? Then why is it not just as true a kindness to want to cure another's fault, even though we have the same fault in ourselves? If we did it in the right spirit it would be. We are bound to seek the welfare of our friends in every possible way, and therefore, if we discover in them things that mar their beauty, we should seek the removal of those things.

But the trouble is we are not apt to look at our neighbor's faults in this loving and sympathetic way. To begin with, we do not know, or at least we do not confess, that we ourselves have beams in our own eyes; we are not even aware that there are motes in our own eyes. It is the self-righteous spirit that our Lord is condemning here. A man holds up his hands in horror at the speck he has found in his neighbor's character; and his neighbor, looking up, sees in him an immensely magnified copy of the speck. Will the neighbor be greatly benefitted by the rebuke?

Suppose a bad-tempered man lectures us on the sin of giving in to bad temper, or a dishonest man on some apparent lack of honesty, or a liar on the wickedness of falsehood, or a bad-mannered person on some discourtesy of ours, or a hypocrite on insincerity. What good will such lectures do, even admitting that we are conscious of these faults? We are only irritated by the unfitness of such rebukes from those in whom the faults are ten times greater than in us. We wonder how people can have the nerve to talk about motes in our eyes when huge beams project from their own eyes. Truly this is not the way to tell others of their faults.

May 19

◆

BEGIN AT HOME

◆

First cast out the beam out of thine own eye; and then shalt thou see clearly to cast out the mote out of thy brother's eye.
Matthew 7:5

Begin at home—that is the teaching; not at home in the general sense, with other members of your family, but very close to home, with yourself. It is a good deal easier, of course, to pull motes out of other people's eyes than beams out of one's own. Yet we are not put in this world to look after other people's faults, to pick the dust out of their eyes, to remove their specks of error. Our first business is to get rid of our own faults. At least we are scarcely competent to take the grain of dust out of another's eye while a beam protrudes from our own. We are not ready to do much toward curing our friend of his faults until we have sincerely tried to rid ourselves of our own.

We all know people whose very presence is a silent rebuke of sin. Their lives are pure and holy, and their unconscious influence is a restraint upon all evil. We are oftentimes told that one of the truest tests of a good friendship is that our friend can tell us of our faults and we shall receive it kindly. That depends first on ourselves, and then upon our friend. If we are proud and vain, it will be very hard for any friend, the wisest and gentlest, to speak to us about our faults, save at the peril of the friendship. Then if the friend treats our faults in a conceited and judgmental way, it will be equally dangerous. He who would truly help to take the motes out of our eyes must come to us in tender love, proving his generous and unselfish interest in us. He must come to us humbly, not as our judge but as our brother, with faults like our own which he is trying to cure. If he approaches us in this way, conscious of his own weaknesses, desiring to be helpful to us, as Christ has been helpful to him, nothing but unpardonable vanity and self-conceit will prevent our accepting his kind offer.

THE PRAYER PROMISE

◇

*Every one that asketh receiveth; and he that seeketh
findeth; and to him that knocketh it shall be opened.*
Matthew 7:8

These are very positive promises, and yet they must be read insightfully, in the light of other Scriptures which explain and qualify the words. It is not every request that receives; for there is asking that is not true prayer. Some ask merely in word, with no real desire in their hearts. Some ask selfishly, that they may consume the divine gift on their lusts. Some ask rebelliously, without submission to the will of God. Some ask without faith, not expecting any answer. Some ask in a lazy fashion, not ready to do their own part. Some ask ignorantly for things which would not be blessings if they were granted. It is very clear that in these cases those who ask will not receive.

So not literally all who seek find. The seeking must be earnest. There is a remarkable word in one of the old prophets: "Ye shall seek me, and find me, when ye shall search for me with all your heart" (Jeremiah 29:13). The seeking must also be for good things. If our quest is for sinful things or for worldly goods that would work spiritual harm in us, God will not give us what we seek. Then we must live right. "No good thing will he withhold from them that walk uprightly" (Psalm 84:11). The request itself must be good; and we must walk in paths of obedience, or there is no promise of reward for our quest.

In the same way, it is not to all knocking that God opens the door. There are timid knocks that indicate neither desire nor faith, as when mischievous children ring a doorbell and then run away, not wanting to enter. It is when we knock at the right door and knock with expectancy and faith and persistence, that the door is graciously opened. Thus in interpreting this wonderful prayer promise we must read into the words their true meaning. The asking, seeking, and knocking must be true prayer.

"GOOD THINGS" FROM GOD

*If ye then, being evil, know how to give good gifts unto
your children, how much more shall your Father
which is in heaven give good things to them that ask him?*
Matthew 7:11

N o father will answer his hungry child's cry for bread with a
stone, or give the child a serpent if he asks for a fish. Even
sinful parents have in their hearts something of the image of
God's own fatherhood. The argument is from the less to the
greater. If a true earthly father, with all his imperfection, will not
ignore a child's cry, but will respond lovingly, how much more
will our Father in heaven do for us?

"How much more?" is a question no one can answer. We can
only say that the heavenly Father is more loving, and wiser, and
more able to give, than is the earthly father. Yet we must explain
this promise also by other Scriptures. The gate of prayer is set
very wide open in this verse, yet those who would enter must
come in the right way and seek "good" things.

While no one who asks for bread will receive a stone, neither will one who asks for a stone receive a stone. And many
times we come to God pleading with Him to let us have a stone.
Of course we imagine it is bread, and that it will be food to us. It
is some earthly thing, some gift of honor or pleasure, some
achievement of ambition, some object of our heart's desire. It
looks like bread to our deluded vision. But God knows it is only a
cold stone—that it would leave us starving if we were to receive
it; and He loves us too well to listen to our weak cries for it, or to
be moved by our intensity or our tears to give it to us. When we
ask for a stone He will give us bread. For this reason many
requests for earthly things are not granted. Yet the prayers are not
unanswered. Instead of the stone we wish, God gives us the bread
we need. We do not always know what is bread and what is a
stone, and we must leave to God the final decision in all our
prayers.

OUR DUTY TO OTHERS

*All things whatsoever ye would that men
should do to you, do ye even so to them.*
Matthew 7:12

This is a wonderfully comprehensive rule of action. It calls us to consider the interest of others as well as our own. It asks us to set our neighbor alongside ourself, and think of him as having the same rights as we have, and requiring from us the same treatment that we give to ourself. It gives us a standard by which to test all our motives and all our conduct bearing on others.

We should at once in our thoughts change places with the person toward whom duty is to be determined and ask, "If he were where I am, and I were where he is, how should I want him to treat me in this case?" The application of this rule would instantly put a stop to all rash, hasty actions; for it commands us to consider our neighbor and question our own heart before doing anything. It would stifle all selfishness; for it compels us to regard our neighbor's interest as precisely equal to our own. It would lead us to honor others; for it puts us and them on the same platform.

The application of this rule would put a stop to all injustice and wrong; for none of us would do injustice or wrong to ourselves, and we are to treat our neighbor as if he were ourself. It would lead us to seek the highest good of all other men, even the lowliest; for we certainly want all men to seek our good. The thorough application of this Golden Rule would end all conflict between ownership and laborers; for it would give the employer a deep, loving interest in the men he employs and lead him to think of their good in all ways. It would also give to every employee a desire for the prosperity of his employer and an interest in his business. It would end all strife in families, in communities, among nations. The perfect working of this rule everywhere would bring heaven here; for the will of God would then "be done on earth, as it is in heaven."

TWO ROADS AND TWO GATES

Enter ye in at the strait gate.
Matthew 7:13

All truly valuable things cost much. Such a glorious privilege as the Christian's, therefore, cannot be gotten without effort. To open the way, and to purchase for us the privilege of becoming children of God, the Son of God had to come from heaven in love and give His own life. Jesus said, too, that any who would reach the glory of His kingdom must go by the same way of the cross. He said that he who will save his life—that is, keep it without self-denial and sacrifice—shall lose it; and that only he who loses his life, giving it away in devotion to God and to duty, shall save it.

In one of His parables Jesus speaks of salvation as a treasure hidden in a field. A man who learns of the treasure and its hiding place sells all that he has and goes and buys the field. In another parable our Lord presents the same truth under the figure of a merchant seeking choice pearls, who, finding one pearl of great price, sells all he has and buys it. We must, in a very deep sense, give up all we have to get Christ and the blessings that come with Him.

Here the truth is put in another way. There are two roads through this world and two gates into the future world. One of these ways is broad and easy, with descending grade, leading to a wide gate. It is not hard to go on this way. The other road is straight and leads to a narrow gate. To go this way one has to leave the crowd and go almost alone, leave the broad, easy way, and go on a hard, rugged path, and enter by a gate too small to admit any bundles of worldliness, or self-righteousness, or any of the fashionable trappings of the old life. All the world is not flowing into heaven; the crowds are going somewhere else.

IN SHEEP'S CLOTHING

*Beware of false prophets, which come to you in
sheep's clothing, but inwardly they are ravening wolves.*

Matthew 7:15

There is something fearful in the eagerness of the devil to destroy souls. He sends his agents and messengers in forms and disguises to deceive the simple-minded and unwary. He even takes the dress of God's own servants and children, hoping to gain the confidence of believers and then destroy their faith and lead them away to death. The world is full now of just such agents of Satan. They profess to be Christians, but in their hearts they are disloyal to Christ and to His cause and kingdom. They win the confidence of the sheep by passing for sheep themselves; but the sheep's covering is only worn outside, while underneath is the heart of a hungry, bloodthirsty wolf.

We need to be on our guard perpetually against the wiles of the devil. Eternal vigilance is the price of spiritual safety and of Christian peace. Many young people, especially those who are intelligent and gifted, fall under the influence of those who have assumed various types of skeptical talk which they drop in the form of sneers or mocking queries in the ears of their listeners. They laugh at the simple cradle-faith these young Christians hold, and ask with pompous airs, "Do you still believe these old superstitions?" Then they go on to cast doubt or to raise questions about this or that difficulty in the Bible, or they caricature some Christian doctrine and hold it up in such light as to make it look absurd.

They poison the minds of these earnest young believers, weaken their faith, and fill them with perplexity. Pastors and teachers of intelligent young people are continually called to try to undo the wicked and destructive work of these wolves in sheep's clothing; but oftentimes it is impossible to undo it. Wrecked infant faith is hard to restore.

DOING THE FATHER'S WILL

Not every one that saith unto me, Lord, Lord, shall enter into the kingdom of heaven; but he that doeth the will of my Father.

Matthew 7:21

It is not enough to believe in Christ intellectually, even to be quite orthodox in creed. It is not enough to seem to honor Christ before men, praying to Him and ascribing power to Him. It is a sad thing that Jesus tells us here—that some who have seemed to be His friends on earth, and who have publicly confessed Him, shall fail at last to get into heaven.

Such a word from the Lord's lips cannot but startle us. We stop and ask, "Are we sure that we shall be admitted to heaven? Why are these confessors of Christ kept out? What are the conditions of entrance?" To these questions the answer is so plain that there is no possibility of mistake if we read the Lord's words with honest care. He tells us that only those shall enter heaven who on earth do the will of the Father. No confession, therefore, is true which is not confirmed and verified by a life of obedience and holiness. "Simply to thy cross I cling" is only half of the gospel. No one is really clinging to the cross who is not at the same time faithfully following Christ and doing whatever He commands. No one can enter into heaven into whose heart heaven has not first entered on this earth. We shall do God's will in heaven if we ever get there; we must do it here now.

Some people have the impression that salvation sets them free from the law; it does do so as a ground of salvation, but it does not as a rule of duty. We pray, "Thy will be done in earth, as it is in heaven"; if the prayer is sincere, it must draw our own lives with it in loving obedience and acquiescence to the divine will. Our confessions of Christ must be confirmed by the earnest doing of the Father's will. All other confession is only an empty mockery.

The Safe Foundation

Whosoever heareth these sayings of mine, and doeth them, I will liken him unto a wise man, which built his house upon a rock.

Matthew 7:24

Everything hinges on doing or failing to do Christ's words. Both these men in this story built houses, but one of them obeyed as well and thus built on the true and immovable foundation. Both men built houses very much alike so far as the super-structures were concerned. But there were two kinds of ground. There was a sandy valley, which was dry and pleasant in the summer days when the men were looking for building sites. Then there were high rocky bluffs. One man decided to build in the valley. It would cost less. It would be easy digging. It was more convenient, for the bluffs were inaccessible. The other man built on the high ground. It would cost more, but it would be safer.

The two homes went up simultaneously, only the one in the valley was finished long before the other was. The families moved into their new residences and were quite happy for a time. But one night there was a storm. The house in the valley was carried away with its dwellers; the house on the bluff was unharmed.

The stories explain themselves. He who built in the valley on the sand is the man who has only knowledge and profession, but who really has never built on Christ as a foundation. The other man, who built on a rock, is the man who has true faith in Christ, confirmed by loving obedience. The storms that burst are earth's trials which test every life, and then later, the tempests of death and judgment. The mere professor of religion is swept away in these storms, for he has only sand under him; he who is truly in Christ is secure, for no storm can ever reach Christ's throne. It will be a terrible thing to cherish a false hope of salvation through life and only find out in eternity, too late to build again, that we have no foundation beneath our hopes.

CHRIST THE GREAT COUNSELOR

John calling unto him two of his disciples sent them to Jesus.
Luke 7:19

John the Baptist was anxious about important things. There were some questions that were worrying him, that he could not figure out himself, and he sent to Christ to ask Him about them. That is just what every one of us should do when there arise perplexities of any kind in our lives or affairs—we should carry them straight to Jesus. Even children have their disappointments and trials. They have discouragements. They should not worry about these matters. Of course they cannot always understand them; how could they expect to understand everything in such a vast world as this? But is it not a great thing to know that Jesus understands it all? He knows what He is doing.

So the true way for us is just to do what John did—tell Jesus whenever anything appears to go wrong or when anything happens we cannot understand. That is the rule Paul gives for keeping clear of anxiety. "Be careful [or anxious] for nothing; but in every thing by prayer and supplication with thanksgiving let your requests be made known unto God" (Philippians 4:6). Then he promises that if we only do this we shall never have to worry— "The peace of God . . . shall keep your hearts and minds."

The meaning of all this is that we should never entertain a worry of any kind even for a moment, but whenever any matter begins to perplex us we should go instantly and tell Jesus all about it, and leave it in His hands, that He may manage it for us.

The leaving it is the hardest part. We can easily take it to Him, but we are so apt to pick it up again, carry it back with us, and keep it just as if we had not taken it to Him. We should practice telling Jesus of our fears and sorrows and then commit all to Him without further anxiety. This is faith and is the way to find peace.

LOSS OF FAITH

Art thou he that should come? or look we for another?
Luke 7:19

John was in prison, in Machaerus castle. It certainly was not a very cheerful place to be. We should not be astonished at his temporary loss of strong faith. Yet a good many people think it strange that the grand, brave John could really have been in doubt, and they scarcely believe it. "It is not possible," they say, "that such a great, heroic man should ever waver in his confidence." They forget that John lived just in the dim dawn of the gospel, before the full light burst upon the world. He had not the smallest part of the light that we have in our day; and yet do we, with all our light, never get depressed? The truth is, there is not one of us who is not sometimes disheartened without a small part of the cause John had.

But that is always the way. We are amazed at every person's blindness or dullness or unbelief but our own. Other people's failures look very large to us, but we never see our own at all. We wonder how Moses once, under terrible provocation, lost his temper and spoke a dozen hasty and impatient words; while we can scarcely get through a single normal day without a much worse outbreak upon a far slighter provocation.

We wonder how the beloved disciple, with all his sweet humility, could once show an ambition for a place of honor, while we ourselves are forever scrambling for recognition. We say, "Isn't it strange that people would not believe on Christ when they saw all His power and love?" Yet we do not believe in Him any more fully than they did. We can scarcely believe that John the Baptist grew despondent when his trials were so great, though most of us are often plunged into gloom by the merest trifles. Many Christian people despair more over the loss of a few dollars or a little pain than John did in his really great trials.

May 29

---◇---

NEEDLESS DOUBTS

---◇---

Look we for another?
Luke 7:19

John did not doubt the messiahship of Jesus that day beside the Jordan, when from the rent heavens the radiant dove descended upon Him and the Father's voice was heard in loving approval. Nor did he doubt in any of the bright days that followed. It was only when it grew dark for John himself that he doubted.

That is just the way still with many people. When everything is bright and sunny they think they have surely found Christ, they believe He is their friend, and their hearts are full of joy. But when troubles come and things begin to go against them, they wonder whether, after all, they have really found the Savior. They begin to question their own experiences. "Am I really a Christian? Was that really conversion when I thought I was saved? Or is there some other experience that I must yet have?" Christ does not do just the things they thought He would do for them. Their religion does not support them as firmly as they supposed it would. If they are indeed Christians, why does Christ let them suffer so much and not come to relieve them? So they sink away down into the Slough of Despond, sometimes losing all hope.

See how unnecessary was John's doubt. Jesus was indeed the Messiah. John's active work was done, and he was now to glorify God by suffering and soon by martyrdom. Just as needless is all anxiety of Christian people in their times of darkness. Of course we must have some earthly trials. Christ does not carry us to heaven on flowery beds of ease. We must expect to bear the cross many a mile. The true way for us is never to doubt Jesus. Suppose there are clouds; the sun still shines behind them undimmed. Suppose we have failures, trials, and disappointments; Jesus is still the same loving friend as when there was not a speck of trouble for us in all the world.

May 30

◇

JESUS ALWAYS ANSWERS

◇

Then Jesus answering.
Luke 7:22

John was perplexed and sent from his prison to ask Jesus if He were indeed the promised Messiah. Jesus patiently answered the messengers. He always answers. Many of our prayers to Him are mixed with doubt; many of them are filled with complaints and fears and murmurings. Still He never grows impatient with us. He never shuts His door upon us. It must grieve and pain Him to have us doubt Him. Joseph wept when his brothers sent a message to him, after their father's death, asking him to forgive them, when he had forgiven them years before, and had proved it by many kindnesses; it almost broke his heart to think how they had misjudged him.

Yet that is the way many of us do with Jesus. After all the sacrifices He has made on our behalf and the blessings His love has bestowed upon us, when some shadow falls upon our heart we wonder whether Christ loves us or not, whether or not He has forgiven us, whether or not He will take care of us in the future. We are half the time perplexed about something—full of worries; and these doubts, fears, and anxieties get into our prayers. They take the joy out of our worship and the faith out of our supplications, and they give a sad tone to our devotions.

Does Jesus never get tired of such prayers? No, He listens, and hears all the disturbances made by the murmurings. His heart must be pained by them too; but He answers us nevertheless. He is very patient with us—He never condemns; He remembers how frail we are, and He sends the sweetest answers that His love can give. It is wonderful indeed how rich and gentle our Savior is. Verily

There is no place where earth's sorrows
Are more felt than up in heaven;
There is no place where earth's failings
Have such kindly judgments given.

THE FOOTPRINTS OF CHRIST

Go your way, and tell John what things ye have seen and heard.
Luke 7:22

John wanted to know whether Jesus really was the Messiah or not. Jesus did not present arguments to prove that He was the Messiah but pointed the messengers to the work He was doing. The best evidence of the divinity of Christ is not any number of proof-texts gathered from all parts of the Bible and arranged in order, but the works that Christ has done and is doing every day. An atheist asked an Arab how he knew there was a God. The man answered by inquiring, "How do I know whether it was a man or a camel that passed my tent last night?" He knew by the footprints. Then he pointed to the setting sun and asked, "Whose footprint is that?"

Look at the footprints of Christ and see whether they are a man's or God's. Whose prints are those by the gate of Nain, by the grave of Bethany, coming away from the tomb of Joseph of Arimathea? Whose prints are those by the doors of sorrow, along the path where the leper, the blind, the lame, the demoniac waited for Him? Or look around at what you see now—churches, missions, hospitals, asylums, joyful homes, cleansed sinners, renewed lives, comforted mourners; whose prints are those? These works, caused by Christianity, are the best evidences of Christ's work. Christ wants to be judged, not merely by His claims, but by His works. The world is full today of the proofs of Christ's divinity.

In the same way we must prove that we belong to Christ, not by getting certificates of church membership, but by showing in our daily lives the unselfishness, the sympathy, the self-denial, the kindness, the love that were the highest proofs in Christ's own life of His divine mission. We must be able, when persons ask us if we are Christians, to say: "Look at my life and my works, and judge for yourselves."

June 1

WAVERERS

A reed shaken with the wind?
Luke 7:24

The picture is of a person wavering and unstable, easily swayed and bent from uprightness. That is what a good many people are. A reed grows in soft mud by the water's edge. It is so frail and delicate that every breeze bends it and shakes it. Jesus did not intimate that John the Baptist was a man of that type but meant just the reverse. John was not like the reed shaken with the wind. He was a man whom nothing could bend or sway. Rather than preaching soft words to please Herod and keeping quiet about sins that the king was committing, John charged home the sins without hesitating, losing his head at last as reward.

Yet there are some persons who are like reeds. Instead of being rooted in Christ, their roots go down into the soft mud of this world, and of course they are easily torn up. Then they have no fixed principles to hold them upright and make them true and strong; and they are bent by every wind and moved and swayed by every influence of fear or favor. The boy who cannot say no when other boys tempt him to smoke, or drink, or do a wrong or mean thing is a reed shaken by the wind. The girl who is influenced by frivolities and worldly pleasure, and drawn away from Christ and from a beautiful life, is likewise a reed bent and swayed by the wind.

They are growing everywhere, these reeds, and the wind shakes them every time it blows. Who wants to be a reed? Who would not rather be like the oak, growing in soil as solid as a rock, which no storm bends or even causes to tremble?

There is one apparent advantage in being like a reed; one seems to escape persecution. John would hardly have met the fate he did meet if he had been easily shaken. People who are like reeds do not often lose their heads on the martyr's block. But they are in danger of losing their usefulness; and that certainly is worse.

THE FRIEND OF SINNERS

A woman in the city, which was a sinner,
when she knew that Jesus sat at meat . . .
Luke 7:37

I t is wonderful how genuine goodness draws to itself the unfortunate, the troubled, the friendless, the outcast, the fallen. Wherever Jesus went, these classes always found Him and gathered about Him. It was because He was the true interested friend of all men. They found sympathy from Him. He would listen to their story. Though He was the sinless One, there was yet no air of "I am holier than thou" about Him. He was just as gentle to an outcast sinner as to a spotless Nicodemus. No matter who reached out a hand for help, He was ready to grasp it. One of the truest things ever said of Jesus was the prophetic word concerning him, "A bruised reed shall he not break" (Isaiah 42:3). He dealt always most gently with hurt spirits and with bruised hearts.

Those who want to be useful in this world must have the same qualities. There is a kind of human "holiness" that draws nobody to itself, but rather repels; genuine holiness, however, wins its way everywhere into men's hearts. The secret of it all is in living "not to be ministered unto, but to minister" (Matthew 20:28), in considering oneself not too good to serve the unworthiest of God's creatures. If we stay in this world to be served, we shall be of no good use. But if we live to minister to others, yearning to be of service to everyone we meet, our lives will be of great worth. The hungry-hearted and the soul-needy will be drawn to us, and God will love to put work into our hands.

We need, too, to train ourselves to exceeding gentleness in dealing with human souls in their spiritual crises. Many earnest people, in the excess of their zeal, do incalculable harm to those whom they greatly desire to help. People with sore and bruised hearts usually need loving sympathy and strong, kindly friendship much more than they need theology.

A BROKEN SPIRIT
◇

Stood at his feet behind him weeping.
Luke 7:38

Those who are familiar with the legend of Paradise and the Peri will remember how the banished Peri sought to gain admittance at the closed gate of Paradise. The angel told the nymph that there was one hope—that the Peri might yet be forgiven who would bring to the eternal gate the gift that was most dear to Heaven.

The Peri wandered everywhere, sweeping all lands with her swift wings, searching for some rare and precious thing to carry up to the barred gate. Amid scenes of carnage she found a hero dying for liberty; and

> *Swiftly descending on a ray*
> *Of morning light, she caught the last,*
> *Last glorious drop his heart had shed,*
> *Before its free-born spirit fled.*

With this she flew up to the gate; but, precious as was the prize, the crystal bar did not move. Next in her quest the Peri came upon a dying lover, over whom his betrothed hung; and stealing the farewell sigh of that vanishing soul, again she sought the gate of bliss; but even to this precious reward the bar did not swing.

Again she wandered far, and came at last upon a wretched criminal, stained by countless deeds of shame and blood, but now weeping in bitter penitence. The Peri with joy caught up the holy tear of contrition as it fell and swiftly took it away to heaven; and the door flew open, admitting her to the blessedness within.

This beautiful Oriental legend is not unrelated to heavenly fact. The Bible tells us the same thing. "The sacrifices of God are a broken spirit: a broken and a contrite heart, O God, thou wilt not despise" (Psalm 51:17). No offerings we can bring are so precious as contrite tears. No song on earth rings with such music up in heaven as the penitential cry, "God be merciful to me a sinner!"

FREE FORGIVENESS
◇

When they had nothing to pay, he frankly forgave them both.
Luke 7:42

A ll of us are in debt. Of course there is a difference in the amount of our debts. Some have sinned far more than others. But whether our debt be little or much, we have nothing at all with which to pay it. We could not more easily pay the fifty than the five hundred pence. He forgave them both. It is just as easy for God to forgive the greatest sins as the smallest. He forgave them. That is the only way we can ever get clear of our sins.

A king owed a large sum to one of his nobles, but he could not pay it. The nobleman made a great feast in honor of his king. A fire of perfumed woods burned on the hearth. During the feast the host brought out all the king's notes and cast them into the fire, thus obliterating beyond possibility of restoration every evidence of his indebtedness. That is the way God does with our sins. Into the fragrant flames of Christ's sacrifice He casts them all, and they will never be heard of anymore.

There is a story of a half-witted boy whose idea of forgiveness was clear. He said that Jesus came and with His red hand rubbed out all his sins. A simple man used to carry a little book, which he took very often from his pocket, and which he called his "biography." It had only three leaves, and there was not a word written on any of them; yet he said the book told the whole story of his life. The first leaf was black; that was his sin; that was his condition by nature. He would shudder when he looked at it. The second was red; that was the blood of Christ, and his face glowed when he gazed upon it. The third was white; that was himself washed in Christ's blood, made whiter than snow. His book told the whole story of every redeemed life. Between the black of our sins and the white of redemption must always come the red of Christ's blood.

June 5

PEACE WITH PARDON

Thy faith hath saved thee; go in peace.
Luke 7:50

Saved! This poor, shame-filled, sin-destroyed person, that the Pharisee would have cast out of his house into the street—saved! Never to go back anymore to her old life! An heir of heaven now, destined to walk the heavenly streets in white! There is an old legend that Mohammed once in passing along the way touched a plant of mallows, and it became a geranium, and has ever since been a geranium, pouring fragrance everywhere. No matter about the legend, but Christ did something far more wonderful on the day of our story. He touched this sinful soul, and it was transformed into beauty. That woman has been in glory for eighteen centuries. That is what Christ does for everyone who comes to His feet in penitence and faith.

Peace came with the forgiveness. There could be no peace until she was forgiven. No one has any right to be at peace while the guilt of sin remains uncanceled. But when Christ has forgiven us, we should be at peace. Why or of what should we then be afraid? What is there for us to fear in this world or the next?

There is a story of someone in the old days who had committed a capital crime. He was the king's friend and favorite; and when his trial came about, although the case went strongly against him, he showed no fear. The evidence accumulated. There was no loophole of escape from conviction. His friends had no hope, yet they marveled at his calmness—he was at perfect peace. He was convicted and was about to be sentenced; still there was in his features no trace of alarm. At the last moment the secret was revealed. He drew from his coat a paper and handed it to the judge. It was the king's pardon. With that in his possession, he had no cause for fear. And with our King's pardon, no matter how guilty we are, we have no need to be afraid and may be at peace.

RIGHT ENTHUSIASM
◇

When his friends heard of it . . . they said, He is beside himself.
Mark 3:21

Even our Lord's relatives did not understand Him. His life was so unworldly that it could not be measured by ordinary standards. Here they could account for His unconquerable zeal only by concluding that He was insane. We hear much of the same kind of talk in modern days when some devoted follower of Christ utterly forgets self in love for his Master. People say, "He must be insane!" They think every man is crazy whose religion kindles into any sort of unusual fervor, or who grows more earnest than the average Christian in work for the Master. Some of Paul's friends thought he was crazy when he went sweeping over land and sea to carry the gospel to every city. But his answer was, "No, I am not crazy; the love of Christ constrains me."

That is a good sort of insanity. It is a sad pity that it is so rare. If there were more of it, there would not be so many unsaved souls dying under the very door of our churches; it would not be so hard to get missionaries and money to send the gospel to other continents; there would not be so many empty pews in our churches, so many long pauses in our prayer meetings, so few to teach in our Sunday schools. It would be a glorious thing if all Christians were "fanatics" as the Master was, or as Paul was.

It is a far worse insanity which in this world never gives a thought to any other world; which, working continually among lost men, never pities them, nor thinks of their lost condition, nor puts forth any effort to save them. It is easier to keep a cool head and a colder heart and to give ourselves no concern about perishing souls; but we are our brothers' keepers, and no lapse in duty can be worse than that which pays no heed to their eternal salvation.

A BEACON-LIGHT

◇

He that shall blaspheme against the
Holy Ghost hath never forgiveness.
Mark 3:29

Few words in the Bible have caused more anxiety and fear than these. Learned men do not agree in their idea as to what it is to blaspheme against the Holy Ghost. But no matter about the exact meaning of the words; they stand here as a warning against a terrible danger. They are like a red light hung over a perilous rock. While we may not know just what comprises the sin, it certainly is our duty to keep as far from its boundary as possible.

And surely all willful and determined resistance to the influence of the Holy Spirit is a step toward this point of awful peril. This saying of our Lord should lead us to treat with the utmost reverence every appeal, persuasion, or bidding of the Holy Ghost, never to resist, but always to yield to His every influence. We have no other Friend in this world who can guide us home. If we drive Him away from us forever, we shall be left in the darkness of eternal night. How long we may continue to reject Him and not go beyond the line that marks the limit of hope we do not know, but the very thought that there is such a line somewhere ought to startle us into instant acceptance of the offered guidance.

> *Oh, where is this mysterious line*
> *That crosses every path—*
> *The hidden boundary between*
> *God's patience and his wrath?*
>
> *How far may we go on in sin?*
> *How long will God forbear?*
> *Where does hope end, and where begin*
> *The confines of despair?*
>
> *An answer from the skies is sent;*
> *"Ye that from God depart,*
> *While it is called today, repent,*
> *And harden not your heart."*

June 8

CHRIST'S RELATIONS

*Whosoever shall do the will of God, the same
is my brother, and my sister, and mother.*

Mark 3:35

This seems too good to be true. To be the brother or the sister of Jesus—did you ever try to think out what it means? Then for every Christian to be taken by Christ into as close and tender a relationship as His own mother sustained to Him—did you ever try to think that out, remembering that you are the one taken into this loving fellowship?

Thousands of women have wished that they could have had Mary's honor in being the mother of Jesus. Well, here it lies close to their hand. They cannot have Mary's distinction in this world, but they can have a place just as near to the heart of Christ as she has. How wonderful it is that sinful creatures can be taken into the very family of God and have all the privileges and joys of the children of God! We cannot understand it, but let us believe it and think of it until it fills our hearts with warmth and gladness.

We do not begin to realize the blessedness and glory of being a Christian. There is a picture which seen in one light shows a poor, weary pilgrim, lying on a miserable pallet in a dreary garret; but seen in another light the same picture shows a saint of God, an heir of glory, arrayed in white robes, surrounded and carried up by angels to heavenly glory. The first view is that which human eyes see in the Christian; the other is the reality—that which heaven sees.

But we must not overlook the first part of this verse, that tells us who are received into this close relationship—"whosoever shall do the will of God." At every point as we go on, we catch more and more distinctly the teaching that obedience to God is part of the faith that saves. We must do God's will, and follow Christ with loving fidelity, if we would obtain the privilege of being the brothers and sisters of Christ.

ALWAYS ON DUTY

A certain Pharisee besought him to dine with him:
and he went in, and sat down to meat.

Luke 11:37

Our Lord was not ashamed to be the guest of publicans and sinners, but neither did He reject the invitations of the rich and influential. He was ready to go wherever there was an opportunity of doing good, even to social feasts and large dinner parties. Of course we are safe in following His example; but we must read on a little further, and then we shall see that He always used these opportunities as occasions for doing good.

We may go to any place where we can do the part of a messenger of God to other souls. We are never to be off duty as Christians, and as Christians we must be always Christ's servants, ready to bear blessings from Him to others. We are to be sure, before we accept an invitation to any place, that our Master has an errand there for us. Then when we go, we are to improve the occasion for doing good in some way to some who are there. Christ never went to any such places of amusement as offer their temptation to young people in these days; and yet this same principle applies to these. "Is it right for me to attend the theater or the dancing party?" Well, can you go there as a Christian? Can you confess Christ there? Can you talk of Him to others? Can you ask His blessing on your going? Can you go as His messenger, sure that He sends you there? It is time we began to look at these matters very honestly and frankly. If we are Christians, we are to be Christians seven days in the week and everywhere.

Then we are to be Christians always on duty. A young clergyman who had been reproved by his bishop for certain unministerial conduct sought to excuse himself by saying that he was not on duty at the time. The bishop replied: "A clergyman is never off duty." This is true of every Christian. Wherever we go we represent our Master.

◇

COVETOUSNESS

◇

Take heed, and beware of covetousness: for a man's life consisteth
not in the abundance of the things which he possesseth.

Luke 12:15

This is one of the red flags our Lord hung out which most people nowadays do not seem much to regard. Christ said a great deal about the danger of riches; but not many persons are afraid of riches. Covetousness is not practically considered a sin in these times. If a man breaks the sixth or eighth commandment, he is branded as a criminal and covered with shame; but he may break the tenth, and he is only enterprising. The Bible says the love of money is a root of all evil; but every man who quotes the saying puts a terrific emphasis on the word "love," explaining that it is not money, but only the love of it, that is such a strong root.

To look about, one would think a man's life did consist in the abundance of the things he possesses. Men think they become great in the proportion that they gather wealth. So it seems, too; for the world measures people by their bank accounts. Yet there never was a more fatal error. A man is really measured by what he is, and not by what he has. You may find a shriveled soul in the midst of a great fortune and a grand, noble soul in the barest poverty.

The first thing is to gather into our lives all the truly great and noble things of character. Here are two texts to ponder, because they settle this question: "Whatsoever things are true, whatsoever things are honest, whatsoever things are just, whatsoever things are pure, whatsoever things are lovely, whatsoever things are of good report . . . think on these things" (Philippians 4:8). "Add to your faith virtue; and to virtue knowledge; And to knowledge temperance; and to temperance patience; and to patience godliness; And to godliness brotherly kindness; and to brotherly kindness charity" (2 Peter 1:5–7).

June 11

◇

HEART-HARDENING

◇

And when he sowed, some seeds fell by the way side.
Matthew 13:4

How are human hearts beaten into a highway? A child's heart is sensitive to every impression. But as it grows older, the thousand influences, feelings, emotions, and imaginations, treading over it continuously, trample it into hardness. Every time a young man feels conviction of sin and does not turn from the sin, his heart is left a little less tender. Every time he feels that he ought to do a certain thing and does not do it, allowing the good prompting to pass, he is left a little less sensitive to good impressions afterward.

The same effect is produced by the common experiences of life. The wheels and carts of business go lumbering over the heart. We ought to have our hearts fenced in and allow none of these heavy wagons to pass over them. A businessman ought to keep his heart soft and warm in the midst of all his business, tender as a little child's, humble, teachable, loving, trusting. He ought to have a sanctuary in his inner life into which no unhallowed foot, none but the priestly feet of heavenly guests, should ever pass. But too many make their hearts an open field till they are beaten into a callousness that nothing can affect.

Another way is by the feet of sinful habits. There was an old legend of a goblin horseman that galloped over men's fields at night; and wherever his horse's hoof struck, the soil was so blasted that nothing would ever grow on it again. So it is with the heart over which the beastly feet of lust, of greed, of selfishness, of passion, are allowed to tread. There is an impression that it does young people no harm to indulge in sin for a time, if they afterward repent. No more fatal falsehood was ever whispered by the tempter into any ear. The heart that is trodden over by vile lusts or indulgences of any kind is never the same again.

June 12

◇

ROOTLESS GRACES

◇

Some fell upon stony places.
Matthew 13:5

There is a thin covering of soil on the rock. The seed sinks in a little way, and the heat radiating from the rock causes it to shoot up at once. This represents a class of people whose religion is emotional. At first they give great promise. They are easily moved by any appeal. The feelings work immediately to the surface. Such persons always seem most affected by sorrow. They repent ardently, but their grief is soon over. In the same way they appear to be most deeply affected by religious appeals. They begin a Christian life with an earnestness that puts older Christians to shame. They attend all meetings; they weep as they sing and pray; they talk of Christ to their friends; their zeal is wonderful. "Immediately it sprang up, because it had no depth of earth."

But such quick growth lacks root and cannot endure the heat of summer. The sun soon scorches such plants, and they wither. In spiritual life, also, the analogy applies. Emotional religion is not apt to be permanent. It bursts up into great full flower today, but we are not sure that it will be found tomorrow in a deeper life. Too often the enthusiasm is only temporary. In the heat of trials, temptation, toil, or sorrow, the rootless graces wilt and die.

Usually the religious life that is most permanent is that which springs up naturally and grows slowly to strength and beauty. It has good soil, and the roots go down deep into the earth and are unaffected by the frequent changes in temperature, by heat or cold, by rain or drought. If anyone finds that his spiritual graces are rootless and that there is a hard rock in his heart underneath the surface, he should seek at once to have the rock broken by penance and prayer, that the plants of righteousness in him may have opportunity to grow.

June 13

◇

WHAT OF THE ROOT?

◇

Because they had no root, they withered away.
Matthew 13:6

A root is very important in a plant or a tree. One may take a green branch from a living tree and set it in the ground, and for a little while it may seem to be living; but soon, under the sun's heat, it will wither. It has no root. The root is not a very beautiful part of a tree—it is hidden away out of sight, and nobody praises it; yet it is essential to the tree's life. In the same way there is a hidden part in every Christian's life. It does not seem to bless the world in any way. It is the heart-life—faith, love, communion with God in His Word and in prayer. No one praises a Christian's inner prayer life; it is secret, and no one sees it; yet it is the root of the whole strong, beautiful life which men do see and praise and whose ripe fruits feed their hunger.

Our Lord says the trouble with these shallow-soil people is that they have no root in themselves; that is, there is not in their heart that root-principle of Christian life which consists of faith in Christ and love to Him. Where there is such a root no persecution can tear it away; no outward circumstances can affect the permanence of its life. It is not kept alive by any external influences. Its source is in the heart. It feeds on heavenly food. Temptations and persecutions only make the true Christian purposes all the stronger.

But it is not so with this superficial religion. It has no inward life of its own. It is not produced by an unconquerable love in the heart for Christ. It depends simply on external excitement—revival meetings, some favorite preacher, some special form of worship, the influence of some friend—something, at least, in the outer circumstances which keeps the emotions active for a time. But it has no root in itself; and in such a religion there is nothing to lead a life very far through experiences of trial.

June 14

WHAT ARE THE THORNS?

Some fell among thorns, and the thorns grew up,
and choked it, and it yielded no fruit.

Mark 4:7

The thorns had been chopped off, but their roots were still in the ground. Then as the seed began to grow, so did the thorns; and growing faster and more wildly than the wheat, they soon choked it out, so that it came to nothing in the end. What are these thorns? Our Lord says they are "the cares of this world, and the deceitfulness of riches" (Mark 4:19). "Cares" are anxieties, distractions, worries.

Martha was in danger of having the good seed in her heart choked out by her distracting thoughts about her household affairs. Many a promising Christian life has been dwarfed and stunted from the same cause. "The deceitfulness of riches": thousands of spiritual lives have been starved into ghostly leanness by the desire for riches. "The lusts of other things entering in, choke the word." We have all seen people who began well; but as cares multiplied or riches increased, their zeal waned. We need, however, to look to our own hearts, and we shall probably have enough to do if we keep out all the thorns and weeds in the one little garden committed to us.

Jesus did not say these people are not Christians, but that they "bring no fruit to perfection." The distractions of this life, the deceitfulness of riches, the lusts of other things, entering in, choke the spiritual life, stunting its graces. They lose the sweet comforts of a healthy faith. The fruits of the Spirit in them are shriveled. They may go on working in the church, preaching, teaching, praying; but the deeper life is wanting. What is the lesson? We need to watch without ceasing these hearts of ours, and let no weed or brier grow there for a day. Sometimes God Himself does the weeding. He lifts out of the bosom the earthly object that is absorbing all the heart's love. The process is difficult, but the results are full of blessing.

GOLDEN GRAIN

The sower soweth the word.
Mark 4:14

The human heart is only the soil. Its natural products are thorns and briers. These grow without sowing and without cultivation. We do not need to be taught in order to be wicked. But if good things are to grow in our hearts, they must be sown and cultivated. The seeds must be brought from heaven. This is just what has been done. The words of the Bible are divine seeds. They have a wondrous power in themselves. Like natural seeds, they grow when planted, and they produce plants of righteousness. Bare like the desert, rather overgrown with foul weeds and briers, like neglected gardens we are, until the Sower comes. Our hearts are this way by nature; yet if we receive the good seed with faith and love, our lives are changed and are made to blossom like the rose.

There is another thought; all of us may be sowers of this good seed. We must take heed that we really sow the Word. There is no other seed that will yield the harvest of spiritual life. The words of God have life in them. "The words that I speak unto you," said the Master, "they are spirit, and they are life." If we get these heavenly seeds into people's hearts, we shall not look in vain for fruits.

It is a holy privilege to be permitted to help the great Husbandman in the sowing of this precious seed. We can carry the golden grains with us and drop them wherever we go. This we can do by being full of the Word, thus having something to give for every circumstance. We can sow the seed by the thoughtful giving of tracts and leaflets. We can do it by writing letters to carry to others some truth suited to their need. We can live so sweetly that our daily influence will be a scattering of heavenly seed all about us. Then someday we shall stand before the great Husbandman, our offering full of golden sheaves.

June 16

◇

HIDDEN LIGHTS

◇

Is a candle brought to be put under a bushel, or under a bed?
Mark 4:21

No one would think of doing such a thing. People always set a lamp where it will give the most light. It would be absurd to cover it up so that its beams could not pour out. Yet that is just what a great many people do with their Christian life. It is a very striking figure, this that our Lord uses when describing Christians. He calls them lights, lamps, candles, which He lights with the fire of His own life when they believe on Him. There is much difference in the brightness of the light in different believers. Some are only little candles, other are great lights. But even a candle makes one spot a little brighter.

The point of our Lord's teaching here is that the light is not to be hidden or covered up but permitted to shine. Yet some people do indeed put their candles under bushels. They carry it so that it never gives light to others. Sometimes they hide it away under an imagined modesty or humility. They do not want to "put themselves forward" —it would seem presumptuous.

Sometimes it is the "bushel" of timidity or bashfulness under which they hide their light. They cannot rise to say a word in the prayer meeting; they cannot even conduct family worship in the midst of their own household. They cannot talk to a neighbor about his soul; they cannot stand up to make a public confession of Christ before the world, or go to call on a poor family or sick person, or offer consolation to someone in sorrow—all because they are "too backward." Some again hide their candle under a very imperfect life. Their faults obscure the light of the religious knowledge they possess, as a dirty glass chimney dims a lamp's shining. There are a great many lamps hidden away under bushels which ought to be shining to some purpose.

June 17

PROFITABLE HEARING

Take heed what ye hear.
Mark 4:24

This is very important counsel. "Take heed what ye hear." The things we hear enter into our souls and become part of our being; they give form and substance to our character. There have come infinite blessings from the printing press. There are thousands of good books whose pages are like leaves from the tree of life, for the healing of the nations. But there are also thousands of evil books whose pages reek with poison and scatter influences of moral and spiritual death. With all this great mass of books, good and bad, it is vitally important that we take heed what we hear. We would not eat poisoned food; why should we take poison into our souls?

If we open our ears to the evil things that are continually spoken on all sides and open our eyes to that which comes to us on vile printed pages, our hearts will become foul and unclean, and our lives will be corrupted. We should shut our ears to all that is unholy. Many a now utterly ruined life dates the beginning of its fall from the moment when an impure word was whispered in a listening ear or when a vile book or paper was secretly read. On the other hand, every holy life has been made pure by what it has heard. We are saved by words. Pure, true words are transforming.

The Bible is simply a book of words; but every word contains a revelation of some holy aspect in character or attainment which we should strive to reach. We should always gladly hear, because we may always safely and profitably hear the words of God. Then we should open our ears to the voice that speaks in every good book. We should take heed what we hear.

Then we must not forget the Master's other counsel: "Take heed how ye hear." We should hear thoughtfully, reverently, obediently, letting the good words of God into our heart, that they may transform our life.

June 18

---◇---

"AFTER MANY DAYS"

---◇---

The earth bringeth forth fruit of herself.
Mark 4:28

Yet the land will not produce without certain other influences upon it. If the sun does not shine upon it, and if there is no rain from heaven, the seed will never germinate, however rich the soil. The human heart is the soil in which the seeds of truth grow; but it must have the sunshine and rain of divine grace upon it before it will produce any spiritual fruit.

A man tore down an outbuilding that had stood for many years in his yard. He smoothed over the ground and left it. The warm spring rains fell upon it, and the sunshine flooded it; and in a few days there sprang up groups of little flowers unlike any that grew in the neighborhood. Where the building had stood was once a garden, and the seeds had lain in the soil without moisture, light, or warmth all those years. As soon as the sunshine and the rain touched them they sprang up into life and beauty.

So oftentimes the seeds of truth lie long in a human heart, not growing because the light and warmth of the Holy Spirit are shut away from them by sin and unbelief; but after long years the heart is opened in some way to the influences of the Divine Spirit, and the seeds, still living, shoot up into beauty. The instructions of a mother may lie in a heart, fruitless, from childhood to old age, and yet at last may save the soul.

When we have sown the heavenly seed, we should continually pray that God would pour His Spirit, like rain and sunshine, upon the heart where it lies to quicken it into life. Then, for ourselves, we should seek always to keep our hearts open to every invigorating influence of the grace of God. We need to pray constantly for the rain to come down, or else our hearts will lie bare and sterile, though filled with the divine seeds.

June 19

◇

PROGRESS

◇

First the blade, then the ear, after that the full corn in the ear.
Mark 4:28

We understand this well enough in nature; but do we in spiritual life? The beginnings of Christian life are very feeble and imperfect. We must not expect in young converts the maturity of character we look for in older Christians. Grace begins in a small way. We have no right to look at once for the ripened fruits of Christian experience. But the wheat does not stop at the tender blade; it shoots up into a strong stalk, at last into ripeness. Christian lives should grow; they should not always stay at the starting point. They should grow in knowledge, in power, in purpose, in achievement, until they bear all the fruits of the Spirit and grow into the ripeness of Christian experience.

We notice here also that while the growth is secret its results are obvious. The processes of spiritual life are invisible, but the results are not. If a Christian is growing in grace, we shall know it by his life. He will wear more and more of the image of Christ, and the "mind of Christ" will appear more often in his character and conduct.

Another thought suggested here is that the beginnings of Christian life in young Christians ought to be most gently nurtured by those who are their spiritual overseers. The tender blades cannot endure a frost. Young converts cannot endure the sharp trials and temptations of this world. A clergyman is reported as saying, "I do not dare to bring too many children into my church—not because I do not believe in their sincerity and piety and fitness for church membership, but because there is no provision for their growth and nurture after they are in the church." Could any sadder confession be made? Something must be wrong with the church when this is true. Let the words remain for the consideration of those whom they concern.

DROPPING SEEDS

The kingdom of heaven is like to a grain of mustard seed . . . the least of all seeds: but when it is grown, it . . . becometh a tree.
Matthew 13:31–32

Many great histories of blessing may be traced back to a very small seed. A woman whose name is forgotten dropped a tract or little book in the way of a man named Richard Baxter. He picked it up and read it, and it led him to Christ. He became a holy Christian and wrote a book entitled *A Call to the Unconverted*, which brought many people to the Savior, among others Philip Doddridge. Philip Doddridge in turn wrote *The Rise and Progress of Religion*, which led many into the kingdom of God, among them the great Wilberforce. Wilberforce wrote *A Practical View of Christianity*, which was the means of saving a multitude, among them Legh Richmond. In his turn Legh Richmond wrote the book called *The Dairyman's Daughter*, which has been instrumental in the conversion of many thousands.

The dropping of that one little tract seemed a very small thing to do; but see what a wonderful, many-branched tree has sprung from it! This is only one illustration of marvels of grace coming from the most minute grains of the heavenly seed. One seed planted in a heart, dropped by some very humble worker, perhaps unconsciously, may not only save a soul for an eternity of blessedness, but may start a series of divine influences that shall reach thousands of other lives. A simple invitation from his brother brought Simon to Jesus; and what a tree has sprung from that seed!

Let us go on, day by day, dropping seeds into as many hearts as we can. We may not always know what comes of them, but from any one of them may spring a history of blessing which shall reach thousands of souls. The branches of the tree from one seed may spread over all lands.

June 21

◇

"THE OTHER SIDE"

◇

He saith unto them, Let us pass over unto the other side.
Mark 4:35

C hrist is continually saying the same to us, though with vary-
ing meaning in His words. He is always calling us to pass
over some boundary into new fields, with their new experiences,
new privileges, new duties, new conflicts, new joys.

He says it to the godless when He graciously invites them to
become His disciples. He wants them to leave the entanglements
of this world, sin and their old dead past, and rise up and go with
Him to the better life which lies beyond. He invites them to His
Father's country, into His Father's family. It is a land of blessing
and of beauty, of plenty and of great riches. True, there is a sea
that must be crossed to reach it. No one can reach the glorious
country on "the other side" without passing over this sea, and no
one can pass over without encountering tempests. There are
fierce temptations, sore self-denials, mighty struggles, and many
losses and sorrows before we can reach heaven; but the reward is
so great that we should be ready to endure any hardship or suffering to win it.

Then Christ gives the same call and invitation to His people
when they reach the end of earthly life and when He comes to
take them home. Before them rolls the sea of death, dark and full
of terrors to the natural sense. They hesitate to cross it. Yet there
is no reason why they should hesitate. On "the other side" glory
awaits. There is the Father's house with the many mansions. And
however dark and terrible may seem the narrow sea that has to
be crossed, there is no danger; for Jesus Himself accompanies His
people, and none of them can perish. But if we would have this
final invitation to come over to the other side into the heavenly
glory, we must accept the first call to come over out of the old life
of sin into the new life of holiness.

June 22

LIFE'S STORMS

There arose a great tempest in the sea.
Matthew 8:24

The disciples had not gone out to sea because of their own suggestion. Had they done so without Christ's asking them, they would not have had the same reason to expect protection and deliverance. The lesson we learn here is this—that storms may arise even when we are in the direct line of duty. We should not be discouraged by the difficulty or trouble that comes and conclude that we are in the wrong path.

We see, too, that Christ's presence with His disciples does not keep the storms away. There are no promises in the Bible that Christian people shall not meet trials. Religion builds no high walls about us to break the force of the winds. Troubles come to the Christian just as surely as to the worldly man. There are the storms of temptation; these sweep down with sudden and terrific power from the cold mountains of this world. Then there are storms of sickness, of disappointment and adversity, of sorrow, that make the waves and billows to roll over the soul.

Travelers say that a boat on the Sea of Galilee will be gliding along smoothly over a glassy surface, unbroken by a ripple, when suddenly, without a moment's warning, a tempest will sweep down, and almost instantly the boat will be tossed in the angry waves. So do many of life's storms come. We are at peace in a happy home. At an hour when we think not, without warning, the darling child we love so much lies dead in our arms. The friend we trusted, and who we thought could never fail us, proves false. The hopes cherished for years wither in our hands in a night, like flowers when the frost comes. The storms of life are nearly all sudden surprises. They do not hang out danger signals days before to warn us. The only way to be ready for them is to be always ready.

FAITHLESS FEAR

They awake him, and say unto him, Master,
carest thou not that we perish?
Mark 4:38

These words imply that the disciples thought Jesus was indifferent to them in their danger—that He was neglecting them by sleeping while they were exposed to such peril. But how unjust was this accusation! They were never safer than they were that moment, in the midst of the wild tempest. The ship that bore the Lord could not sink in the sea. Faith should have trusted even in the darkness.

Yet do we never, at least in our hearts, make the same complaint of our Lord? When we are in some difficult trial, and the trial grows very strong, and He does not come to deliver us; when we seem about to be engulfed by the waves of adversity, and no relief comes down from Him—do we never say, "Jesus does not care though I perish"? When we pray long and with persistence for the lifting of some heavy cross, or the lightening of some painful burden, and no answer comes, does the thought never arise in our minds that Jesus does not hear us, or that He does not come to us?

But this complaint is never just. Sometimes He may seem not to care. The disciples had some lessons to learn. One was how helpless they were in trusting themselves in the world's dangers. Another was that Christ alone could deliver them. They could not learn these lessons except in the storm with the Master asleep. So there are similar lessons that we never can learn until Christ withholds His help for a time. And sometimes He hides Himself for a time just to teach us faith. But He is never indifferent to us. He never neglects or forgets us. His heart always wakes and watches, and at the right moment He comes and brings deliverance. We should learn to trust our Lord so confidently that in any hour of danger we can nestle down in His bosom, without fear or anxiety, and let Him take care of us.

THE HEARER OF PRAYER

And he arose, and rebuked the wind.
Mark 4:39

The roar of the storm He did not hear in His sound sleep; but the moment there was a cry from His disciples for help He instantly awoke. What a revelation of heart have we here! He is never asleep to His children when they call Him. Amid the wildest tumults of this world He always hears the faintest cry of prayer. Nor is He ever too weary to listen to the supplications of human distress.

We have another illustration of this same quickness to hear prayer in the hours of our Lord's sufferings on the cross. His life was fast leaving Him. His own agony was intense beyond description. Around Him surged a storm of human passion. Curses fell upon His ears. But amid all this tempest of hate He was silent. To all these bitter insults and strong reproaches He answered not a word. Then amid the derision and jeers of the multitude there came a voice of prayer. It came from one of the crosses beside Him. It was the penitential cry of a soul— "Lord, remember me." In all the tumult of the hour He heard this feeble supplication. In His own agony He gave instant answer. Do not doubt that this Jesus always hears prayer. His love is always watching, ready to catch the faintest note of human distress.

Though aroused so suddenly in the midst of such scenes of terror, Jesus awoke calm and peaceful. Dean Trench says: "It is such cases as these—cases of sudden, unexpected terror, met without a moment of preparation—which test a man what spirit he is of, which show not only his nerve, but the grandeur and purity of his whole nature." Here we have an illustration of what Christ's peace was, and of what He meant when He said, "My peace I give unto you" (John 14:27). He acted this way through all the turbulent scenes of His earthly life.

CHRIST IN THE STORM

He . . . rebuked the wind, and said unto the sea, Peace, be still.
Mark 4:39

He spoke to the storm and to the tossing sea as if they were intelligent beings—just as a man would speak to his servants. The truth we learn here is that He is Lord of nature, that the elements recognize His voice and obey Him even in their wildest moods. If we only fully believed this, it would bring a great deal of peace to our lives. No tempest ever breaks from the control of Him who is our Lord and Redeemer. No wave ever rolls any farther than He permits. There is nothing in this world that is not under the sway of the hand that was nailed on the cross.

There is a story of a Christian army officer at sea with his family in a storm. There was great terror among the passengers, but he was calm. His wife, in her consternation, chided him, saying that he ought to be concerned for her and the children, if not for himself, in such danger. He made no reply, but soon came to her with his sword drawn, and with a stern countenance pointed it at her heart. She was not the least alarmed but looked up into his face with a smile. "What!" he said, "are you not afraid when a drawn sword is at your breast?"

"No," she replied, "not when I know it is in the hands of one that loves me."

"And would you have me," he asked, "to be afraid of this tempest when I know it to be in the hand of my heavenly Father who loves me?"

Thus even in the wild tumults of nature we should be at peace, since our Savior is Lord of nature.

Someone tells of being at sea in a terrible cyclone, and of seeing a little bird flying down when the storm was at its height, and lighting on the crest of a wave, where it sat as quietly as if it had been perching on some green bough in the quiet forest. So should the believer in Christ rest in quietness and confidence in the wildest terror.

"DEPART FROM US"

They began to pray him to depart.
Mark 5:17

This is one of the saddest sentences in the Gospels. We can scarcely conceive of any person asking Jesus to go away. He had come to their coast to bring them rich blessings. His hands were full of golden gifts. He had power to heal the sick, to open blind eyes, to make the lame walk, to scatter all kinds of blessings among the people. He had begun His work of grace as soon as He landed by curing their most terrible case of demon possession. He would have gone on performing other works of mercy and love if they had not asked Him to leave. It was probably all because of the loss of the swine. If that was the way Christ's work was going to affect them, they did not want Him to go any further.

Some people feel the same way when a work of grace begins in their community. They are opposed to Christianity because it interferes with their business. Those who sell immorality oppose revivals because when the devil is cast out of men they stop their bad behavior, and so these men's businesses suffer; they are against Christianity because Christianity is against them. So all of us are apt to want Christ to depart from us when He interferes with our cherished plans. We need to be careful lest we send Christ altogether away from us.

For He did not stay after these people asked Him to go away. He would not stay where He was not wanted. He carried back the gifts He had come there to leave. The lame continued lame, and the demon possessed remained possessed, and the dying whom He would have restored passed away. Does anyone now ever ask Christ to depart when He comes with blessings? Does Jesus ever turn away from any heart now because He is not wanted, because He is rejected?

June 27

◇

THEY THAT ARE SICK

◇

*They that are whole have no need of
the physician, but they that are sick.*
Mark 2:17

That was the answer of Jesus to those murmuring about His
presence among the disreputable people at Matthew's feast.
The Pharisees thought He was compromising Himself in sitting
down at the table with such characters. Their insinuated remarks
were that He must belong to the same class Himself. But Jesus
gave them a wise and good answer. These wicked and sinful ones
were the very classes that needed Him most. It was the same with
Him as with a physician. The physician does not go about visiting
the people who are in excellent health. Those who are well do
not need the physician, but the sick and downcast need him; and
the worse their sickness, the more they require his presence and
his service.

No one would ever find fault with a physician for going into
sickrooms and into hospitals, and into plague-infested districts.
No one would ever suggest that he must have low standards and
values because of the kind of people among whom he spends his
time. It was just the same with Him, Jesus said. He had come to
this world expressly to save sinners. Surely, then, He could not be
blamed for going where sinners were; and the worse the sinners,
the more reason there was that He should be found there. Good
people, like those who criticized Him, did not need His services;
but wherever He found a poor, lost sinner, there was one of the
persons He had come to help and save.

One possibility is that, like their Master, Christ's disciples
should try to carry the gospel to the lowest classes. We should not
mingle among the wicked as companions; but when we strive to
save them we are becoming Christ to them. Another lesson is that
no sinner need ever despair of hope, since the worse he is, the
more surely is Christ willing to save him.

June 28

—◇—

JOY IN THE LORD

—◇—

Can the children of the bridechamber fast,
while the bridegroom is with them?
Mark 2:19

This was our Lord's answer to those who thought His religion was too optimistic and joyous—that it had not fast-days enough in it. They thought that religion was genuine only when it made people sad and that its quality was just in proportion to its sadness. But Christ's reply showed that mournful faces are no essential indicators of true piety. Should His disciples be mournful and sad when He was with them, filling their lives with the gladness of His presence? Should Christians profess to be heavy-hearted, wearing the emblems of grief, when they are really filled with joy, and when there is no occasion for sorrow? Why should one who has been saved by the Lord Jesus, and who is rejoicing in full assurance of hope, go about in sackcloth and ashes? Is there any piety in a sad face? Does God love to see His children always in mourning? Is human joy displeasing to our Father?

All these questions are answered here in our Lord's words. He does not wish His disciples to go mourning and fasting when they have no reason for such behavior. His words are an explanation of Christian joyfulness. Christ wants His friends to be glad. There is an utter contradiction in a sad and mournful Christian life. By its very nature true religion is joyous. Our sins are forgiven. We are adopted into God's family. We are heirs of God and joint heirs with Christ. The covenant of love has its shelter over us all the time. All things in this world work together for our good, and then glory waits for us beyond death's gate. With all this blessed heritage, why should we be mournful and sad? While we enjoy the grace of God, the consciousness of His love, the assurance of His forgiveness, and the hope of heaven and eternal life, what should make us sad? We should have radiant faces.

A NEW GARMENT

No man also seweth a piece of new cloth on an old garment.
Mark 2:21

Christ did not come into this world to patch up any old religion, merely to mend a hole here, and beautify a spot there, and add a touch to this part or that; He came to make all things new. He did not come to add a few moral deeds and human kindnesses to lives otherwise devoid of His influence; He came to make men new creatures all the way through. When He saves a sinner, He does not propose to mend him a little here and there, to cover over some bad spots in him, and to close up rents in his character by strong patches of the new cloth of grace. The gospel is not patchwork. Christ does not sew on pieces; He weaves a new garment that has no seam throughout the fabric.

When the weather began to get cold, a woman put her summer clothing in a box on a closet shelf. The next summer she brought out the clothes and discovered one dress was badly stained and discolored. It had *looked* clean when she put it away, but it had actually been dirty, and the stain had worked its way into the fibers of the dress. So we may try from without to make human character perfect, but there is sin in its very fiber, and the blemishes will always work out and corrupt all. The only way is to have a new heart, and then the beauty will be real and will endure. No outward reform is enough, for all the while the heart is evil within, and it sends up its foul odor, staining the fairest beauty. The change that is permanent must be completed in the heart.

June 30

◇

AT THE POINT OF DEATH

◇

There cometh one of the rulers . . . and besought him greatly,
saying, My little daughter lieth at the point of death.

Mark 5:22–23

There is nothing like trouble to drive people to Christ. So long as things go on prosperously, many men do not ask any favors of Him; but when sickness or great need comes, He is the first one to whom they turn. This is one of the most obvious uses of trouble. God stirs up many an earthly nest in which His children are reposing too softly, that they may be compelled to try heavenward flights. There are many in heaven now who would never have left the old earthly life had not God sent troubles, sorrows, and adversities.

This father said his little daughter was "at the point of death." This is one point to which everyone must come. The paths of earth run in very diverse ways, but they all pass at last to the "point of death." It is a point that lies hidden from view; no one knows the day or hour when he will come to it, and yet somewhere along the happy years it waits for everyone. Sometimes this point is reached in early youth. Here is a little girl of twelve who lay "at the point of death." Even children should think about dying, not as a sad and terrible thing, but as a point to which they must come, and for which they should prepare.

It is a touching sight to see this father falling at Christ's feet. The strongest men break down when their own children are sick or in danger. A man may seem very cold and stern as he carries on his business, or has his struggle with the world, or presses toward the goal of his ambitions. You think he has no tenderness in him—that he is a man of iron or rock. But let one of his children be stricken down, and your man of iron melts like wax. Behind his stern aspect and all his severity there is a warm spot in his heart where he is gentle and willing to give all.

THE TOUCH OF FAITH

*Jesus . . . turned him about in the press,
and said, Who touched my clothes?*
Mark 5:30

How did He know that one touch amid all the pushing of the crowd? The multitude were close about Him, pressing up against Him. The disciples even thought it strange that He should ask such a question. The people could not help touching Him. Yet there was one touch different from all the rest. A heart's cry was in it, a pitiful, earnest request. It was not like the jostling of the crowd, an accidental or a thoughtless touch, the mere touch of proximity; there was an emotion and a need in it. So, amid all the rude crowding of the multitude, He recognized it.

In every church service all are near to Christ, but all are not blessed. All press up against Christ, but some go away as they came, carrying with them unhealed sores, weakness left as it is, heart-hunger unfilled. Others, sitting close by, receive rich help. The first, though near, reach out no hand of faith, while the others touch the hem of Christ's garment.

The ordinances of the church may be compared to telegraph wires, through which messages are all the while passing. You may climb up and put your ear to the wire or hold it in your hand; but you will not hear a word of all the important messages that are flashing through it. But let an operator come with his instrument and attach it, and he hears every word. So in the ordinances we touch the invisible wires that bind heaven and earth together. Along these wires messages are flying: up from earth to heaven—prayers, praises, heart-cries, faith-filled desires; down from heaven to earth—answers of comfort, encouragement, joy, help, blessings of pardon, healing, life, peace. But many know nothing of all this—no surge of healing, new life, joy, or help comes to them; they are close by, but have no faith-attachment. The others receive by prayer and faith.

THE CHILD OF JAIRUS

While he yet spake, there came . . . certain
which said, Thy daughter is dead.

Mark 5:35

So it seemed that Jesus had delayed too long on the road. It may appear that He should not have stopped at all to heal or talk with the woman. The child of Jairus was dying, and there was not a moment to lose. Why did the Master not hurry on and get to her bedside before she died? But when we read the story through to the end, we are glad that He did stop to heal and help the woman.

One thing we learn from this incident is that Jesus is never in a hurry. He is never so much engrossed in one case of need that He cannot stop to give attention to another. He is never so pressed for time that we have to wait our turn. No matter what He is doing, He will always hear instantly our cry of need.

A little child's idea of God's listening to her was that when she began to pray God bade all the angels be quiet, saying, "I hear a noise—a little girl's noise"; and then all the angels kept perfectly still till she said Amen. The angels need not be hushed for God to hear the humblest little one pray; yet the child was not far from wrong.

Another thing we learn from this delay is that Jesus never comes too late, never waits too long. It certainly seemed that He had tarried too long this time; but when we see how it all came out, we are sure that He made no mistake. True, the child died while He lingered; but this only gave Him an opportunity for a greater miracle. He waited that He might do a more glorious work. There is always some good reason for it when Christ delays to answer our prayers or come to our help. He waits that He may do far more for us in the end. So we have one more lesson on letting our Lord have His own way with us, even in answering our prayers. He knows best when to answer, and what answer to give.

NOT DEAD, BUT SLEEPING

Why make ye this ado, and weep?
the damsel is not dead, but sleepeth.
Mark 5:39

The Christian should not grieve as others do. Christ has brought the truth of immortality out into clear light. We ought to familiarize our minds with the Christian idea of death. Christ wrote no truer lines anywhere than He wrote over the gateway of the believer's grave. We ought to learn to look at death in the light of Christ's teachings. Too many Christians, however, never seem to have entered into the blessedness of the Savior's victory over the grave. Here, in the account of this miracle of the raising of the ruler's daughter, we have a beautiful illustration of the way our Lord would have us look at death.

When we lament over our dead He says, "They are not dead, but sleeping. Why do you make all this bitter grief?" Our Christian friends who have died have only passed out of our sight. They have not ceased to be. Even their bodies only sleep. And as a mother in the morning calls her children and awakes them, so Christ will some day call up from their graves all who sleep in Him.

Sleep is not a terrible experience; it renews and strengthens the weary body. So the sleep of death is a time of rest and renewal. The calling of this child back from death, and her restoration to her friends, represented what Christ will do for all His people at the end. He will restore friend to friend and bind up again the broken relationships of households.

There is one point, however, in which the raising of this young girl does not illustrate the final resurrection of believers. She was brought back to resume the old life of toil, struggle, temptation, and sorrow, and to die again. But in the final resurrection believers shall rise to a new, glorious, and immortal life, without sorrow or sin, in the fullness of life, joy, and blessedness.

July 4

◇

WORDS OF WONDER

◇

Many hearing him were astonished, saying,
From whence hath this man these things?
Mark 6:2

They could not help being astonished, for Christ's words were full of wisdom. "No man ever spake like this man," they said. Yet, although they were astonished, they did not grant Him their confidence and their love. The result of their amazement was only scornful and unbelieving rejection. It is oftentimes the same yet. People cannot help confessing that Christ is wonderful—that He is the most glorious figure the world ever saw; that His teachings are infinitely above all human teachings; that His power is majestic; that His love passes all comprehension. Yet while they grant all this, they do not give Him the homage of their hearts. It is as if a drowning man in the sea were to be amazed at the beauty and the adequacy of the lifeboat that came to offer him rescue and should still reject the rescue and stay in the waves to perish.

"From whence hath this man these things?" they asked in derision and contempt. They knew Him. Some of them had been His playmates and schoolmates in earlier years and then later His workmates. They knew that He had never been to any but the village school, where they had all attended. How did this plain, untaught young man have such wisdom as He now seemed to have, and do such works as were reported of Him? They could not explain it, and so they treated the whole matter with contempt.

We may ask the same question today in sincerity of those who reject Christ. Here is a man who spoke the wisest words ever spoken on this earth, and who did the most wonderful works ever performed. Yet He was only a village carpenter and had only a village school education. How do you account for His wisdom and His power? "Where did this man get these things?" Can it be that He is more than human?

◇

ONLY A CARPENTER

◇

Is not this the carpenter?
Mark 6:3

Certainly; yet that refutes nothing. It only helps to prove the claims of Jesus to be the Son of God. If He had been a learned rabbi or philosopher, it might have been said that He had received His wisdom from men; but as He was only a poor village carpenter, He must have been taught of God.

There are other thoughts which this question suggests. It tells us how wisely Jesus spent His youth and early manhood—not in idleness, but in useful toil, no doubt helping thus to provide for His mother and her family. The example has its inspiring lesson for every young man growing up in the home of his childhood. He should make the years bright with earnest work and the conscientious use of every moment of time.

There really are no pictures of the Christ; yet there are on the pages of the evangelists pictures of the Christ in certain perspectives which have deep meaning for us. Once we see Him with a whip in His hand driving the profaners of the temple from their unlawful work. Another time we see Him with a basin and towel. Again we see Him on the cross dying. All these pictures are richly suggestive. Here we see Him as a carpenter, with the saw and the chisel in His hands, and this picture is rich in meaning.

It teaches us that there is no disgrace in working at a trade, since the Son of God worked as a carpenter. No hands are so beautiful as working hands. Marks of toil are stronger symbols of honor than jeweled rings and delicate whiteness. The picture shows also the voluntary humiliation of Christ. Though He was rich, He became poor, and He even toiled for His daily bread. It assures us, therefore, of His sympathy now with those who toil. It is a pleasant thought that the hands that now hold the scepter once wielded the hammer and the saw.

THE SECRET OF POWER

Then he called his twelve disciples together, and
gave them power and authority over all devils.
Luke 9:1

The first thing is always to come to Christ Himself. We can do nothing until we have been to Him. We should take every command from His word and go out always with the blessing of His hand upon our heads. It is told of one of Wellington's officers that when commanded, during a battle, to do some dangerous duty, he seemed to hesitate. He did not for a moment shrink from the hazardous service, but he said to the duke, "Let me, before I go, have one touch of your all-conquering hand, and then I can do it." There is no duty too perilous, no toil too heavy, no task too difficult, if, as we start, we have the inspiration of Christ's hand and His inspiring words.

Christ alone can give power for the work He asks us to do. His followers are to have authority over devils. Anyone who tries to cast out devils in his own strength, whether the devils be in himself or in some other, will meet only miserable failure. A man may rule nations and conquer kingdoms and yet be unable to eject one devil from his own heart. Alexander conquered the world, but he was overthrown by appetite and passion. Men are forever foolishly trying to battle without God's help with the evil of their own natures; but they fail in the struggle.

The same is true of power over devils in others. Once the disciples, in Christ's absence, tried to cast out an evil spirit, and could not do it. Yet they ought to have been able in Christ's name to cast out the demon. Jesus said afterward that the reason they could not do it was that they had no faith. He wants every follower of His to have power over all forms of evil in this world—not miraculous power, such as He gave the apostles, but real power. And if only we have faith in Him, He will always give us power.

WHAT CAN WE DO FOR OTHERS

He sent them to preach.
Luke 9:2

Apostles are not the only persons to whom Christ gives this same commission. He wants everyone that He saves to go out and preach the gospel to others. Christian men and women can preach by living a holy and good life at home, at school, among companions. Christlike living is the most eloquent of all preaching. There is a story of one who became a Christian; when asked under whose preaching he had been converted, he replied, "Under nobody's preaching, but under Aunt Mary's practicing." Everyone ought to preach by faithful practicing.

But there are other ways. There is in the Bible a story of a little captive girl far away from home, who told in her master's house what the God of her own nation could do; and her words led to the healing of at least one leper. We can all tell something about Christ—what He has done for us, what He can do for others; and our words may fall upon some ear that will be glad to hear them, and upon some heart that will turn to Him with hungry faith and prayer.

This is a missionary text, and there are a thousand ways in which we can help to give the gospel to the world. What a pity it is that we should keep to ourselves something so precious, that has such power to bless the world, and that men, women, and children everywhere need so much, the very gospel of Jesus Christ! Think of a rich man in the time of famine, when his neighbors are all starving, keeping his great full barns locked up, and not dealing out bread to the hungry. We who have found Christ have bread for human souls, not only enough for ourselves, but enough for all about us; for giving out does not waste this bread of life. All around us are perishing sinners whom we may save. Shall we keep to ourselves that for want of which souls are dying?

July 8

HOME MISSIONS

Whatsoever house ye enter into, there abide.
Luke 9:4

The place to carry the gospel is right into people's homes. We must take it down along the streets and alleys, and over the fields and hills, entering every door, and telling the old, old story by the firesides and at the household tables. It should be the aim of every church to reach every house in its parish with the gospel. Christians should go themselves to this work, and not merely send a hired carrier to put tracts under people's doors. Tracts are good; but we should take them ourselves and add to them the gifts of our own warm love and eager sympathy and interest. We should get the wonderful gospel into every home by telling it from our own experience.

Did you ever think what a wondrous blessing it is to a home when the salvation of Christ comes to it? Think what a dark and sad place a godless home is, with no prayer, no recognition of God's love and mercy, no shelter, no comfort in sorrow, no hope in death. Then think what Christ brings when He is admitted. Peace comes with Him, for sin is pardoned. God's love builds protection over the home, for they are His children who dwell there now. There is direct communication from heaven, a ladder running up, with angels upon it, and God above it. There is comfort in sorrow, help in trial, strength in weakness, hope in dying.

For illustration of the two homes—the godless and the godly—we can picture an Egyptian and a Hebrew home on that night when the angel of death came to slay the firstborn. The blood on the doorpost made the difference. Christ's blood on the door of a home is a shelter from every woe. Would it not be a great thing if we could carry Christ's gospel into every home about us where Christ has not already been received? Do you know a home where there is no prayer? Will you not try to open that door for Jesus?

THE MISSIONARY SPIRIT

◆

They departed, and went through the towns,
preaching the gospel, and healing every where.
Luke 9:6

A great many people do not do this. They come to Christ and hear His command, but they do not go, or at least they do not preach and heal. They do not carry to other homes and to other lives the sweet blessings of mercy and restoration they have themselves received. Surely this is very ungrateful to Christ, when we remember all He has done for us. Then it is also very selfish, when we have found such joys, not to try to share them with others who need them.

Christ wants to get the gospel into every home in the world; and the way He wants to do this is through the hearts and hands of those whom He has already saved. If we do not carry the good news, the lost will not receive it at all. It is told of a boy who was converted that at once he started to walk—for he was poor, and could not buy a ticket on the railroad—away to a place in the West, more than a thousand miles from his home, to tell his brother about Christ. History relates that the early Christians, many of them, were so eager to carry Christ's gospel everywhere that they even hired themselves out as servants or sold themselves as slaves, that they might be admitted into the homes of the rich and great among the heathen, to live there and thus have opportunity to tell in those homes of the love of Jesus and of His salvation.

It would have great power in shaping our lives for usefulness for us to consider ourselves under a divine commission to advance the kingdom of our Lord by bringing others under its holy way. So long as we merely regard ourselves as sinners saved by grace, with no further responsibility, we shall be of very little use. But when we become conscious that we are apostles, every one of us, sent to witness for Christ, we shall become blessings.

HERODIAS'S REVENGE

◇

The daughter of Herodias danced before them, and pleased Herod.
Matthew 14:6

It seems disgraceful even in that country and in those days for a woman to show herself at all in a hall of partying and carousing. Then to perform such a dance in such a place for the entertainment of the revelers was regarded as a most debasing and shameful act. The dance was indecent, and only those who had lost all sense of modesty and womanly propriety would debase themselves this way. That a mother should send her own daughter into such a scene to perform such a part seems almost incredible. The act reveals the kind of home life and the ideas of womanly purity that prevailed in the court of Herod—also the strength of Herodias's passion for revenge upon John. She would even send her own daughter to play this shameful part in order to accomplish her purpose.

While this lesson is before them, young women should learn that they cannot be too careful of their behavior and bearing in public. A young woman's reputation is a precious jewel, which she should prize above all wealth or pleasure. If she loses it, neither wealth nor pleasure will be of much use to her afterward. Her name once sullied can never be altogether white again.

Sometimes young girls think their parents unreasonable in the restraints which they put upon them with regard to appearance or conduct in public; but someday they will see how wise and loving is such restraint. It may very fairly be questioned whether young ladies can take part in certain fashionable dances of today and not pass beyond the bounds of pure female modesty and decency. At least, heart-purity is so holy a thing, and so easily tarnished, and the harm when done is so irreparable, that one had better deny oneself a fascinating pleasure rather than risk the loss of anything so precious.

A ROYAL COWARD

*For the oath's sake, and them which sat with
him at meat, he commanded it to be given her.*
Matthew 14:9

Herod called himself a king, and yet see what a poor slave he was, what a terrible coward! He was sorry he had made the oath, exceedingly sorry. His conscience was not altogether dead. He did not want to kill John. He was afraid of public opinion, which he knew would condemn him. He was afraid of avenging wrath. Then he hated himself for having been caught by Herodias in her plot to have her long-cherished revenge. Yet he was so much a slave that, although he claimed to be a king, he had not the courage to refuse such a request.

True, he had made an oath, but no promise or oath is binding which requires one to sin. Of course, Herod did very wrong to make such a reckless oath, not knowing what his promise would involve. After he had made it, he was bound to keep it, at whatever cost to himself, provided nothing sinful was involved. If Herodias had asked for half his kingdom, he would have been bound to grant her request; but he was under no obligation to grant any desire which required him to commit sin.

It was not the oath, however, that really influenced Herod. He had not the courage to do the heroic thing he ought to have done. He was afraid of the ridicule of his guests; and he was so under the power of Herodias that he dared not refuse what she demanded. It was his weakness that ruined him. Rather than be a moral example of a leader, he stained his hands in holy blood; and the stains are not yet washed out.

There are some things we have no right to give away. Things that are our own we are always to do with as we have sworn. According to the Scriptures, a good man, having sworn to his own hurt, does not change. But no oath binds anyone to give away another man's life. This is not his to give.

◇

DEATH OF JOHN THE BAPTIST

◇

And he sent, and beheaded John in the prison.
Matthew 14:10

This seems a sad end for this glorious man's life. After a few months of faithful preaching he was cast into a dungeon, where he lay for a year and where he was beheaded as a criminal. To us it is very mysterious. Why did God permit such a fate to come upon so faithful and noble a servant? Our Lord Himself said that no greater man ever lived than John. Why then was his life allowed to go out in such darkness?

We know, first, that it was no accident. There are no accidents in this world over which our loving Father presides. John would not have chosen such a destiny for himself, so brief, with such a tragic ending; few of us would choose just the life we live in this world. There are no chances, no accidents. Our ways are those of the Lord's choosing—ways sadder, perhaps, but safer; rougher, perhaps, but surer; narrower, perhaps, but better than those of our own dreaming.

John finished his work. If there had been anything further for him to do, he would not have been left to die so shamefully to gratify the revenge of a wicked woman. His work was done when Christ began to preach. Then when he died, it was for faithfulness to the truth. It is not long years that make a complete life. A life is complete, whether long or short, that fulfills the purpose of its creation. And the longest life is incomplete and a failure if it does not do the work for which it was made. It is better to die in youth with a life unspotted than to live on to old age in sin and crime. It was a thousand times better every way to die as John died than to live on as Herod and Herodias lived.

> *He liveth long who liveth well—*
> *All else is being flung away;*
> *He liveth longest who can tell*
> *Of rue things truly done each day.*

TELL JESUS

*The apostles gathered themselves together
unto Jesus, and told him all things.*
Mark 6:30

That is just what we should always do when we have been trying to do any service for our Lord. We should do it as well as we can, and then go and tell Him what we have done. At the close of each day we should go to Him and tell Him of all that we have done or tried to do during the day. We should tell Him how we have lived, how we have done our work, how we have endured temptations, how we have treated our friends and those with whom we have been associated, how we have performed our mission as His servants, what words we have spoken for Him, what efforts we have made to do good or to give comfort or help, and how we have met the calls upon us for sympathy and aid.

We must not forget to tell Him about the day's failures. Did we lose our patience? Did we yield to temptation? Did we neglect to speak the word for the Master that we ought to have spoken? Were we unkind to anyone? We must tell Him of the efforts to do good which seemed to come to nothing. Oftentimes we are like the disciples who had toiled all the night and caught nothing. At many a setting sun we come, weary and sad, with empty hands. Then sometimes we are tempted to stay away from the Master and make no report; what have we to report? Nothing but a fruitless day. But we should not keep away from Him who sent us out. Jesus had days in His own life that seemed fruitless, and He can understand our sadness when we come with no sheaves.

So let us tell Him everything. That is the kind of evening solitary prayer that will bless us. It will make us very watchful all day if we remember that we must report to Jesus all we say, or do, or fail to do; it will keep us in more intimate relations with Him. Then His sympathy will strengthen us for better service each day.

QUIET RESTING PLACES

*He said unto them, Come ye yourselves apart
into a desert place, and rest a while.*

Mark 6:31

How concerned Jesus is for the comfort of His disciples! He never wants to overwork them. He provides times and places of rest for them all along the way. One of these "quiet resting places" is the night, coming after each day of toil. Then our emptied reservoirs are refilled. Another resting place is the Sabbath, after a week of tense battle and strife. Then it is that we should seek the renewal of our spiritual life by communing with God, by lying on our Lord's bosom. The Lord's Supper is another resting place. The Master leads us into the supper room to sit with Him at His table, to feast our souls on the provisions of His love and grace.

Then there are many other quiet places to which our Lord invites us to come apart with Him to rest awhile—the sweet hours of prayer, alone, or in the house of God, the communings with friends, the sacred hours we spend in home joys. Sometimes the Master calls us to rest awhile in a sickroom, away from the noise and struggle of the busy world. It may be in pain or in suffering, and there may be no bodily rest; but our souls are resting, and we are learning lessons we never could have learned in the midst of life's exciting toil.

One thing about all these "rests" to which Jesus invites us is that we are to rest *with Him.* He never says, "Go apart and rest," but always His word is, "Come with me apart." The resting is always to be with Him. It is His loving presence that makes the blessedness of the rest. There is no true soul-refreshing for us anywhere, even in the most sacred ordinances, if we do not find Christ there. It is lying on His bosom when we are tired or sorrowing or penitent that rests us. Rest apart from Christ brings no refreshment. So we must be sure that we go apart with the Master.

DIVINE COMPASSION

◆

Jesus . . . saw much people, and was moved with compassion toward them, because they were as sheep not having a shepherd.

Mark 6:34

Here we have a window through which we catch a glimpse of the heart of Jesus. Every scene of sorrow touched Him. It is a great truth that the heart of the Son of God is actually moved at the sight of human distress or want. It was this compassion that brought Christ from heaven. It was because our Father loved the lost world that He gave His Son to save the world. Does God care now if we are in suffering or in need? "Like as a father pitieth His children, so the Lord pitieth them that fear Him" (Psalm 103:13). Does Jesus, since He has gone up into glory, have any compassion for human sorrow on the earth? "We have not a high priest who cannot be touched with the feeling of our infirmities" (Hebrews 4:15).

It is worthwhile to notice what kind of trouble it was that so stirred the compassion of Jesus at this time. It was because He saw the people as sheep not having a shepherd. It was not their hunger, nor their poverty, nor their sickness, but their spiritual need that so deeply touched His compassion. There were no wise, gentle, thoughtful pastors watching over the higher interests of their immortal natures, feeding them with heavenly bread, protecting them from the wolves of sin and lust, and leading them in right paths.

We learn here that no condition is so sad as that of spiritual neglect. Soul peril is far more pitiable than bodily danger or distress. Nothing moves the divine heart so deeply as a soul exposed to the world's pain, wandering from the fold amid sin's pitfalls and uncared for. Happy are those people, old and young, who are safe in the Good Shepherd's keeping! If we have "the mind of Christ," we also shall be moved with compassion for all souls that have no shepherd.

BARLEY LOAVES

He . . . took the five loaves.
Matthew 14:19

We are not surprised that a disciple asked, of the five loaves and two fishes, "What are these among so many?" What a little way they will go in feeding such a multitude! Why bring out this poor, paltry store at all? Surely Christ can feed the hungry people without these poor, little dark loaves.

Still, Jesus asked the disciples to bring the loaves to Him, and He used them. Is it not strange that the mighty Christ should need us and our little barley loaves to feed people's hunger? Yet He does; He wants our gifts, and then He wants our ministry in dispensing the gifts. He passed the bread to the multitude through the hands of the disciples; He channels salvation through His saved ones to the unsaved.

> *Only one talent small,*
> *Scarce worthy to be named;*
> *Truly he hath no need of this—*
> *O soul, art thou ashamed?*
> *He gave that talent first;*
> *Then use it in his strength;*
> *Thereby—thou know'st not—he may work*
> *A miracle at length.*
>
> *Many of the starving souls*
> *Now waiting to be fed,*
> *Needing, though knowing not their need*
> *Of Christ, the living Bread.*
> *Oh! hast thou known his love?*
> *To others make it known;*
> *Receiving blessings, others bless!*
> *No seed abides alone.*
>
> *And when thine eyes shall see*
> *The holy, ransomed throng*
> *In heavenly fields by living streams,*
> *By Jesus led along.*

"TOILING IN ROWING"

*He saw them toiling in rowing; for
the wind was contrary unto them.*
Mark 6:48

Jesus always sees our toils and distresses in this world. We do not see Him, and sometimes we think He has forgotten us; but that is never true. He is not indifferent for even a moment.

On the heights, while a battle was in progress, stood a group of men watching the struggling armies in the plain below. In this group was the American Civil War general Sheridan, who watched the mighty strife with the keen eye of a soldier. King William was also there, but his interest was different from Sheridan's. His son was in the thick of the fight, and he watched the battle with the eye of a father as well as of a king.

Christ looks down upon our struggles in this world. He sees us toiling; all our battles and strife He watches. He sees us in the waves and in the storm. He sees us, not with the eye of the calm spectator merely, but with the eye of tenderest love. This is a wonderful thought; if we can only get it into our hearts, it will give us tremendous courage in the hour of toil, sorrow, or struggle. Jesus knows when the battle is hard, when the night is dark, when the temptation is more than we can bear.

Here the winds were contrary, though Christ sent His disciples out to sea. We learn that even when we are doing the things God has bidden us do, we may encounter opposition and sore difficulty. We may even be beaten back and find the resistance too great for our strength. Many of the Lord's disciples have to make their voyage over very stormy seas on their way to glory. For some people, duty is hard; indeed, a true, holy, positive, strong life must always exist in the face of opposition and contrary winds. "The law of head-winds in life is doubtless in the secret love of God. When the voyage is over, perhaps we shall be let see the charts, and know why it had to be."

NEVER FORGOTTEN

*About the fourth watch of the night he cometh
unto them, walking upon the sea.*

Mark 6:48

It was a long night for the tempest-driven disciples; they were in great distress. But Jesus was only trying them; He had not forgotten them. From His mountain seat, unseen by them, He was watching them. He saw their struggle and danger. He sent up prayer for them. Then finally He came to rescue them.

It is the same in every Christian's life. Sometimes Christ seems to have forsaken His people. For a long while they are left to struggle alone and to be driven back by contrary winds. They call and get no answer. The night wears away, and it is almost morning. Then at last He comes.

When people are in serious trouble of any kind they are like those disciples that night out in the midst of the sea. No human aid can reach them. Human friends eagerly want to help, and they come to offer sympathy and consolation. But in such hours even the most helpful of us are only like people standing on the shore of a dark and stormy sea, while our friends are far out on the wild waves. We cannot go to them to give help or rescue. Our little boats cannot ride in the surges of the waves. All we can do is to stand on the shore, as it were, and look with pitying eye and heart at the struggling ones in the angry sea. That is the very best that the richest human love can do.

A father stood on the shore opposite the wild waves, and with unutterable anguish saw the boat that bore his own son swept into the angry torrents, but he could do nothing. Thus it is in all life's deep needs. It is in such hours that we realize the blessedness of Christ's power to help. He can go out on any wave, into the wildest sea, to reach those who are driven and tossed. He can carry help to all who are troubled. He can comfort in any sorrow and give victory in any strife.

—◇—

CHRIST WALKING ON THE SEA

—◇—

When they saw him walking upon the sea, they
supposed it had been a spirit, and cried out.

Mark 6:49

I t seems strange that the disciples should ever have been afraid of their own Master. They had been in great distress all night because He was not with them. They had greatly desired all those long dark hours that He would come to them. Yet now, when He came, they were in terror at the sight of Him. It was because they did not know it was Jesus Himself that His presence so frightened them.

It is oftentimes the same with us. We are in some need or danger, and Jesus does not seem to come to us. We call upon Him, and we most earnestly desire His coming; yet He does not come. Finally He comes; but it is not as we expected, in beautiful appearance and gentle manners, but in a type of anguish. It is in some great trial that He sometimes comes. Death enters our door and carries away a loved one. We experience loss or some misfortune—at least it seems to us loss or misfortune. We cry out in pain. We do not know it is Christ, veiled in the dark robe, who has come. We do not know that this is the answer to our prayer for His presence and His help. We are frightened at the form that moves over the waters in the dark night. We think it is new danger, when really it is the very divine love and divine help for which we have been longing and pleading.

We ought to learn that Jesus is in every providence that comes to us. He does not come in the sunshine only; quite as frequently it is in the shadow that He draws near. It is our duty as Christians to train ourselves to see Christ in each event. Then, whether it be sorrow or joy that knocks at our door, we shall give it a loving welcome, knowing that Jesus Himself is veiled in whatever form it is that enters. Then we shall find that when we welcome Him in the somber garments of pain, He has always a rich blessing for our lives.

July 20

---◇---

PEACE IN STORM

---◇---

He went up unto them into the ship; and the wind ceased.
Mark 6:51

When Jesus comes to us, our trouble ceases. At His bidding the wildest storm instantly becomes calm. The trouble itself may not go away from us, but it is no longer a trouble when He is with us. The wind may not cease to blow without and beat upon our lives, but He makes peace within. It is far better to have so much grace in order that our hearts shall be calm and quiet in the fiercest storm, rather than to have the storm itself quieted, while our hearts remain as restless as ever. Peace within is far better than any mere calm without.

In a gallery in Italy there are two pictures side by side by different artists. One represents a sea tossed by storms. Dark clouds hang over it, the lightning bolts pierce the sky, and the powerful waves roll in fury. In the seething waters a dead human face is seen. The other represents a sea similarly storm-tossed; but in the midst of the angry waters is a rock. In the rock is a cleft with green herbage and flowers, and amid these a dove quietly sits on her nest.

These two pictures tell the whole story of human life in this world. The first is the story of life without Christ, unblessed by His presence and peace. There are storms everywhere, with no quiet shelter. The other picture paints the peace which Christ gives. There is no less of a storm. The waves roll as high. But there is peace. The rock represents Christ; it is in the cleft of the rock that the peace is found.

Rock of ages, cleft for me,
Let me hide myself in thee.

It is in the redemption and atonement of Christ alone that we can have peace. "In me ye shall have peace." If, therefore, we take Christ into our boats on the storm-swept sea, we shall glide on in safety through earth's tempests to glory's shore.

July 21

❖

ONE THING NEEDFUL

❖

Labour not for the meat which perisheth, but for
that meat which endureth unto everlasting life.
John 6:27

We should call a man very foolish who, in building a great and costly house, should look only after the outside, spending large amounts of money in exterior decoration, while he left the interior in a rough, unfinished state, the walls unplastered, the rooms filled with rubbish and without furniture or decorations of any kind. No one can get comfort from a beautiful exterior in his home and from fine grounds if within all is bare and crude. The wise person will think more of the inside than of the outside of the house in which he is to live. He will provide beauty, warmth, and comfort, and thus make a true home, in which he may dwell in peace and in real enjoyment.

Even more foolish is the man who thinks only of the needs of his physical nature and gives no thought to the needs of his immortal soul. He is looking after the outside and neglecting the inner life. He is providing for his body, which will soon perish, and giving no care to his soul, which will endure forever. He is planning only for the present and neglecting the interests that are eternal. How pitiful is such a life, deliberately turning away from all the best, holiest, most beautiful, and most enduring things, and seeking only the poor, miserable, worthless things that are impediments, not enriching him who has them!

Our Lord's counsel is that we should look first after our spiritual necessities. It is a fearful mistake to toil all one's days for bread and raiment, or for wealth and honor, and never do anything for the inner life. At the end there will be nothing left to show for all the toil and pain and sacrifice. If we look after the interests of our souls, then when this life is ended we shall find ourselves in possession of eternal life. A good motto for life is, "Live for the immortal things."

THE WORK OF FAITH
◈

This is the work of God, that ye believe
on him whom he hath sent.
John 6:29

People are curious to know how they can eat spiritual bread. They cannot see it or take it into their hands. When they are told to work for the food which gives eternal life, they ask how they can do it. Here Christ says that the way to work for the spiritual food is to believe on Him.

Of course, believing on Christ must be taken in its fullest sense. Merely believing that bread will satisfy hunger will not in itself satisfy any hungry man; he must eat of the bread, its nourishing qualities being then assimilated in his system. And merely believing that Christ is able to meet all our soul's needs will not in itself bring to us spiritual satisfaction. Christ must be received into our lives.

There are different ways of believing. One may read in a book on astronomy that the sun is some ninety million miles away. One believes the statement, but it has no particular effect on his living tomorrow; it is not calculated to have any effect of this kind. But when he reads that whosoever believeth on the Lord Jesus Christ shall be saved, the truth is meant to bless him by leading him first of all to entrust himself to Christ for salvation, then to follow Him as his Master, then to have his unholy life transformed into holiness like Christ's. It is the same with all spiritual truth. The mere receiving it is not enough; it must be assimilated, as food is assimilated in the body. The bread of today is the laborer's strength, the orator's eloquence, the artist's skill tomorrow. The Bible verses of the morning must become the Christian's joy, or refuge, or inspiration, or warning, or transforming influence in the day's struggles and toils. It should be noticed also that we are not to get this spiritual food by working for it, but by believing on Christ. We live by faith.

July 23

◇

"THE BREAD OF LIFE"

◇

The bread of God is he which cometh down from heaven.
John 6:33

No bread that comes from the earth will furnish food for a human soul. In all our worldly strivings and ambitions we are thinking only of our perishing part, we are looking only after the poor, frail tabernacle while we are allowing the dweller within to die of hunger. Recently in a well-furnished house a family was found starving for food. There are many souls starving in bodies that are luxuriously cared for. A soul cannot feed on grains and fruits. The finest luxuries of earth will never quench a soul's hunger.

Manna is called once in the Bible "angels' food," but this was only a poetical designation, referring to its falling from the sky. Manna did not really come down from heaven. It was not angels' food. It was food for bodies, not for spirits. Angels could not have lived on it. Imagine an angel taking up his abode in some millionaire's palace on the earth. Would he care for the magnificent things filling every room? Would he sit down and feed at the rich man's luxurious table? Souls and angels are much alike in their needs; both are spirits, unable to subsist on material food. Yet many people live as if their souls could be clothed in earth's finery and fed and satisfied with earth's delicacies.

Bread for souls must literally come down from heaven. It is the nature of the soul to feed upon immortal things. Its hungers and cravings are for pardon of sin, for peace, for communion with God, for holiness of character, for Christlikeness, for restoration to the divine favor. The bread for these spiritual hungers must come down from heaven. It must come in the form of mercy, of grace, of love, of divine friendship, of gifts of life. Such food is found on no table on earth; it grows in no earthly climate; it can come only from God. It is for God, the living God, that our souls hunger and thirst.

July 24

SPIRITUAL FOOD

I am the bread of life: he that cometh to me shall never hunger.
John 6:35

How is Christ bread? We understand what the bodily needs are which common bread satisfies. What in the soul corresponds to these cravings? The most intense of the soul-cravings is for pardon. All men sin, but sin satisfies no one. Nor has the world any power to give peace to a troubled conscience. We cannot forgive ourselves, and no man can really forgive us. How is Christ bread to satisfy this hunger? He was the Lamb of God, taking away the sin of the world; and because He bore our sins He is able to forgive us. We remember how the guilty sat at His feet when they saw Him and, looking up into His face, heard the word which gave them peace.

Another craving is for holiness. The world has no way by which human souls can be restored to moral beauty. Men can restore paintings, and buildings over which fire has swept can be erected again into more than their original nobleness; but there is no human hand that can replace the glory of a ruined soul. Yet this very craving Christ satisfies through the Holy Spirit, who enters the heart of everyone who believes and builds up anew the holy beauty which sin has destroyed.

Another of the soul's cravings is for spiritual life here, and then everlasting life. Again, earth has no bread to meet the hunger. The vain searches for hope are among the most pitiable of this world's efforts. But those who receive Christ have eternal life. He has opened the doors clear through into the glory beyond. He said, "Whosoever liveth and believeth on me shall never die" (John 11:26). He is the hope of glory to everyone who receives Him. Said a martyr as he was led to execution: "I have only two stiles to get over to reach my Father's house—one, the steps up the scaffold; the other, the ladder let down from heaven."

◇

A WELCOME FOR ALL

◇

All that the Father giveth me shall come to me; and
him that cometh to me I will in no wise cast out.

John 6:37

We need not worry ourselves trying to harmonize the two parts of this verse; we can believe them both and find great comfort and joy in them. Together they bring to every Christian a glorious and double confidence. Surely it is a blessed thing to know that God has thought about our salvation and planned for it, and then given us to Christ to be His.

If this is true it is easy to understand the other part of this verse. Of course, Christ will not cast out any whom His Father gives to Him. They are His own; He knows them by name, and He loves them, for He died for them. Surely He will not pass by one of His own when He finds him lying by the wayside or among the thorns, wounded, bleeding, dying, but will take him up and bear him home in safety. We need not give ourselves any anxiety about the first part of this sentence; the latter part is all that really concerns us. If we truly come to Christ, we are here assured that He will in no way cast us out; but we must come. Then we shall find room enough and a most loving welcome.

No father's house is full,
    E'en though there seems no resting place for more;
Forgiving arms and doors do open wide,
    If one repentant child implore
    Outside.

No mother's heart is full,
    Unless it be with longing, burning wild—
Heart throbbings that no cheerful face can hide—
    The wish to clasp her sinning child
    Outside.

God's flock is never full:
    Fear not to enter boldly at his door;
None ever were refused who there applied;
    He hath abiding place for more
    Inside.

◇

OUR SECURITY

◇

*This is the Father's will which hath sent me, that of
all which he hath given me I should lose
nothing, but should raise it up again at the last day.*

John 6:39

There is not a shadow of doubt in the Christian's hope. There is not a broken link in the chain that binds the believer to eternal blessedness. There is not a step wanting in the ladder that reaches up from the depths of sin to the heights of glory. "Whom he did foreknow, he also did predestinate to be conformed to the image of his Son . . . Moreover whom he did predestinate, them he also called: and whom he called, them he also justified: and whom he justified, them he also glorified" (Romans 8:29–30). These are the links in the Christian's hope as St. Paul saw them; in the words of today's text we have the same links as they appeared to our Savior's eye.

The assurance is that Christ will never lose any soul that entrusts itself to Him for salvation. "Yet Christians die, just like other people," says someone. Yes; but they are not then lost; their spirits pass at once into glory with Christ, and their bodies will only rest in the grave until the resurrection. An old Christian sailor put it well. When asked if he was not afraid when the storms were very high, he answered that according to the Bible God held the waters in the hollow of His hand; and even if the ship were wrecked, and he should fall into the sea, he would but drop into his Father's hand. That is what death is to a Christian, however and wherever he may die—committing his soul into the hands of God.

The grave seems dark, but we have Christ's own pledge here that not one of His own shall be lost or left in the grave. No matter where we die, or where our bodies lie, we have the Savior's word—which we had better receive in simplicity, without questioning or doubt—that He "will lose nothing, but will raise it up again at the last day."

PHARISAISM

The Pharisees . . . except they wash . . . eat not.
Mark 7:3

The religion of the Pharisees consisted not in love of God, or in disposition, character, and conduct, but in certain ceremonial rites which they observed with great scrupulousness. They washed their hands before meals because ceremonial uncleanness in their hands contaminated the food. Yet they took no pains to wash their hearts of evil or uncharitable thoughts and feelings toward others. They washed when they came in from their shops, because worldly business defiled them; but they were not careful in their dealings with others to be just, honest, and true. They saw that every pot and kettle, every vessel, and all household arrangements were ceremonially cleansed; but they did not stop to look within their own hearts to see if all was clean there for the indwelling of God's Spirit.

We all need to watch concerning making our religion consist in forms of worship. We may pray many times a day, and read a regular number of chapters, and go through many and laborious devotions, and yet not have a particle of true religion. We are truly religious just in the measure in which we have the spirit of Christ in our disposition, heart, and character. "The kingdom of God is not meat and drink, but righteousness, and peace, and joy in the Holy Ghost" (Romans 14:17).

Loving God and our fellowmen is the sum of all duty. Unless we have this twofold love in our hearts, manifested in life and character, our profession of religion is vain. Not a word should be said against external cleanliness; a clean heart should make the life clean to the tips of the fingers and in all tastes, feelings, habits, words, and actions. But clean hands and well-scrubbed floors and shining dishes and careful ceremonial observances will never please God, if in the heart there is no love for Him and no love for men. "Blessed are the pure in heart: for they shall see God" (Matthew 5:8).

"CORBAN"

Making the word of God of none effect through your tradition,
which ye have delivered: and many such like things do ye.

Mark 7:13

It is a good thing to dedicate one's property to God. But when we have done this we must take good heed that we use it in the ways marked out for us by the divine commandments. It will not do to cover miserliness and greed by a pretense that we have given our money to God and therefore cannot use it for charitable purposes.

For example, if a man has needy parents, one of the first uses of consecrated money is to provide for their wants. He may say that he is gathering means to build an orphanage, or an asylum for old men or old women, and that he has consecrated his property to this great charity; but if meanwhile he allows his own aged parents to suffer, his consecration of property is not acceptable to God. He who sets aside the fifth commandment that he may use his money for the poor is playing a miserable farce before God. No amount of service in the work of the church avails when one is neglecting the duties he owes to his own family.

The case is still worse when, as under the rabbinical rules, the money or property was never really used at all for God, the plea of "Corban" being only a pretext to evade the requirements of family duty. The consecration of money to God implies always the use of the consecrated money in the service of God as He may call for it. God does not want money hoarded up; He wants it put to work doing good. We apply the parable of the talents to everything but money, when there surely is nothing to which the parable applies more certainly than to money. At least we may never pretend that we have given our money to God, and therefore cannot give it away. Giving it away for wise use is the very thing God wants us to do with it.

July 29

◇

WHAT DEFILETH?

◇

*Not that which goeth into the mouth defileth a man; but
that which cometh out of the mouth, this defileth a man.*
Matthew 15:11

There are many applications of this principle. The food we eat
does not affect our moral character. No external ceremonies
really touch the soul. Indeed, nothing in this world has any
power to defile a heart while it remains outside and is not
allowed to enter. A man may be a coal miner, always dirty and
grimy, and always working in dirt, and yet he may have a soul
clean and unspotted. This is dirt of living amid temptations. So
long as we keep them outside, they have no power to injure us.

Luther says somewhere that we cannot prevent the birds flying about our heads, but we can prevent them building their
nests in our hair. We cannot prevent a great many evil things
buzzing around us continually, but we can keep them from entering our hearts and nesting there. And so long as we do this, the
worst things in the world cannot lay a spot upon our souls.

Our Savior says further that it is what comes out of the
mouth that defiles. So, then, there may even be evil in the heart
which does not defile us unless it is allowed to shape itself in
thoughts, words, or deeds. The suggestion of wrongdoing is not a
sin until the suggestion is accepted and entertained. Temptation
to sin is not itself sin. Jesus was tempted. Suggestions of evil were
made to Him by Satan; yet He never sinned, and because these
suggestions never found any place in His heart, they never found
any expression in word or act, or even in thought. So temptations
come to us from without. These things we cannot help; we are
not responsible for them; there is no sin in merely having these
suggestions. But the sin begins the moment we open the door to
one of these sinful invitations. That which comes out defiles us.

July 30

◇

HE IS HERE

◇

He could not be hid.
Mark 7:24

The fame of Christ had gone out too widely over the whole country for Him to travel anywhere without being recognized. No doubt there was something in His appearance and bearing that distinguished Him from other men and soon revealed His identity. There must have been a rare sweetness in His face, the outpouring of the great love of His heart. There was no halo upon His features, as artists represent Him in their pictures; yet there must have been a glow of grace that revealed Him to sad and hungry hearts.

But really Christ never can be hid. He can be in no place in this world very long and His presence not be recognized. You may hide sweet flowers so that they cannot be seen, but soon the fragrance will disclose their hiding place. So the sweetness of the Savior's life and love will always tell when He is near. When He enters a human heart He cannot be hidden; for soon His Spirit begins to breathe into all the words, actions, and life of the new followers. When He enters a home He cannot long be hidden, for the home is changed—worldliness, bitterness, and sin giving place to prayer and praise, to the spirit of love and gentleness, and to purity and holiness. When He enters a community He cannot remain concealed. The stories of missionary work illustrate this. Cannibal islands are changed into God-fearing, brotherly-loving settlements. Christ will always reveal His presence in this world.

The same is true also of all faithful discipleship. A Christian cannot be hidden. If the love of Christ is in His heart, people around Him will very soon know it. They will see it in His bearing, in His disposition, in the way He honors God, in the way He treats His fellowmen. When a man can hide His religion, He has not much of it to hide. True religion breathes out its fragrance, shines out in light.

SILENCE NOT DENIAL
◇

But he answered her not a word.
Matthew 15:23

There is something very remarkable in this silence of Christ. Usually He was quick to hear every request made to Him by a sufferer. Scarcely ever had anyone to ask twice for a favor. His heart was sensitive, as is a mother's heart to her child's cries, and He instantly responded to every petition for help. Yet now He stood and listened to this woman's pitiful pleading and answered her not a word. Like a miser with hoards of gold, at whose gates the poor and suffering knock, but who, hearing their cries of need and distress, keeps his gates locked and is deaf to every entreaty, so Jesus stood unmoved by this woman's cries, though He had all power in His hands.

Why was He silent? It was not because He could not help her, for His arm was never weak. The best of us have our weak moments, our days of ineffectiveness, when we have nothing with which to help; but His fullness was never exhausted. It was not because He was so engrossed in His own approaching sorrows that He could think of no one else's sorrow, for even on the cross He forgot Himself to show kindness to others. Evidently the reason for His silence was to try this mother's faith, and to draw it out into still greater strength. He was preparing her to receive in the end a better blessing than she could have received at the beginning.

Our Lord sometimes still seems to be silent toward His people when they cry to Him. To all their earnest supplications He answers not a word. Is His silence a refusal? By no means. Oftentimes, at least, it is meant only to make the supplicants more earnest, and to prepare their hearts to receive richer and greater blessing. So when Christ is silent toward our prayers, it is that we may be brought down in deeper humility at His feet and that our hearts may be made more fit to receive heaven's gifts and blessings.

August 1
◇
CRUMBS FROM THE MASTER'S TABLE
◇

The dogs eat of the crumbs which fall from their masters' table.
Matthew 15:27

Both the humility and the quick, eager faith of this woman appear in this response. She was not offended by the figure our Lord had used. She was willing to be as a little dog under the Master's table. The children were first served, and then the pieces they let fall belonged to the dogs. All she asked for was the portion that ordinarily went to the dogs. Even the crumbs from that table were enough for her, more than the richest delicacies from any other table.

Thus both humility and faith were shown in her answer; and in both she is an example to us. We should come to Christ with a deep sense of our unworthiness, ready to take the lowest place. It is such a precious thing to be permitted to take even the crumbs from the Master's table that we should exalt the privilege. Even the crumbs of His grace and love are better than all the richest feasts of this world.

> *Not worthy, Lord, to gather up the crumbs*
> *With trembling hand that from thy table fall;*
> *A weary, heavy-laden sinner comes*
> *To plead thy promise and obey thy call.*

> *I am not worthy to be thought thy child,*
> *Nor sit the last and least at thy board;*
> *Too long a wanderer, and too oft beguiled,*
> *I only ask one reconciling word.*

Yet we are not fed with crumbs; we are seated at the full table, with the richest provisions before us. The prodigal, returning, asked only to be made a servant, as he felt unworthy to be restored to a son's place. But father-love knew no such halfway restoration as that. The white robe, the ring, the shoes were given to him, insignia of sonship. God puts the lowliest and unworthiest at once into the children's place and feeds them abundantly.

DIVINE SYMPATHY
◇

Looking up to heaven, he sighed, and saith unto him, Ephphatha.
Mark 7:34

How it must have saddened the heart of Jesus to walk through this world and see so much human misery! There is a story of a sculptor who wept as he saw at his feet the shattered fragments of his breathing marble, on which he had spent years of patient, loving toil. Jesus walked through this world amid the ruin of the noblest work of His own hands. Everywhere He saw the destruction caused by sin. So His grief was twofold—tender sympathy with human suffering and sorrow over the malignant work of sin.

It is a precious thought to us that we are so dear to Jesus that the observing of our grief touches and stirs His heart. What a wonderful revelation it is to us that we are thought of tenderly by Him and that He cares enough for us to be moved to sorrow by our woes and sufferings!

But Christ's help does not end in the expression of sympathy. That is about as far as human help usually goes. People stand over us when we are in misfortune or trouble, heave a sigh, and then pass on. Sometimes this is all they can do. Human sympathy in suffering is a wonderful help; but the assurance of divine sympathy is infinitely more uplifting. Christ gives real help. He was moved with compassion as He saw the widow of Nain in her lonely sorrow, and he restored her dead son to her. He wept with Mary and Martha, and then He raised their brother. He sighed as He looked on the misfortune of this deaf man, and then He opened his ears. He is "touched with the feeling of our infirmities," and He gives "grace to help in time of need" (Hebrews 4:15–16). Not only does He pity us when He finds us deaf to all the sweet voices of love and grace, but He is ready to open our ears. We have only to bring to Christ our infirmities, and He will take them and give us back in place souls with all their lost powers restored.

DEAF AND DUMB

*His ears were opened, and the string of his tongue
was loosed, and he spake plain.*

Mark 7:35

I t is a great thing to have deaf ears opened. In many places in the Bible we find the words, "He that hath ears to hear, let him hear." This suggests that there are people who have no ears, and also that there are those who, having ears, hear not. He who cannot hear is a great loser. The world is full of harmonies of sound. The deaf man misses all the pleasure which others derive from the songs of the birds, the tones of human speech, the charms of music. It is a great thing when closed ear-gates are opened.

Souls have ears also—ears fitted to hear the voice of God and the harmonies of heavenly music. Yet there are many who are utterly deaf to these spiritual utterances. They hear God neither in the voices of nature, in the whisperings of conscience, nor in the sacred words of Holy Scripture. Christ is also able to open these spiritual ears, that our souls may listen on this earth to the music of heaven.

It is a great thing also to have our tongues loosed, that we may talk of these things to others. Some people, however, who seem to have their ears opened still have their tongues tied. They do not speak of God's love. They have such an impediment in their speech when they talk of spiritual things that they stammer and hesitate and break down altogether, although on other themes they can talk plainly and fluently. There are Christian men who are eloquent when they talk of business, of science, of farming, or of whatever may most occupy their thoughts and hands; but the moment the subject of religious experience is approached, their eloquence forsakes them. They are tongue-tied Christians. What a blessing it would be to them if Christ would someday loose the reins of their tongues, so that they could speak plainly!

"THE LORD WILL PROVIDE"

They have now been with me three days, and have nothing to eat.
Mark 8:2

This word of Christ shows first how earnest the people were in their desire to be with Christ. They had been three days with Him, and even when their provision was exhausted they would not leave Him. They would rather stay with Him hungry than leave Him to go away to seek bread. It would be wonderful if there was such devotion to Christ in these days. Some people can scarcely sit through one short hour with Jesus in the church, or spend a few minutes with Him morning and evening, communing with Him. If we had real spiritual hunger, we would not weary so soon of waiting upon Christ.

Another thought suggested by these words is that Christ will take good care of those who are earnestly following Him. The reason for this multitude being so long in the wilderness was their desire to be with Jesus; and it was this fact especially that stirred His compassion when He saw them growing hungry. "They came here to find Me, and they have lingered here, forgetting their own needs, that they might be near Me." We may draw the lesson that Jesus will take care of those who are enduring hardness for His sake. He may not always save them from suffering, but He will always watch over them and provide for them in the best way. His heart is just as tender now in the midst of heaven's glory, and as thoughtful of His friends in their need, as it was when He was on the earth.

We must not overlook the fact that it is care for the people's bodily wants that we find here in our Lord. We are constantly in danger of limiting our faith in Christ to spiritual things; but He looks just as lovingly after the supply of our physical wants as after the needs of our souls.

HELP IN TIME OF NEED

Having eyes, see ye not? . . . Do ye not remember?
Mark 8:18

There is nothing unreasonable in expecting a man with two eyes, when walking through an art gallery, to see the beautiful pictures that hang upon the walls. Why were his eyes given to him, if he is not to see with them? And it was nothing unreasonable that our Lord looked for when He expected the disciples to understand His spiritual teachings. They had eyes with which they might have seen spiritual things, yet they failed to use them. Many people never learn to see much with their natural eyes. They walk over the fields in summer days and never see a lovely thing; while in every wildflower and in every grass-blade there is beauty enough, if perceived, to fill the dullest heart with rapture. It is still more true in spiritual things: we walk in a world full of the glories of God's love; yet how much do we see of this ineffable splendor? At best, in this world we see only through a glass, darkly. Should we not train our eyes to see?

Then there was another wonderful faculty which the disciples did not use. This was memory. "Do ye not remember?" They did remember the facts of the miracles very definitely, but the spiritual lessons they did not recall. They had forgotten the spiritual meaning of the miracle. This is what all of us are too apt to do; we remember the things God has done for us in the past, but we fail to draw the lessons from these experiences which they are meant to teach us; we fail to profit by the experience. Every deliverance in time of danger, every help in time of need, ought to write upon our hearts its new lesson on trusting in the Lord. When we come again to similar points of need or danger, we should not be afraid, but remember how God helped us before and believe that He will give us the same help in the new experiences.

LED APART

He took the blind man by the hand, and led him out of the town.
Mark 8:23

That was a very gentle thing to do. Look closely at the picture—Jesus leading a poor blind man along the street. What thoughts does it bring to our minds? The blind man represents each one of us in our sinful state—in the midst of a world of beauty, but seeing nothing; groping in the gloom, unable to find the way alone; doomed to perish forever in the darkness, unless someone takes us by the hand and leads us. As Jesus came to this man in his blindness, so He comes to each one of us, offering to take us by the hand and be our guide, to lead us, through the gloom and the dangers, home to light and glory. We can never stumble in the darkness if He leads us.

The blind man entrusting himself, without fear or questioning, to be led by this stranger, and quietly and confidently going with Him, is a picture of what true faith in Christ always does. It is in this same way that we are to commit ourselves to Christ. It is not enough to lay our sins on Him; we must entrust our whole life to His guidance. We can never find the way ourselves in this world's paths, but we may entrust ourselves with unquestioning confidence to Christ's leading.

> *I do not try to see my way,*
> *Before, behind, or left or right;*
> *I cannot tell what dangers gray*
> *Do haunt my steps, nor at what height*
> *Above the sea my path doth wind:*
> *For I am blind.*
>
> *Yet not without a guide I wend*
> *My unseen way, by day, by night;*
> *Close by my side there walks a Friend—*
> *Strong, tender, true: I trust his sight;*
> *He sees my way before, behind,*
> *Though I am blind.*

"WHAT THINK YE OF CHRIST?"

But whom say ye that I am?
Matthew 16:15

It is to us a great deal more important question what we think personally about Christ than what the world thinks about Him. We may be able to state the doctrines of all the creeds of Christendom concerning His person; and yet the question remains: "Whom do you say that I am? What do you think of Christ?"

It is vitally important that we have right views of Christ. Who is He? Is He divine, or only human? If He is only human, we may get much profit from His teachings and from His example, but that is all. In our days of struggle and temptation we cannot turn to Him for personal help. The holiest saints in heaven cannot impart to us any strength in our weakness. They cannot reach down their hands to lead us, to defend us, to help us over the hard places. If we fall, they cannot lift us up again. We can get no help from John or from Paul. If Jesus was no more than a good and holy man, He can do nothing for us now except through His teachings and His example; but if He is divine, He can be to us all that we need as friend, helper, guide, comforter, refuge. So we see that it does matter what we believe concerning the person of Christ. Doctrines are important.

Then, when the doctrinal question has been answered, there are other questions that come still more closely home: "What is Christ to you personally? Is He only in your creed? Is He only a person about whom you believe a great many blessed and glorious things? Is He in your thoughts only as the mighty Savior of all who believe on Him? Is He anything to you personally? Is He your Savior, your Friend, your Helper?" These are the questions that tell just where we stand with regard to Christ and eternal life. Opinions about Christ, though perhaps true and orthodox, are not enough; only living faith in Him saves.

THE SHADOW OF THE CROSS

*He began to teach them, that the Son of man must suffer . . .
be rejected . . . be killed, and after three days rise again.*

Mark 8:31

Peter had made a noble confession of his faith in Christ as the promised Messiah, and now Jesus tells him what the role meant, how He was to fulfill His mission. It was not as the disciples expected. They were looking for His manifestation as an earthly king. But He told them that the way to His throne was through suffering and by the Cross.

It is to be noticed that while the way He marked out lay through darkness and sorrow, at the end there would be glory—"after three days rise again." Thus there was to be no failure in His mission. An apostle said to believers in Christ: "Ye must through much tribulation enter into the kingdom of heaven." The tribulation was hard, but they would go through it; and beyond was the kingdom of heaven. In the twenty-third Psalm there is a verse often quoted: "Yea, though I walk through the valley of the shadow." In these words there is a suggestion of darkness—but the Christian is going through it; then comes "the house of the Lord forever." So here the dying of the Savior seemed to be failure; but the rising again meant glory, victory, and eternal blessedness. He was simply going through death as the appointed way to His throne.

This quiet announcement by our Lord of what was in store for Him reminds us of an element of sorrow in Christ's life from which we are mercifully spared. He knew beforehand every inch of His path of woe. The shadow of His cross lay upon His soul through all the years. We sometimes rashly say that we wish we could see our future; but it is really a most gracious provision for our own life that we cannot see an hour ahead of us. To know the future would only darken the present and make us unfit for our duty. It is better by far that it is hidden.

August 9

---◆---

PETER REBUKED

---◆---

He turned, and said unto Peter, Get thee behind me, Satan.
Matthew 16:23

I t was Peter's love for Christ that made him rebel so strongly at the thought of such a fate before Him. In his love he sought to hold the Master back from throwing away His life. But in doing this he was acting the part of Satan in seeking to tempt Jesus from His great work of sacrifice. This way of the Cross was not an accident; it was the way marked out for Christ; to turn from it would be to fail in His mission.

Our best friends may become our tempters in the same way. In their love for us they may seek to keep us from entering paths of duty which will lead to sacrifice. Mothers may seek to restrain their children from going to foreign fields. Any of us, in the warmth of our affection for our friends, may seek to dissuade them from perilous or costly service which it may be their duty to undertake. We need to guard ourselves at this point. The path of true success does not always lie along the sunny hillside; sometimes it goes down into the dark valley of self-sacrifice. And if we try to hinder anyone from beginning hard duties, urging them to choose easier ways, we may be doing Satan's work. We may be plucking the crown from the brow of our friend by holding back his feet from the way of the Cross.

We all need to guard, too, against the counsels of friends who would restrain us from costly or perilous service. In matter of duty we must know only one Guide and follow the call of only one Voice. We are not put in this world to have a good or easy time; we are not put here to consult our own inclinations at all. We are here to go where Christ leads; to follow Him to sacrifice and to death if He leads us in these paths. We dare not allow ourselves to be turned aside by any tenderness of human love. It is the way of duty, however hard, that takes us home.

SELF-DENIAL

If any man will come after me, let him deny himself.
Matthew 16:24

There are few things at which people play more ill-disguised farces than in their efforts at self-denial. Very few seem to have the remotest conception of what it is. One does without meat on Fridays, eating fish instead, and thinks he has denied himself in a most commendable way. Another gives up over-indulgence for forty days in Lent and is complacent over the merit of great self-denial. Others make themselves miserable in various ways, inflicting pain, making useless and uncalled-for sacrifices, as if God were pleased when they suffer. But these things do not equate with self-denial. There is no merit or virtue in giving up anything, suffering any loss or pain, or making any sacrifice, merely for its own sake.

True self-denial is the renouncing of self and the yielding of the whole life to the will of Christ. It is self coming down from one's own throne, laying crown and scepter at the Master's feet, and then submitting one's whole life to His rule. It is living all the while, not to please ourselves, not to advance our own personal interests, but to please our Lord and do His work. It is denying ourselves anything that is sinful in His sight. It is the glad making of sacrifices that loyalty to Him requires. It is the giving up of any pleasure or comfort for the good of others which the living out of His spiritual life may demand. The essential thing is that self gives way altogether to Christ as the motive for living.

Nothing, therefore, is true self-denial which is done merely as self-denial. True self-denial, like all other traits of Christlikeness, is unconscious of itself, does not know that its face shines. We deny ourselves when we follow Christ with joy and gladness, through cost and danger and suffering, just where He leads.

August 11

◇

NO CROSS, NO CROWN

◇

And take up his cross, and follow me.
Matthew 16:24

The cross is to be taken up, not simply borne when laid upon the shoulder. This implies willing, cheerful suffering for Christ. Some people endure trials, but always with complaining. The spirit of these words requires cheerfulness in suffering for Christ. Half the trial is gone if we meet it willingly.

Notice again, it is his own cross and not some other man's that each one is to take up. It is the particular cross that God lays at our own feet that we are to bear. We are never to make crosses for ourselves, but we are always to accept those which are allotted to us. Each one's own cross is best for him. Sometimes we think our lot is peculiarly hard, and we compare it with the lot of this or that other person and wish we had his cross instead of our own. But we do not know what other people's crosses really are like. If we did we might not want to exchange. The cross that seems woven of flowers, if we put it on our shoulders, we might find filled with sharp thorns under the flowers. The cross of gold that seems so bright we should find so heavy that it would crush us. The easiest cross for each one to bear is his own.

God has measured it specifically for our stature and strength. He has fit it to our circumstances and though we suffer with it, He will cause us also to suffer through it. Even Jesus in His weakness was assisted by Simon of Cyrene. We now have the Risen King who tells us that when we are heavily yoked He will help us carry the cross appointed for us. The way to receive the crosses is therefore always gladly to accept, through love to Him, whatever trial, pain, or loss God sends.

August 12

LOST, YET FOUND

Whosoever will save his life shall lose it: and whosoever will lose his life for my sake shall find it.
Matthew 16:25

It seems to be saving one's life to be governed by self-interest, to avoid self-denial and sacrifice, to live to gather into one's hands as much as possible of the things that give comfort, pleasure, or power. But if this is the motive, that life is really wasted. That is the deep meaning of our Lord's words. Self-seeking is self-losing. We have not really learned to live at all until we have learned to live for Christ. What we keep for ourselves we lose; it is only what we give away that we really keep. Selfishness is not only a sin; it is always spiritual death.

The way to save one's life, says the Master, is to lose it. Christ Himself lost His life, poured it out in loving self-sacrifice for the good of others. It seemed a waste; but was it a waste? He found it again in greater glory. Paul lost his life for Christ, renounced everything for His sake, suffered everything, and gave his very life at the end, but did he lose anything by his self-sacrifice? A young girl, who was beautiful, cultured, honored, with a lovely home and many friends turned away from ease, refinement, and luxury and went to teach the freed slaves after the Civil War. She lived among them and gave of her rich young life in efforts to help them and save their souls. One day she got sick and died, and her friends said: "Oh, what a waste of a precious life!" But was it a waste?

All who truly follow Christ make this choice between saving and losing their lives—that is, between making self-interest or Christ the motive in living. In following Christ, we may never be called actually to make great sacrifices; but the fact that we are ready to make them, even to the utmost, is implied in our covenant of discipleship. Yet this losing is saving; it is sowing the golden wheat in the ground—losing it for a time—to reap from it a rich harvest in the future.

AN UNANSWERED QUESTION

*What is a man profited, if he shall gain the
whole world, and lose his own soul?*
Matthew 16:26

That is putting the case in its most favorable light. The whole world is the largest possible gain. But suppose a man gets it—it cannot keep him from trouble; it cannot give him peace of conscience; it cannot comfort him in sorrow; it cannot make a soft pillow for him when he is dying; it cannot purchase heaven for him when he is gone. All he can do with the world, after he has it, is to keep it until he dies; he cannot carry any part of it with him to the other life. "How much did he leave?" asked one, referring to a millionaire who had just died. "Every cent" was the reply. He left all. So it is easy to see that there is no profit, but rather a fearful and eternal loss, in gaining even all the world at the price of one's soul.

Then think for how much smaller price than "the whole world" many people sell their souls. Some do it for a few hours' guilty pleasure; some for a political office; some for money; some for honor which fades in a day. In a newspaper this advertisement appeared: "Wanted—A nice cottage and grounds in exchange for a lot of choice liquors." No doubt many people answered the advertisement. Men are continually giving home and property and peace and love for strong drink. They are selling their souls also in many other ways for pitiable trifles. They are bartering their heavenly birthright for a mess of pottage like Esau.

What shall a man give in exchange for his soul? Ah, that's the trouble. When the soul is lost, there is no way of recovering it. When we have made our choice, and lived our life, whether right or wrong, there is no possibility of changing the results. Life is given to us only once; and if we live it wrongly, there is no chance to live it over again. A soul lost cannot be gotten back; no money will redeem it.

August 14

CHRIST'S SPECIAL FRIENDS

Jesus taketh Peter, James, and John.
Matthew 17:1

These three disciples belonged to the inner circle of our Lord's friends. There must have been something in them that peculiarly endeared them to Him. We know that Peter was a leader among the apostles and also a bold confessor; that John was "the disciple whom Jesus loved"; and that James was the first of the band to die as a martyr.

It is encouraging to look at Peter, a man with so many faults, and who made so many mistakes, at last shamefully denying Christ, and yet remember that he was one of our Lord's closest friends, admitted to such high privileges. It gives encouragement to us that with all our faults we too may yet be very dear to Christ, as Peter was.

It does not seem strange that John was allowed to enter the inner circle. His disposition was gentle and amiable, very much like the Master's. Yet probably John owed his sweetness and gentleness of character to his being with Jesus. He was not always a man of love. There is a Persian fable of a piece of clay made fragrant by lying on a rose; the perfume of the rose passed into the clay. So it was with John. He laid on the Master's bosom, and lay close to His heart; and his Master's spirit of love and gentleness passed into his life and transformed it. In this way we have a lesson from John: constant and loving communion with Christ will change us into His likeness.

The lesson from this choosing of three out of the whole band for peculiar privileges is that while Jesus loves all His friends, there are certain ones whom He takes into closer confidence than the others. There are degrees of nearness to Him, even in this world. Should we not strive to be among those who, by commitment and by service, win their way to the closest places? *We must remember that those who serve most are the greatest among all.*

HEAVENLY MESSENGERS
◆

There appeared unto them Moses and Elias talking with him.
Matthew 17:3

These two heavenly men of God were conversing with Jesus; they were talking with Him about His death. Several thoughts are suggested by this. One is that the death of Jesus was part of the divine plan. It was no disaster, no defeat. It was understood in heaven that He was to die on a cross.

Another thought is that Moses and Elijah had been sent to talk with Jesus, as He was now about to turn His face toward Jerusalem, that they might strengthen Him for the sad journey and for the bitter sorrows at the end of it. Before Jesus went to the wilderness there was a vision of glory, and a voice spoke, uttering the divine approval, to strengthen Him to endure His temptation. Now again, when He is looking toward His cross, there is a vision and a voice, to prepare Him for the darkness and the agony.

In these heavenly visits we have a hint of the role of the redeemed in heaven. These two men are sent all the way to earth to comfort and cheer a weary spirit in its mission of suffering. Perhaps it will be true that all the saved shall be used in this way in glory (Revelation 22:3). It is delightful to think that we shall be sent from heaven on errands of love. The idea that in heaven we shall do nothing forever but rest on green banks and sing praises to God receives no support in the Scriptures. We are to be like Christ; and He is never idle, but ever busy in loving service. "His servants shall serve him" is one description of the employments of heaven. It will still be the pattern there to minister rather than to be ministered to. They will still be first there who serve. Our poor work here is only a training for work in heaven and forever.

August 16

---◇---

DUTY AFTER PRIVILEGE

---◇---

Lord, it is good for us to be here . . .
let us make here three tabernacles.
Matthew 17:4

We should know that it was Peter who said this, even if his name were not given; it is just like Peter. He wanted to hold the heavenly vision on the mountaintop and not go back any more to the cold, struggling life of earth. It seemed such a heavenly place that he did not want to leave it. It certainly was good to be there; but they could not stay there long and yet be faithful to their duty and their mission. There was work waiting in the sad world below which they must hasten to do. There was a poor demoniac at the foot of the mountain whom the disciples could not cure; the Master was greatly needed there. Then farther off were Gethsemane, Gabbatha, and Golgotha for Jesus; He must make an atonement for the world. Then for Peter there was Pentecost, with many years of earnest service and martyrdom in the end.

Devotion is good. It is very sweet to commune with God in the closet, in the church, at the sacramental table; but we must not spend all our time in these holy exercises. While the raptures thrill our souls we must not forget that outside there are human wants crying out for help and sympathy; and we must tear ourselves away from our warmest devotions and most exalted experiences to go down to answer these cries. Religion is not for enjoyment only; God gives us spiritual enjoyment that we may be strong for much loving service.

> *Hark, hark! a voice amid the quiet intense!*
> *It is thy duty waiting thee without.*
> *Open thy door straightway, and get thee hence;*
> *Go forth into the tumult and the shout;*
> *Work, love, with workers, lovers all about;*
> *Then, weary, go thou back with failing breath,*
> *And in thy chamber make thy prayer and moan.*
> *One day upon his bosom, all thine own,*
> *Thou shalt lie still, embraced in holy death.*

BRIGHT CLOUDS

A bright cloud overshadowed them.
Matthew 17:5

The cloud was a symbol of the divine presence. One of the writers says the disciples were afraid as they saw the cloud come down over the Master and the heavenly visitants. God still comes to us often in thick clouds, and we too are afraid. But the cloud meant no harm to the disciples. No cloud means any harm to a disciple when God is in the cloud; and always, if we only listen, we may hear words of love.

> *Sorrow touched by love grows bright*
> *With more than rapture's ray;*
> *And darkness shows us worlds of light*
> *We never saw by day.*

There was a voice out of the cloud testifying to the divine sonship. The disciples had been staggered at what Jesus had said about His rejection and death. Now they are assured that He is the Messiah, and that they must hear Him. Even if they could not understand, and if the things He said seemed to destroy all their hopes, they were still willing to hear.

At times God's ways with us seem very hard, and we think disaster is coming to every fair prospect in our life. In all such hours we should remember that He who rules over all is the Son of God, our Friend, and our Savior; and our trust in Him should never fail. We should always listen to what He says; and when everything seems strange and dark, we should never doubt nor fear. What so staggered the disciples then, we now see to have been the most glorious and loving wisdom. So in our most difficult trials there are the best wisdom and the richest love. Hereafter we shall know. It was out of the cloud that this voice came. Out of the clouds that hang over us come often the most tender voices of divine love, the most precious disclosures of divine grace.

FAILURES

I brought him to thy disciples, and they could not cure him.
Matthew 17:16

A great many teachers in our Sunday schools have had similar experiences. Children have been brought to them possessed by "evil spirits," and they have failed to cast out the "demons." They have tried every device, gentle and severe; they have prayed and labored, they have talked and wept; but the "evil spirits" in their students have defied all efforts to dislodge them. Teachers of such incorrigible scholars may learn some lessons here.

It may be a little encouragement, first of all, to know that even Christ's apostles met at least one case that they could not do anything with; it is no wonder that common people like us fail now and then. Failures like this in the apostles show us that they lived at our level. If we saw them victorious and successful at every point, we would be discouraged. But when we find them baffled and defeated, we see that they were human, just like us, and could do nothing by themselves. We get far more real help from St. Paul's experience with his "thorn" than we get from his "third heaven" exaltation. In this latter he is so far beyond us that we cannot follow him; in the former we are on familiar ground.

It may be instructive also to study the reasons for the apostles' failure. For one, the Master was absent; the disciple cannot do anything without his Lord. This is a lesson we should deeply impress on our own minds. Unless we have Christ with us, all our Christian work will utterly fail. We cannot of ourselves ever change a heart. Another reason was want of faith in the disciples; unbelief makes anyone fail. Though absent, Christ's power would have been theirs had not their faith failed. Still another reason was the hardness of this particular case; all cases are not the same, some requiring more faith and spiritual power than others.

August 19

◇

THE UNFAILING HELPER

◇

Bring him hither to me.
Matthew 17:17

The disciples had failed in their effort to cast out the demon, but there yet was hope. The Master Himself was now at hand, and He could not fail. There should be a great deal of encouragement in this for all who are trying to change people's lives toward spiritual growth. When parents have done all they can to make their children true and strong in their character, and have failed, they can take them to Jesus. He can cast out the evil that is in them. He can give them new hearts. He can put His own Holy Spirit within them, and thus transform them into Christ-likeness.

When teachers have incorrigible students in their classes, on whom they can make no impression, their discouragement and failure should lead them to bring them to Jesus, for He is yet able to take them and change them into noble character. When troubled souls have sought in vain for comfort and help from the church and from Christian ministers, they should go to Christ Himself, for He can comfort. No matter that we have been defeated, Christ stands ready to take our humiliation and turn it into victory. The disciples had toiled all night in vain, but when they dropped their net at the Lord's bidding, great was their success. So in the shadows of our human failure He stands to give blessing.

There is another thought here. It is to Christ, and not merely to the school or the church or the minister, that we should try to lead our children and our friends. The teacher cannot regenerate the child. The church cannot renew its nature. The minister cannot cast out the evil in the child's heart. Unless we bring our children truly to Christ they must remain unchanged. Baptism does not wash the heart. The Lord's Supper does not put grace into the life. We must bring our friends and ourselves directly to Christ.

◇

DESIRE FOR PLACE AND POWER

◇

*They held their peace: for by the way they had disputed
among themselves, who should be the greatest.*

Mark 9:34

Sometimes we have done something through the day which we are ashamed to tell Christ about when we come home in the evening and bow at His feet, or we have said something which we are not willing to repeat to Him in our prayers when we come to talk face-to-face with Him. But this failure to confess is cowardly and wrong. Someday we shall be asked what we said and did as we came along through life; let us be careful to say or do nothing which we shall be ashamed to confess before our Lord and the angels and all the universe.

The disciples' ideas of position and rank were altogether earthly. They wrangled for places in the kingdom Christ was going to set up, very much as a company of modern politicians wrangle over perks of office. Peter thought he ought to be president, for he was the best speaker. Judas thought he would certainly be secretary of the treasury, which would give him a prominent place. John was Christ's favorite, and he felt sure he would be the greatest. Andrew had been first called, and he claimed that this fact ought to give him precedence. So they bickered. So Christians sometimes do today. They want official places in the church—want to be elders, deacons, or trustees; or want positions in the Sunday school, as superintendents; or want to be presidents or vice presidents or something else of missionary societies, or charitable societies, or Dorcas societies, or of some other organizations; or want to be pastors of popular city churches. The desire to be useful is not the problem; the problem is that too often believers want the higher places and are unwilling to take the lower. It is the same old spirit—the idea that the way to be a great Christian is to be prominent in some official position, to have honor and power among men. It is a shame to see such scrambling in the church of Christ, but sometimes we see it; perhaps we sometimes scramble ourselves.

THE CHILD IN THE MIDST

◇

Jesus called a little child unto him,
and set him in the midst of them.
Matthew 18:2

The child preached the sermon. It said to those ambitious disciples, "Shame on all your quarreling about prominence and high place. Look at me. I am much higher up in the kingdom of heaven than you. You must get clear of all your proud thoughts and become lowly and simple-minded and childlike, or in the new kingdom you will have no place at all, much less a high place." Little children are all preaching sermons to us, if only we have ears to hear. Young children, in their innocence, their simplicity, their naturalness, their sweetness of soul, wherever they go exert an influence upon other lives which no words can describe. They are at once the greatest preachers and themselves the most eloquent sermons.

This picture of Jesus with the little one in His arms is very beautiful. In all the Bible there is scarcely another scene which so well represents the attitude both of the soul and of the Savior in salvation and in all Christian life. Jesus takes the child in His arms; there is love, tenderness, protection. The bosom is the place of warmth, of affection, of intimacy, of confidence. The encircling arms imply safety, support, shelter. He lifted up the child and held it in His arms; so He carries His people through this world; He does not merely tell them how to go, but He takes them on His shoulders, carrying not only their burdens, but themselves. He bears them through life and through death.

Then look at the picture the other way—the child in the Savior's arms. Its attitude speaks of trust, confidence, repose, peace, love, joy—just the feelings which belong to the true Christian. What a place the bosom of Christ is in danger, in storm, in sorrow, in death! Shall we not learn to just nestle in our Savior's arms in all our experiences?

"FOR HIS SAKE"

---

*Whosoever shall receive one of such
children in my name, receiveth me.*
Mark 9:37

This saying of Christ is rich enough to be studied carefully and intently. To receive a child in a certain way is to receive Christ Himself. How must a child be received? In Christ's name—that is, out of love to Him, for His sake, just as we would receive Christ Himself if He actually came in person. So it is not enough to love children, to care for orphans or those that are destitute. It must be for the sake of Christ that we do these things. Thus in every child we see Christ standing before us, and we may have the honor of receiving Him in this way.

The Christmas legends are full of illustrations of this truth. One of the most beautiful of these tells how on a Christmas Eve a poor man, coming homeward through the forest, heard a cry and found a little child, cold and hungry. The good man stopped and sought the little one and took him with him to his house. His children gladly welcomed the stranger and shared their evening meal with him. Then, while he sat there at the table, suddenly a change came over the child's appearance, and then it was the Christ-child whom unconsciously the family had received in this needy, suffering little one. Christ is always coming to our doors in the person of some poor or suffering one, and the reception we give the one He sends we give to Him. This ought to make us careful how we treat those who need sympathy or help, lest at some point we slam the door in the face of Jesus.

Those words of Christ have their precious lesson for parents. The child who comes to them comes in Christ's name, comes in His wake. It brings blessings to them and to their home if they receive it in the right way. But they must receive it in Christ's name, with love, with thankfulness, with reverence. If they do not receive it with welcome, as from God, it is as if they rejected Christ Himself.

LITTLE DEEDS OF LOVE

*Whosoever shall give you a cup of water to drink
in my name, because ye belong to Christ, verily
I say unto you, he shall not lose his reward.*

Mark 9:41

I t seems wonderful indeed that God should keep note of such a little thing as the giving of a cup of water to a thirsty Christian. It shows how dear to Him are His people, since the smallest things done to one of them He accepts, remembers, and rewards. The mention here of the giving of a cup of water suggests that this promise is for little, commonplace acts, rather than for great deeds. We are too stingy with our service. God has put His gifts of love into our hearts, not to be kept locked up and useless, but to be given out. We would call a man selfish who should refuse a cup of water to one who was thirsty; yet many of us do this continually. It is the heart that thirsts, and the water we refuse to give is human kindness.

> *'Tis a little thing*
> *To give a cup of water, yet its draught*
> *Of cool refreshment drained by fevered lips*
> *May give a shock of pleasure to the frame*
> *More exquisite than when nectarine juice*
> *Renews the life of joy in happiest hours.*
> *It is a little thing to speak a phrase*
> *Of common comfort, which by daily use*
> *Has almost lost its sense, yet on the ear*
> *Of him who thought to die unmourned*
> *'Twill fall like choicest music.*

Kindness is the proper word for these small acts. Kindness is love flowing out in small gentle acts. We ought to conduct our lives so that they will be perpetual blessings wherever we go. All we need for such a ministry is a heart full of love for Christ; for if we truly love Christ we shall also love our fellowmen, and love will always find ways of helping. A heart filled with gentleness cannot be miserly in its giving.

August 24

◇

WISE SACRIFICES

◇

*It is better for thee to enter into life halt or maimed, rather than
having two hands or two feet to be cast into everlasting fire.*
Matthew 18:8

This life is so full of peril that even its best advantages may become stumbling blocks. Our very qualities of strength may become fatal forces driving us to ruin. Human beauty is a token of unfallen life, and yet beauty has proved a snare to many a woman, drawing her away from God. Power to make money is a perilous gift, which has led many a man to spiritual ruin. The appetites, desires, and affections are part of the glory of humanity, and yet unbridled they have whirled many a good life to destruction. These are illustrations of our Lord's meaning when He speaks of cutting off the hand or the foot which causes us to stumble.

It is better to throw away altogether the ability to make money and go poor through life with the talent wasted and shriveled, and reach heaven, then to exercise the gifts and grow rich, and be lost forever.

A steam vessel came into port which had long been out to sea. An accident had happened which caused delay. The coal gave out; then all that would burn—cargo, stores, furniture—had to be burned up to bring the vessel home. At last she gained the shore, but stripped of everything of value. Yet it was better to burn up all her cargo and stores than perish at sea.

Some men can get to heaven only by sacrificing every earthly pleasure and crucifying every desire; but who will say the prize is not worth the sacrifice? The hand had better be chopped off than steal or strike down another. The foot had better be cut off than carry one into crime or sin. The eye had better be put out than by its lustful gazing set the soul on fire. A man on a wrecked vessel had better throw his bags of gold into the sea and have his life saved than hold onto the gold and sink into the waves.

August 25

"THE JOY SET BEFORE HIM"

When the time was come that he should be received up.
Luke 9:51

There were a great many painful steps to take before our Lord could reach this blessed hour and be received up to glory. The immediate future was full of struggle, loss, and pain. On the far heights His eye saw the radiancy of heaven, with its opening gates and its welcome home; but before His feet could enter the shining portal there was a broad battle-plain to pass through, and it was full of enemies. There were days of toil and nights of loneliness. At last He must pass through Gethsemane's gloom and all that via dolorosa which led to Calvary. He must die and go into the grave. All this before He could be received up.

But He did not think of any of these painful steps. He did not let His eye rest on the shadows that lay in the valley, but He lifted His gaze up to the mountaintop beyond, where the splendors of heaven blazed. Keeping His thoughts distantly forward on the glories that were to be His when He had ended the journey, He forgot the toils and the tears and did not faint.

This is a wonderful secret which all of us ought to learn—not to think so much about the toil and hardness of the way, but to look beyond to the brightness of the end. It doesn't matter how rough the road is if it only brings us home at last. Many of us continue worrying all through this life, keeping our eyes always downcast on the path we are treading. We see all the troubles, the difficulties and discouragements, but we never raise our eyes to see the joys and the blessings that are waiting for us. We ought to learn this secret of life which made Christ forget the shame and sorrow of His cross and see only the glory beyond. Learn to look up toward heaven. Think of its joys, its blessedness, until earth's trials shall melt away in the brightness, and its griefs and losses be forgotten in the hopes of glory.

"GO FORWARD"

He steadfastly set his face to go to Jerusalem.
Luke 9:51

We do not know what lies before us in life. Some great sorrow or anguish may be awaiting us tomorrow, but it casts no gloom over our spirits today, because we are ignorant of it. This is a merciful provision in our lives. If some of us knew all that we must pass through in the future, it would make our lives very bitter, even while our present joys remain. It is a great deal better that we should not know until God leads us to the edge of the experience.

But there was no such merciful veiling of the future from Christ's eyes. He saw every step of the sorrowful way right to the close of His life. Yet this makes the scene of this verse all the more moving. Knowing all, observe how eager He is to press on in His path. He could not be held back. He steadfastly set His face to go and directed His steps with intense haste to His journey, which He knew would lead Him to Gethsemane, Gabbatha, and Golgotha. In this, as in all things, He left us an example, that we should follow His steps. It is in this way that we should always go forward in the path of duty, no matter what the dangers, the sufferings, the sacrifices that lie in our path. We are too apt to hesitate and count the cost, when hard tasks are assigned to us, instead of eagerly pressing on in duty's path.

That walk to Jerusalem, every step a step toward the cross which was always in plain view, is the finest heroism of all history. Let us not forget why the walk was taken. That cross meant salvation and eternal blessedness for millions of lost souls. Love was the heart of that heroism. Jesus pressed on with intense earnestness, because the accomplishment of His mission would be life for the world and glory for the Father. We ought to bow our heads in reverence as we see Jesus pressing on to His cross; it was for our sakes He set His face steadfastly to go to Jerusalem.

August 27

◇

AN OPEN FOUNTAIN

◇

If any man thirst, let him come unto me, and drink.
John 7:37

Every word here is full of meaning. "If" marks the one condition to which the Savior's invitation is addressed. Of course if we do not thirst we will not care to come to the well and drink. Souls are dying all around us, not because there is no water near, but because they are not thirsty. Intense thirst is a pitiable condition; but the lack of soul-thirst is infinitely more pitiable. It is hopeless. The words "any man" show us how universal is our Lord's invitation. The cry was not to "any Jew," nor to "any man of good character," but to any person. No one is left out.

The word "thirsty" describes the need which Christ is able to supply. It is not bodily thirst, but thirst of the soul, which He offers to quench. For the soul as well as the body has its own thirsts, and there is no spring of earth at which they can be satisfied.

The words "let him come" show us the gate to the fountain flung wide open. There is no barrier in the way. "Let him come" reminds us, however, that if we would have our thirst quenched by Christ we must really come to Him. We must leave the dry wastes of our souls, where no water is, and come to Christ.

The word "drink" tells us that we must receive Christ Himself into our hearts if we would have our thirst satisfied in Him. Merely going to a spring and looking at its sparkling waters will never quench anyone's thirst; we must drink of the waters. So, looking at Christ is not enough to bless us; we must take Him into our life and let His Spirit fill our hearts. This new picture of Christ presents Him as a great well in the desert. The water gushes from a cleft in the rock. We understand the meaning of the cleft—Jesus died that there might be water for our soul's thirst.

WORDS FOR LIFE

Never man spake like this man.
John 7:46

In all literature there are no words like those which Christ spoke. We remember what wonderful power His words had. One of them dropped upon the wild sea and quieted it in a moment; another touched the blind man's eyes and opened them; another fell on the sparkling water and changed it into wine; another fell into a dark grave and caused a dead man who lay there to arise and come forth.

Then we remember how His words comforted sorrow and gave peace to troubled ones; how they reached men's hearts and changed the whole purpose of their lives. Those who heard His words rose up from their business and from their sins, and left all to follow Him in His homelessness and loneliness. Demons listened trembling when He spoke, and they instantly recognized His power, cowered, and obeyed.

These words of Christ still have the same power. They are still calming tempests, opening blind eyes, expelling evil spirits, and raising the dead. They are still giving comfort to hurting people, hope to those in despair, and forgiveness to penitents. They are still changing hearts, sweetening bitter fountains, and making flowers bloom where thorns grew before. If you lean upon a word of Christ, you will find the everlasting arm underneath it. If you are sinking in the waves of trial and grasp one of these blessed words, you will find the divine hand within it, and will be upheld by it. If you are pursued by spiritual enemies and take hold of the word of Christ, you will find in your hand an all-conquering sword, before which all foes will fly. If you are weary, or in sorrow, and pillow your head on one of these precious words, you will find that you are lying on your Father's bosom, close to His warm, beating heart. The world's richest treasures today are the words of Christ. "Never man spake like this man."

◇

EXPERIENCE THE BEST EVIDENCE

◇

Doth our law judge any man, before it
hear him, and know what he doeth?
John 7:51

Nicodemus asked justice for Jesus, and pleaded that He should not be condemned without a fair hearing. The same principle of justice should appeal now to men who are uttering hostile opinions of Christ. His enemies are never really those who have by experience proved His promises unworthy of confidence. The world has never yet known of a true follower of Christ who has honestly sought for Christ's salvation and has been disappointed.

All who have trusted Him have found every word true; they did not hope in vain. No one who has tried Him as Savior, Deliverer, Helper, and Friend has ever become His enemy. Those who oppose Christ are those who know nothing about Him through experience. They judge Him before they hear Him. But is this fair? Is it right to condemn any man if we really have no knowledge of the facts alleged against him? Would it be right to condemn a book we had never read and of which we had no actual knowledge?

Surely no one has any right to be an enemy of Christ without having honestly and conscientiously examined Christ's claims and then proved them untrue and unworthy of confidence. No one should reject Christ until he finds something better than Christ—something that will do more for him, that will bring him better help in trouble, a better salvation in his lost condition, that will make a better man of him, lifting him up to greater heights of holiness and strength of character.

The best evidence of Christianity always is experience. "Come and see" was all the eager disciple asked, when the man invited doubted. "Come and see" is sometimes better than argument. If we can only get people to try Christ's religion for themselves in the way the gospel lays out, there is no danger that they will condemn it.

August 30

◇

NO LONGER CAPTIVES

◇

Ye shall know the truth, and the truth shall make you free.
John 8:32

Even among the followers of Christ there is still much bondage because of ignorance of the truth. Superstitious people are in terror of certain imagined dangers, but their terror instantly vanishes when they learn the truth. They are slaves of ignorance until knowledge makes them free. So it is in spiritual things. There are Christians who are in perpetual distress about their sins, thinking that God's wrath still rests upon them, when in reality they passed long since from under wrath into blessed forgiveness. They do not know the truth about divine forgiveness, and therefore they miss all the joy. If they but knew the truth, the truth would make them free.

At the end of a war between France and Great Britain there were a number of French ships that had been out for some years. They did not know that peace had been proclaimed in their absence, and they wanted to get back to their own country without meeting any British men-of-war. A gale scattered them, one vessel was carried away from the others, and when the morning broke she found herself opposite the coast of England, with a British war vessel lying close by. The French captain was greatly perplexed and in terror. His first thought was to sink his vessel rather than allow her to fall into the enemy's hands. At length his ship was hailed from the man-of-war, and he was told that peace had been proclaimed between Great Britain and his own country. When he had been assured of this fact his fear vanished.

So the truth of the gospel makes us free, by telling us of the peace which has been made for us by Christ's cross. The moment we truly accept Christ we are free forever from sin's curse and condemnation. We are no longer captives, but free.

CHRIST'S YOKE TRUE FREEDOM

We be Abraham's seed, and were never in bondage to any man.
John 8:33

Self-confidence is the peril even of the truest piety. We are in danger of forgetting that we are nothing and that Jesus Christ is our all in all. This very day children of godly parents need to be on their guard against the sin of these ancient Jews. By what species of mental hoodwinking they fancied themselves "free," when at that very time Roman soldiers stood guard about their city, we cannot understand.

But both these errors are common enough. Some people boast more of their nationality than of anything else. It truly is a great privilege to have good ancestors; it is a good advantage with which to start life; but beyond a certain point it does not count. The first question may be, "Who is your father?" but the next question will be, "Who are you?" Parents may lead a child to Christ in infancy, but when the child is old enough for moral accountability it must accept Christ by a personal faith. Nothing else really avails for salvation. We must enter Christ's kingdom as individuals. Abraham had some descendants who were quite far away from his virtue and whom he would scarcely wish to recognize as his children; and many a godly father nowadays has worthless sons.

The illusion of freedom, while one is really in chains, is not altogether rare. A great many people living in sin imagine they are the only free people there are. They have thrown off the restraints of religion and of law, and they think they are free, while they regard those who follow Christ as slaves. Sin plays strange tricks with people. Insane people sometimes deck themselves out in tinsel and imagine that they are some great personages. The devil often puts similar notions into the heads of his deluded followers. None are free but those who wear Christ's yoke.

SERVANTS OF SIN

Whosoever committeth sin is the servant of sin.
John 8:34

So the people who boast of their freedom are really slaves after all. They look upon a Christian with a sort of pity, because he cannot do the wicked things they do. "Oh, I forgot! You have to obey the Ten Commandments, have to go to church, and have a narrow creed. You are a Christian. I would not be so bound up; I want to be free." So these people talk while they enjoy their license—which they call liberty! They do not imagine that they are the slaves, and that the Christians whom they so pity are really the only free people there are in the world.

Everyone is a servant of some master, the only difference being in the master. There is no dishonor in having a master, if the master be worthy of us, able to lead us up to glory. The Christian has Christ for his Master; while he who lives in sin has sin for his master. Christ is a blessed Master; serving Him lifts one up to eternal glory. What sort of a master is sin? We need but to look about us to see. What does sin do for its slaves? What life did it ever enhance or lift up?

It is said that one of the great prisons of this country was built by the prisoners themselves. They dressed the stones and built the walls which afterward shut them in. The legend is familiar, too, of the man to whom the devil came ordering a chain of a certain length. Coming at the appointed time, he ordered the chain made longer, and then he went away. When at last it was finished he came again, and with it he bound the poor man who had fastened its links at his command. In the same way sinners are everywhere building their own prison walls and with their own hands fashioning the chains to bind themselves forever. We need to be on our guard perpetually against little sins of thought, of habit—mere thin threads at first, which will become cables at last if we allow them to be wrapped about our souls.

◇

PASSING BY

◇

*By chance there came down a certain priest that way:
and when he saw him, he passed by on the other side.*
Luke 10:31

We must not suppose that all priests were cold and heartless. Ministers are generally warm-hearted men; they should all be so; they ought to set the people an example of kindness and sympathy; they ought to be like Christ—and He was always ready to help anybody in trouble. No doubt many of the Jewish priests were kind and generous; but here was one who was not. This shows us that being a priest or a minister does not make anyone tender-hearted; one may hold a very sacred office and yet have a cold and hard heart. But it is very sad when it is so.

This priest did not even stop to look at the sufferer, or to ask him how he came to be injured, or to inquire what he could do for him. He kept as far to the other side of the road as he could get; perhaps he even pretended not to see the wounded man. No doubt he had excuses ready in his own mind. He was in a great hurry, or he was very tired, or he could not do anything for the poor man if he should stop, or he was sensitive and could not bear to look on blood.

No matter about his motives; it is more important to avoid repeating his fault. Do we never pass by human wants that we know well we ought to stop to relieve? Do we never keep out of the way of those whose needs strongly appeal to us? Do we never have trouble conjuring up excuses to satisfy our own insistent consciences because we passed by someone we ought to have helped? Some people look the other way when they are passing a blind man on the wayside. Ministers have refused to go to see sick people because they were weary. Persons have stayed away from church because there was to be an appeal for money for a needy cause. This verse is an ugly mirror, isn't it? It shows us blemishes that we didn't know we had.

◇

MY NEIGHBOR

◇

A certain Samaritan . . . had compassion on him,
and went to him, and bound up his wounds.
Luke 10:33–34

Now we must conclude that the half-heathen Samaritans were better as a class than the highly favored Jews. Our Lord uses a Samaritan in His parable because He wants to teach the law of love. No matter who the sufferer is that we come upon in any of life's paths, he is our neighbor. He may be a very worthless sort of man, but it does not matter; he is our neighbor. As we look closely at him, we may see that he is an enemy. Once he did us a bitter, cruel wrong, and he has no claim whatever on us for sympathy or for help, but no matter; he is our neighbor. The person of the human race that we find suffering or in need of any kind becomes for the time our neighbor—the one neighbor to whom for the present we owe love.

There is more definition here: we learn what the word "love" means. You say, "I can't love hateful people; I can't love criminals; I can't love a poor tramp." Nobody expects you to love such people the way you love your wife, your child, your friend. It is not likely that this Samaritan had a tender affection for this wounded Jew while he was helping him. Samaritans were not in the habit of loving Jews very deeply. But he did not look at the man and consider whether he loved him or not before he began to attend to his wounds. Yet he loved him precisely as the commandment meant he should love him. His love was not a warm emotion; it was a very practical affection.

First it was pity; he had compassion on him. But pity is sometimes a very useless emotion—merely a tear that comes easily and costs nothing. This good wayfarer had more than a tear. His pity was found in his hands and in his pockets. He went to the man and bound up his wounds, helped him to an inn, and gave attention to him until he was restored.

September 4

SPIRITUAL BLINDNESS

As Jesus passed by, he saw a man which was blind from his birth.
John 9:1

The blind man illustrates everyone's natural condition. For one thing, he had never been able to see. Men are born in a state of sin. Whatever we may say about the sweetness, innocence, and purity of childhood, the Scriptures plainly teach that no one is born by natural birth in the kingdom of heaven, but that all must be born again to enter it.

Another analogy is that this man's blindness shut off from him a whole world of beauty. There were lovely things all around him—green fields, sweet flowers, blue skies, bright sunshine, shining stars; but he never saw any of these things. So also there is a whole world of spiritual beauty lying about the unregenerate person and above him—the love of God, divine promises, blessed hopes, the heavenly kingdom, all the joys of salvation; but he sees nothing of all this glorious world.

It is said that a lady looking at one of Turner's pictures, which depicted some scene of nature, said to the artist, "Mr. Turner, I cannot see in nature what you put in your pictures." The artist's quiet answer was, "Don't you wish you could, madam?" Men of the world observe the raptures of Christian faith and Christian hope, read the joyous words of Christian experience, and say with a sneer, "We cannot see any such joys as these in religion." The only proper answer is, "Don't you wish you could?" It takes the artist's eye to see the glory of nature; it takes the opened eye of Christian faith to see the glories of God's spiritual kingdom.

For another thing, this blind man's condition was incurable. In this, too, his case illustrated the condition of every sinner. The sinner is incurable, and none but Christ can remove his spiritual blindness. "Except a man be born again, he cannot see the kingdom of God" (John 3:3).

September 5

◇

"THE NIGHT COMETH"

◇

I must work the works of him that sent me, while it is day: the night cometh, when no man can work.
John 9:4

Even Jesus felt the pressure of time's brevity, and the necessity for doing promptly and quickly the work which had been given Him to do. How much more should we feel this pressure, and hasten to improve the moments as they fly. We have all some work given us by God Himself. We are in the world on divine missions—sent from God to take some specific part in blessing the world.

To do this work we have just a "day" of time. Each one's day is his lifetime. A day is a brief time; it is not long from the rising to the setting of the sun. It is a fixed time; when the sun comes to its time for going down, no power in the universe can prolong his stay for one moment. When death comes he will not wait one instant. Unfinished at that time, then unfinished forever.

Yet the day is long enough for God's plan. The sun never sets too soon for His purpose. Each little life is long enough for the little part of the world's work allotted to it. This is true even of the infant that lies only an hour, merely coming into this world, smiling its blessing, and flying away. It is true of the child, of the young man or young woman, of him who dies in the maturity of his powers, with his hands yet full of unfinished tasks. No one can ever offer as an excuse for an unfulfilled lifework that the time given to him was too short. It is always long enough if only every moment of it is filled with simple faithfulness.

To have our work completed at the end, we must do it while the day lasts. Mr. McCheyne had on his watch-dial a picture of the setting sun, and over it the words, "The night cometh." Every time he looked at his watch to see the hour he was reminded of the shortness of life, and of the urgent necessity for discipline in duty. We should all comprehend the lesson.

September 6

---◇---

SIGHT TO THE BLIND

---◇---

When he had thus spoken . . . he anointed the
eyes . . . and said unto him, Go, wash.
John 9:6–7

I t is related that one day, several summers ago, the empress of
Austria was riding over the country in her carriage and saw a
woman a little distance from the road acting in a strange manner.
She soon discovered that the woman was blind, and further, that
she was close to a precipice—that another step might hurl her to
death. The empress quickly left her carriage and hurried to the
woman, just in time to save her life. The world admires the act;
but here is one still more amazing. The King of glory sees a poor
blind beggar sitting in the darkness, is moved with compassion for
him, and stops to open his eyes.

We may trace here the course of Christ with this blind man. He
saw him and was touched by his condition. So the sight of a
sinner always touches Christ. He came unasked to the blind man
and brought the healing unsought to him. He touched his eyes,
bringing Himself as the light of the world into contact with the
man's darkness. So Christ comes first to us, not waiting to be
sought. In His incarnation He brought Himself in contact with our
fallen nature to save it. By His Spirit He touches each blind soul
that believes and brings light and salvation to it.

He used means, making clay with the spittle, anointing the
man's eyes, then sending him to wash. Christ uses means in the
opening of men's spiritual eyes. He sends His grace to us through
His Word, through the ordinances, through the touch and love of
human friends.

He gave this man something to do, something requiring obedience and action. So He gives the sinner something to do, asking
him to believe, to rise up, to wash in the fountain, to confess his
Savior, and to follow Him into lowly service. Thus the curing of
this blind man illustrates the opening of the spiritual eyes.

September 7

—◇—

THE BLIND MAN'S OBEDIENCE

—◇—

He went his way therefore, and washed, and came seeing.
John 9:7

We must mark the promptness of this blind man's obedience. We observe him rising from his place, and led by some attendant, walking along the street with the patches of mud upon his eyes. People probably laughed at him as he went along, but he did not mind it. Christ had told him to go to the pool of Siloam and wash, and he was going to do it. Was not the great blessing of sight a gift enough to compensate for any trouble in going after it? He would not be laughed out of the cure that was so near to his hand.

Perhaps some people told him it was all nonsense—that mud never cured anyone's blindness, and that the Siloam water had no such wondrous power. Still he pressed on through the long streets, amid the hooting and laughing people, until he came to the pool. There he washed and as he washed, his eyes, which never had seen before, now saw clearly. For the first time in all his life he saw the beautiful things about him—the skies, the hills, the buildings, the colors, the faces of the people. So his faith was rewarded.

In all this there is an analogy which is so obvious that it scarcely need be written out. This man's faith in taking that walk through the streets to the pool illustrates the kind of faith every sinner must exercise in obeying Christ, if he would have his spiritual eyes opened and be saved. People sneer at the Christian and ask, "What good is it going to do you to trust in Christ and unite with the church?" Then the result—the opening of his eyes to see the world of natural beauty never seen before, though lying close all the years—illustrates the revelation which faith in Christ brings to the believing soul. God's face and heaven's invisible things burst upon the spiritual vision of him whose soul's eyes are opened. So faith has its reward.

September 8

THE GOOD SHEPHERD

He calleth his own sheep by name.
John 10:3

There is a great difference between the care which the owner gives and that which a servant or hireling gives. There is a difference between the way a true mother looks after her child and the way a hired nurse does it. This is seen especially when the child is sick or in danger. The nurse serves for pay; the mother serves for love. Christ the Good Shepherd is the owner of His sheep.

There is something very sweet in the thought that Christians are Christ's own. It suggests how dear they are to Him. "Having loved his own which were in the world, he loved them unto the end" (John 13:1). The thought also brings with it the assurance of love and care. His will is that "His own" shall be with Him in heaven forever. The thought suggests also much about our duty to Christ. If we are of "His own," He has the entire right to the disposal of our lives and our services.

There is something very wonderful in the thought that Christ calls His sheep by their individual names. Some pastors do not know their people by name when they have but a few hundred to know. Christ has millions scattered over all the world; it is hard for us to realize that every one of these He knows personally by name. The Bible tells us that He calls the stars by their names, but then the stars are so big that it does not seem so strange. But here is a poor widow, one of His own, living in a desolate garret in the heart of a great city, amid thronging thousands. Does He know her name? Here is a little orphan child, one of His own, left with no home, no friend to protect. Does He know this little one? Certainly He does. This ought to be a very precious truth to everyone who loves Christ and belongs to Him. He knows if any of His own are suffering or in need, or if they are in danger; and He will never neglect even the least of them.

September 9

◇

FOLLOWING JESUS

◇

He . . . leadeth them out. . . . He goeth
before them, and the sheep follow him.
John 10:3–4

The Eastern shepherd does not drive his sheep, but leads them wherever he wants to take them. At night he leads them into the fold for safety. In the morning he leads them out to pasture. So Christ never drives His people; He goes before them and leads them, and they follow Him.

Sheep need to be led. They have no such instinct for finding their own way as most other animals have. Christ's people are just like them. Sheep wander away, and a lost sheep never finds its way back. "All we like sheep have gone astray" (Isaiah 53:6); and we never could find the way home again if the Good Shepherd did not seek us and lead us back. Christ leads His people gently. He goes before His sheep. He is very thoughtful for the weak ones. "He gathers the lambs in His arms, and carries them in His bosom." He never leads His sheep too fast. He takes them sometimes over rough and dangerous ways, but He never loses any of them. Not a sheep of Christ's was ever yet lost by the way under His guidance, even in the most perilous paths.

An old guide said to a tourist in the Alps, who was afraid to trust himself to the guide's hand to be helped over some perilous ledge, "This hand never lost a man." Christ never lost a man. He has led missions home over this world's paths, but not one of them ever perished in the way. "Those that thou gavest me I have kept, and none of them is lost" (John 17:12).

Christ leads His sheep to the pastures and by the still waters. Sometimes He leads them over deserts, and along thorny paths, and through dark gorges; but He is always just before them, and where He is they are safe. At the last He leads them through the valley of the shadows into the heavenly fold. There they shall be safe eternally and be blessed in His love.

GREEN PASTURES

By me if any man enter in, he shall . . . find pasture.
John 10:9

The shepherd takes care that his sheep are well fed. Christ also feeds His people and leads them out to find pasture. *The Bible is His pasture-land*, and the pasture there is always good. Every chapter is a field of rich grass. Some of these fields seem at first to be bare and sterile; but even in the barest there is enough pasture to feed a hungry soul.

Then there are the pasture-fields of *prayer*. These lie very close to the border of heaven. They are always up in the quiet valleys among the mountains. The Good Shepherd leads us to them through the gates of prayer. We bow down in lowly humility, and enter with Him into the great pastures, and feed our souls until their hunger is satisfied.

The *church* is another of our Shepherd's pasture-fields. We enter the gates of the sanctuary, and at once we find spiritual food. We find it in the services, in the preaching, and in the ordinances.

In our coming life in this world, if we are faithfully following Christ, we are continually in fields of rich pasture. Christ never leads us into any places in which there is nothing to feed us. Even in the hot deserts of trial and sorrow there is food. We sometimes think there is only barrenness in our toilsome life, filled with temptations, cares, and sacrifices; but the Good Shepherd is ever with us, and there is always pasture.

Thus the whole world is a rich field when Jesus leads His flock. If any Christians are not well fed, it is because they will not feed. The trouble is that they do not hunger for spiritual food. The saddest thing in this world is not a passionate cry for bread but a soul that has no hunger. Many souls die in the midst of the provision made by the Good Shepherd, not for want of food, but for want of appetite.

CHRIST KNOWS HIS OWN

I . . . know my sheep.
John 10:14

The Eastern shepherds had certain marks by which they knew their own sheep. Even in this country the farmers put marks on their sheep—their own initial, or an "ear-mark," or some other particular sign by which they will know them anywhere. Christ knows His people by certain distinguishing marks.

He knows them by their faces. There is something in every true child of God which shows where he belongs—some family likeness, some feature of the divine image shining out. The prodigal's father knew his son when he saw him a long way off. In his rags, the poverty, amid the pangs of hunger, the eye of love recognized the child. Christ knows His own, however dim the likeness, by their faces. The crowds do not recognize heaven's princes in the humble Christians they meet; but every angel knows them. Not only does Christ know His own by their faces, but also by their voices. The mother knows her child's cry anywhere, even in the darkness, and can distinguish it among a thousand voices. Christ knows the voices of His own wherever He hears them speak or cry.

He knows them also by their character. Even if the outside is rough and uncultured, it does not hide from His eye the inner life, the spirit, the heart. He saw the future Peter with all his grandeur of character in the rude Simon who was brought to Him. He knows His friends by their obedience. He knows the white garments of righteousness which His redeemed ones wear. He knows His disciples by their following where He leads. He knows the penitent heart by the fragrance it emits. It is an altar of incense. It is a box of ointment broken open. As we discover the hiding places of flowers by their odors, so God knows the home of the penitent heart by the sweetness that comes from its prayers. He knows His own.

THE HOME OF BETHANY

A certain man was sick, named Lazarus, of Bethany.
John 11:1

This home at Bethany was wondrously favored. The family seems to have been wealthy. It was a loving home, the three members named being bound together by very close and tender ties. This we know from the fact that Jesus found it such a congenial home for Himself. He surely would not have chosen a quarrelsome household for His own abiding place. He could not have found a refuge there if it had been anything but a home filled with love's sweetness.

We know that it was an affectionate household, also, from the sorrow of the sisters when their brother was dead. As we read the matchless story we are sure it was no ordinary tie that bound the family together. In too many homes brothers and sisters are not to each other what they might be. Oftentimes there is a lack in the display of love. Brothers and sisters should not only love one another, but they should be kindly and affectionate in their relationship together.

It was a favored home, also, because it was the one which Jesus chose to be the resting place for His heart in the still evenings after the fierce strife with His enemies in the temple. It was His love for the members of this family, and the honor He put upon their home, by which the little town of Bethany was immortalized.

Yet, highly favored as was this home in these ways, sickness came into it. We receive a lesson from this. No home can be made which will shut sickness out of its chambers. Wealth cannot keep it away, love cannot. Yet we learn, also, that sickness in our home is no proof that Christ does not love us. Into the households that are dearest to Him pain and sorrow come; but we shall see that in the end blessing to the family and glory to God come from the trial. These thoughts should comfort us when sickness comes into our households.

◆

THE SISTER'S MESSAGE

◆

His sisters sent unto him, saying, Lord,
behold, he whom thou lovest is sick.
John 11:3

In their trouble the first thought of the sisters was of Jesus, and they sent at once to Him. This lesson we should not overlook. No doubt they sent for the physician; but they sent also for Christ. We should never fail to send word to Christ when anyone is not well in our home. We should want Him always at the bedside when our loved ones are suffering.

We must also notice the message which the sisters sent to Christ. It was very short and simple. They did not beg and plead with Him to come—indeed they made no request whatever; they merely told Jesus that His friend was sick, and left it to Him to decide what He would do. They knew that He would do the right thing from the prompting of His own heart. Notice also the plea. They did not say, "He who loves thee is sick," but, "*He whom thou lovest* is sick." They made their appeal to Christ's own heart rather than to any personal claim. This is always our best plea with Christ—His love for us, not our love for Him.

There is something also in this message which speaks of a deep feeling of peace in the midst of danger. Many persons in such experiences lose all their courage and often their faith; but these sisters, though in such deep distress, maintained their composure. They had learned lessons of peace from Christ in the bright, happy days beforehand, and when the trouble came they were ready for it and were not disturbed. If we would get Christ's sweet comfort when sorrow comes, we must welcome Him in the days of gladness. If this Bethany family had shut Christ out of their home when they were all well and happy, they could not have had His blessed comfort in their great distress. We must take Christ in the bright days if we would have Him when it grows dark.

MARTHA GOING TO JESUS

*Martha, as soon as she heard that
Jesus was coming, went and met him.*
John 11:20

The coming of Jesus to this Bethany home was never so welcome as on that day. It is the same yet in people's homes, even in those where He is most loved; Christ is never so dear and precious to us as when we are in trouble. Need reveals His preciousness. Many persons who do not desire the minister's presence during their days of prosperity and gladness are quick to send for him when sorrow comes. This was not Martha's way, however; she had welcomed Christ to her home in the happy days when there was no sorrow, and that was what made His coming such a blessing to her now.

We understand this lesson—that the only true preparation for trial is personal friendship with Christ. If we never turn to the Bible for comfort until some great grief is upon us, it will not give us much light; but if we have it in the bright days, and its words are hung up then like lamps in our heart's chambers, when it grows dark the beams will shine out and change night into day.

When visitors to the Mammoth Cave are preparing to enter that magnificent cavern, the guide puts into the hand of each tourist a lighted lamp. It is noonday, perhaps, and it seems very foolish to walk down the green bank carrying little lamps in the bright sunshine. But when the party members enter the mouth of the cave and go a little distance, they understand the use of their lamps. In the darkness they would perish except for their pale light. Some people do not think, when they are moving along in joy and gladness, that they need Christ; but by and by it grows dark in some path of sorrow, and then they learn the blessing of having Christ beforehand. If they have Him in their hearts, they find it light all about them; if they have Him not, the gloom is turned to despair.

September 15

UNBELIEVING "IF"

Lord, if thou hadst been here, my brother had not died.
John 11:21

Would Lazarus not have died if Jesus had been there? Do we not read that because Jesus loved the Bethany family, and because He learned of the sickness of Lazarus, therefore He remained two days after the messenger came? Did He not also say that He was glad He had not been there before Lazarus died?

One thing at least we know: it was better as it was—better that Lazarus should not be cured, but should die, and then that Christ's power should be shown in his resurrection. It was therefore an unbelieving "if," and a groundless one, which fell from Martha's lips. But we are all apt to let similar "ifs" drop from our lips when trouble comes to us. If we had only tried another doctor, or taken the matter in hand a little sooner, our friend would not have died. We feel sometimes that sorrow is an evidence that God did not hear our prayers; if He had only heard our cry the trial would have been averted. Yet we have but to read this story through to the end to see that Christ's way was the better way here, as it always is the better way.

> *We sadly watched the close of all,*
> *Life balanced on a breath;*
> *We saw upon his features fall*
> *the awful shade of death.*
> *All dark and desolate we were;*
> *And murmuring nature cried—*
> *"Oh, surely, Lord, hadst thou been here,*
> *Our brother had not died."*
>
> *But when its glance the mourner cast*
> *On all that grace had done,*
> *And thought of life's long warfare passed,*
> *And endless victory won,*
> *Then faith prevailing wiped the tears,*
> *And looking upward cried—*
> *"Oh, surely, Lord, thou hast been here,*
> *Our brother has not died."*

LIFE IN CHRIST

*I am the resurrection, and the life: he that believeth in me,
though he were dead, yet shall he live: And whosoever
liveth and believeth in me shall never die.*

John 11:25–26

Martha believed in the resurrection at the last day; but that seemed far away, while her heart craved immediate comfort. It was to this feeling, which many another mourner besides Martha has experienced, that our Lord spoke these wonderful words. His answer shows that He Himself is the bridge of life that unites the shores of eternity and time, filling up the dark chasm, and bringing the resurrection and life eternal close to earth's death.

The resurrection is not far away, for it is all in Christ's hands. When His believing ones die they only sleep in Him. They are not really dead; indeed, those believing on Him never die at all. What we call dying is only passing through the gate into the immediate presence of Christ. Christ has abolished death. To Him death was real and full of terrors. But because it was so terrible to Him, it is only an entrance of glory for His people. He absorbed the blackness and the gloom in His own soul, as He passed though the valley, and He left it a vale of brightness for His followers.

If we could all get into our hearts the truth of the immortal life as revealed in the gospel, it would take away all the gloom related to the death of our loved ones. Those who live here are in Christ, and those who have passed over are with Christ; thus in Him we are still united. There is but one family in Christ—part gone over, part crossing now, soon all to be together.

This truth of the endless life is one of marvelous power when we have, even in the least measure, realized it. Death is not the end of anything but mortality, imperfection, and sin. Life goes on fuller, richer, with enlarged capacities, beyond the incident which we call death. We shall never die.

THE SEEKING SAVIOR

*What man . . . if he lose one [sheep] . . .
doth not . . . go after that which is lost?*
Luke 15:4

Does the shepherd care when one of his sheep has left the fold? He has a hundred in his flock; does he care that one of them has gone? Does he miss one among so many? Christ has millions of holy beings about Him—angels and redeemed saints—who never go astray. Does He care when on earth, in the heart of a great city, or out in some lonely country town, one soul wanders away into the darkness?

> *There were ninety and nine that safely lay*
> *In the shelter of the fold;*
> *But one was out on the hills away,*
> *Far off from the gates of gold,*
> *Away on the mountains wild and bare,*
> *Away from the tender Shepherd's care.*
>
> *"Lord, thou hast here thy ninety and nine;*
> *Are they not enough for thee?"*
> *But the Shepherd made answer: "This of mine*
> *Has wandered away from me;*
> *And although the road be rough and steep,*
> *I go to the desert to find my sheep."*

Christ misses even one, no matter who, that strays away. Did any mother ever have so many children that if one of them wandered from home she would not miss it? We have strange thoughts of Christ's love if we think He loves us only as a race, and not as individuals. The father of a stolen child said, "So long as I live I will continue to go up and down the country, looking into the face of every boy I meet, trying to find my own lost child." Think of that weary, broken-hearted father going from city to city and giving up everything in this one sad search! Then think of Christ seeking the lost one that has wandered away from His home of love. Behold Him, weary, with bleeding feet, as He goes on and seeks until He finds!

September 18

◇

BROUGHT HOME

◇

When he hath found it, he layeth it on his shoulders.
Luke 15:5

H e does not drive the poor weary sheep home. This is not the way the gentle Eastern shepherd does. He stoops down and lifts it up, and lays it on his own shoulder and carries it back. There is a wonderful revelation in this little touch in the picture. Let us be sure that we understand just what the words say.

We all know that Christ carried our sin when He went to the cross. We know, too, that we may cast our burdens upon Him. But here we learn that Christ wants to carry, not our sins only, not our burdens and cares only, but ourselves. The shepherd took up the sheep itself and laid it upon his shoulder.

> *I am the Burden-bearer; I*
> *Will never pass the o'erladen by.*
> *My feet are on the mountain steep;*
> *They wind through valleys dark and deep;*
> *They print the hot dust of the plain,*
> *And walk the billows of the main;*
> *Wherever is a load to bear*
> *My willing shoulder still is there.*

He does this with "rejoicing." Can this be true? Has Christ really interest enough in any human being on this earth to be made sad by his wandering and glad by his recovery? The thought overwhelms me. We can understand a shepherd's rejoicing when he bears home a sheep that has been lost. We can understand a mother's joy when her lost child is brought to her door. But that the heart of Jesus rejoiced when He found us, and carried us back toward home, seems too amazing to be true. Yet here the word stands. Then listen to Zephaniah: "The Lord thy God in the midst of thee is mighty; he will save, he will rejoice over thee with joy, he will rest in his love, he will joy over thee with singing" (Zephaniah 3:17). How dear we are to Christ!

THE FAR COUNTRY
◇

The younger son gathered all together,
and took his journey into a far country.
Luke 15:13

Once a man has shaken off his subjection to God he begins his departure from Him. He first gets the reins into his own hands, and then the old paths are too straight and limited for him. He has taken all his "goods" into his own control—that is, he has assumed charge and direction of all his own powers, gifts, and energies; and now he will go out and try life in his own way—the way of license and self-gratification. Everyone has departed from God into the far country who is not at home with God, who is not living as a child in the Father's house.

The "far country" is a costly place to live. When the prodigal got there his property soon began to go; and it was not very long till it was all gone—wasted in riotous living. This story is the literal history of a great many young men. There are thousands of them who are wasting large fortunes every year in this same riotous living—in drinking and all kinds of excesses.

But how must we interpret this in its spiritual application? The "substance" of the sinner consists in his gifts, talents, powers, opportunities, and possibilities. He "wastes his substance" whenever he does not use it for God and for the good of the world—the uses for which God bestowed it. He wastes it also when he squanders it in sin. Here then is the picture: a man endowed with powers fitting him for advancement and usefulness, rushing into evil ways, spending his strength in sin, destroying his body, mind, and spirit in revelry and dissipation. The man with one talent, who only hid it away and did not use it at all, keeping it as it was, to be returned in the end, was condemned to outer darkness. How much worse will be the doom of those who squander their talents in sin, and use them to curse the world and drag down other souls!

THE PRODIGAL'S RETURN

When he was yet a great way off, his father saw him.
Luke 15:20

The boy had, in the faraway country, a vision of his old home. As he sat there and thought of his dishonor and his ruin, there flashed before him a picture which made him very homesick. The vision brought back the old home in all its beauty and blessedness. There was plenty there, while here the once happy, favored son was perishing with hunger.

It was a blessed moment for the prodigal. It was God's message to him, inviting him to return home. When a child is stolen away from a lovely and tender household, it may be kept among wandering gypsies or savage Indians even to old age, but there are always broken fragments of sweet memories that hang over the soul like trailing clouds in the sky—dim, shadowy memories of something very lovely, very pure, reminiscences of that long-lost, long-forgotten past, when the child lay on the mother's arms, and was surrounded by beauty and tenderness. So there is something in the heart of everyone who has wandered from God that ever floats about him, even in sin's revels—a fair, ethereal vision, dim and faraway perhaps, but splendid as the drapery of the sunset. It is the memory of lost innocence, of the Father's love, the vision of a heavenly beauty with the potential of falling to the worst state possible, with the possibility of restoration to the original state.

When the prodigal reached home he found his vision realized. His father was watching for him—had long been watching for him. It is a picture of the heavenly Father's loving welcome of every lost child of His that comes back home. Thus He receives the worst who comes penitently. Our sweetest dreams of God's love are a thousand times too poor and dim for the reality. A great way off God sees the returning prodigal and runs to meet him. No matter how far we have wandered, there is a welcome waiting for us at home.

September 21

❖

THE BEGGAR'S ESCORT

❖

The beggar died, and was carried by
the angels into Abraham's bosom.
Luke 16:22

Nothing is said about his funeral—of course it was only a pauper's. Earth had no honor for the beggar, no splendid coffin, no flowers; but the angels came and were his bearers and escort to glory. Notice also that nothing is said about what became of his body; but little matter, for the man himself was no longer in that old, worn-out, battered frame. He was soon far away in a realm of brightness. While the body was dropped to the grave, the beggar, the real man, was carried away to heaven; and we see him there, a beggar no longer, enjoying blessedness.

There is another important thought here. We dread death. It seems the end of existence. But really to the Christian it is only an incident in his life. It is just a moment's passage through an experience we never can understand; and then—glory. One minute this poor beggar lies at the gate, despised, suffering, hungry; the next, a strange sensation passes over him, and all is confusion; then he awakes flying through the air with angel-escort, and in a little time he is inside the gate of pearl and lives on. There is no break in his life.

Death came also to the rich man. His riches could not save him from that. No doubt he had a splendid funeral. There would be a long procession, many mourners, great waste of luxuries, every show of honor. But who would not rather have the beggar's escort after death than the finest funeral earth ever gave to mortal? There have been funerals of rich men at which there was genuine sorrow, where those who had been blessed by their benevolence came and wept by their coffins. But in this case there were no sincere mourners, for the man had allowed the needy to lie hungry at his gates. He had lived for himself only, and no one really missed him when he was gone.

September 22

"CONTINUE IN PRAYER"

Men ought always to pray, and not to faint.
Luke 18:1

A great many people get discouraged in praying because the answer does not come at once. It should be settled in the mind, first, that God always hears the true prayer, and that He will always send an answer, though it may not always be the answer we desire. He never despises or disregards the cry of one of His children; but sometimes for wise reasons He delays His answer. Perhaps it cannot be prepared at once. God's plans reach out widely, and He works slowly. Look at Joseph in Egypt—a slave, then a prisoner. No doubt he was praying every day for release; and he may have thought at times that the answer was long in coming. But when it came, he could see that one reason for the delay was that all things might be gotten ready. It took years to prepare the answer that came at last with such blessing.

Or the reason of God's delay may be to draw out our faith, to increase our earnestness. The story of the Syrophenician woman illustrates this. At first Jesus "answered her not a word"; but it was for her sake that He kept her waiting. She received a far better answer later than she could have received at first. Suppose she had "fainted" after her first apparent refusal, think what she would have lost.

No doubt thousands of prayers are never answered because men faint at God's delay. Perhaps you have lost many a joy and blessing because you lost heart and faith before the answer came. A little longer patient perseverance would have brought you a great reward. After spending thousands of dollars in drilling for oil, the operator became discouraged and sold out for a trifle. The purchaser started the drill, and in six hours found a flowing well. We see what giving up cost the first owner. Many Christians lose heart just when the answer is about to be granted.

TWO PRAYERS

God, I thank thee, that I am not as other
men are . . . God be merciful to me a sinner.
Luke 18:11, 13

Here we have two kinds of prayer set side by side for our instruction. The first really is no prayer at all; it is only a bit of self-congratulation in the presence of God. Yet it was not much comfort, after all, that the Pharisee found. He was better than certain other men, he said. He never thought of comparing himself with God, the only true thing to do.

This Pharisee has many followers. A great many people's whole stock of piety consists in not being as bad as someone else. The dishonest man soothes his conscience with the reflection that he is sober and temperate. The false-tongued man is thankful that he pays his debts. The gossiping woman finds great comfort in the fact that she is not a heathen like her neighbor, who never goes to church at all. But it is a poor kind of virtue which has nothing better to build on than such imperfect relative goodness. One may be clear of a great many ugly faults that his neighbors have and yet not be a saint himself.

The other man's prayer was different altogether. There was in him no measuring of himself with other men to see whether he or they were the worse. There was no going over sins he had not committed. He said nothing about his neighbors' sins, but was very free in speaking of his own sins. He stood before God burdened with the awareness of his own personal guilt and cried to God for mercy—mercy wholly undeserved, to be granted only through grace. It is very obvious which was the true and acceptable prayer. It is the penitent's prayer that reaches heaven. God wants honesty in our supplication; he wants humility. It is not enough to be worried about other people's sins; the particular sinner with whose sins each man ought to be most concerned is himself.

September 24

◇

THE CHILDREN'S FRIEND

◇

Then were there brought unto him little children,
that he should put his hands on them, and pray.
Matthew 19:13

Those children must have been glad in later days to remember
that Jesus had laid His hands upon their heads and blessed
them. Sometimes the remembrance even of a human hand laid
on the head in childhood stays all through life and is a blessing.

A Christian man said late in his life that he could still feel the
touch of his dying mother's hand on his head as she told him
farewell and asked him to promise to follow Christ. A boy was
brought to his father's bedside and was "kissed and blessed and
given to God." All through his youth, when there came any
temptation to do wrong, the thought would come, "No, I must
not do this, for I am the boy who was kissed and blessed and
given to God." When, later in life, burdens pressed and he was
about to yield to despair, he would remember his father's acts and
words, and the remembrance would support him: "No; am I not
the boy who was kissed and blessed and given to God?"

In the stress of life his mind at last gave way, and he spent
years in the dark rooms of an insane asylum. And there in his
brighter moments he would write to his daughter: "Here I am
shut away and very lonely. I have no one to sing to me as you
used to do—

"'Jesus, lover of my soul,'

or

'Rock of Ages, cleft for me.'"

"It seems very dark and hard; but yet I am the boy that was
kissed and blessed and given to God." Thus all through his life he
was sustained and strengthened by the remembrance of his
father's last blessing. If all who have been consecrated to Christ,
and have had His hand laid on them, would ever remember that
holy touch, how pure and true would it make their lives!

"FORBID THEM NOT"

Suffer little children, and forbid them not, to come unto me.
Matthew 19:14

The love of Christ for children was one of the most beautiful qualities in His life. It revealed His true human-heartedness. But we must remember too that it revealed His divine interest in the children.

Jesus was much displeased when His disciples rebuked those who brought the little ones and would keep the children away. "Suffer them to come to me, and forbid them not," He said. So we have the caution for ourselves. We must be very careful that we never keep any children from coming to Christ.

We may do this in many ways. We may do this, if we are parents or older Christians, by our own worldly example. Worldly parents are likely to keep their children away from the Savior, even unintentionally, by the influence of their own life. We may do it also by telling them they are too young to come to Him; by simply doing nothing, allowing them to grow up uninfluenced toward the right; by allowing their minds to become preoccupied with other things to the exclusion of Christ.

Christ stands yet and calls upon us to clear every hindrance out of the way that the children may come to Him, and besides to do all we can to bring them to Him. It must be noticed that it is to Christ Himself the children are to come. Suppose they cannot understand "the plan of redemption," or cannot know the doctrines of the church, or cannot answer the hard questions we sometimes put to inquirers; shall we therefore keep them back? No, Christ says, "Let them come to me." No matter how little they know of the way, we are to put up no barriers, we are to make no artificial standards of knowledge or experience; we are only to be sure we do not hinder them, and that we let them come to Him. After that there will be time enough to teach them.

THE YOUNG RULER

◇

There came one running, and kneeled to him, and asked him,
Good Master, what shall I do that I may inherit eternal life?
Mark 10:17

This was a young man, with all his powers primed and full. He was rich, with all the honor, ease, distinction, and influence that riches give. He was a man of good reputation among his fellows; for he was a ruler of the synagogue. His character was above reproach; for he had scrupulously kept all the commandments. He was a lovable man, with many fine qualities, attractive and winsome; for Jesus loved him when He saw him. Yet he was not satisfied. His heart-hunger was also very strong, driving him irresistibly in all haste to Christ.

There never was a more important question asked than he put to Jesus. Eternal life is the most glorious prize in the universe to be gained. It embraces all the blessings of salvation in this world, and then a place in the family of God forever. It is no wonder this young man ran to ask Christ this question. The wonder is that so few people ever do run to make the same inquiry. Men run to seek earth's poor prizes, but they are slow in their pace when they are seeking eternal life.

It is a prize which can be gained. It lies within the reach of everyone. There is no one who may not obtain it. It is a prize, however, that cannot be obtained merely by doing anything. There is plenty of room for doing in the Christian life, but this is not the place for it. Eternal life cannot be gained by saying so many prayers, or fasting for so many hours, or being baptized in a certain way, or joining a particular church, or by giving so much money to charity, or by any other kind of religious act or service. Eternal life is the gift of God; it is obtained through Jesus Christ. It is bestowed upon all who will accept it. The way to get it is to take Christ as Savior and Lord.

---◇---

"Not Far From The Kingdom"

---◇---

Jesus beholding him loved him, and said unto him, One thing
thou lackest: go thy way, sell . . . give . . . and follow me.

Mark 10:21

Jesus loves everyone, but there was something in this young man that especially drew out His affection. He saw in him many amiable qualities, many signs of beauty of character, many things that by divine grace could be made into great loveliness and power. There are many thoughts suggested by this statement. Here are a few of them: Christ loves those who are not His disciples; some people think He loves only those who have begun to love Him. Christ is deeply interested in every young person's life; He beholds the possibilities in every young life. He sees lovable things even in the unsaved, but good qualities are not enough to save one.

Our Lord's answer to the young man's question is very instructive. What is the one thing which, besides all we can do for ourselves by obedience and cultivation of character, makes one a Christian? It is important to be able to answer this question, for it is often asked. A man says, "I live as well as Christians do. I attend church; I keep the commandments; I am kind to my family and generous to the needy and poor; I live conscientiously in all things. What do I lack?"

What shall we answer him? Shall we tell him to sell his farm or his property and give all he has to the poor? Was that the one essential thing in the Master's counsel to this young man? No: the essential thing was following Christ; the selling and giving away were but parts of this. The young man's heart was attached to his wealth, and the "one thing" was to take Christ instead of his wealth. So we should answer our inquirer by telling him that he must accept Christ as his Savior and Lord, that he must lay his money and all that he has at Christ's feet, to be used only for Him, and as He directs, and must take Christ as his sole portion forever.

September 28

◇

SERVING OTHERS

◇

Not to be ministered unto, but to minister.
Matthew 20:28

The art of photography is now so perfect that the whole side of a great newspaper can be taken in miniature so small as to be carried in a little pin or button, and yet every letter and point be perfect. So the whole life of Christ is photographed in this one little phrase. He came not to be served; if this had been his aim He would never have left heaven's glory, where He wanted nothing, where angels praised Him and ministered to Him. He came to serve. He altogether forgot Himself. He served all He met who would receive His service. At last He gave His life in serving—gave it to save others, to redeem lost souls.

You say you want to be like Christ. You ask Him to print His own image on your heart. Here, then, is the image. It is no vague dream of perfection that we are to think of when we ask to be like Christ. The old monks thought that they were in the path to become like Christ when they went into the wilderness, away from men, to live in cold cells or on tall columns. But surely that is not the thought which this picture suggests. "To minister"—that is the Christlike thing. Instead of fleeing away from men, we are to live among men, to serve them, to live for them, to seek to bless them, to do good, to give our lives.

Christ tells us also that this is the stairway to the highest reaches of Christian life. "Whosoever of you will be the chiefest, shall be servant of all" (Mark 10:44). To worldly men this seems indeed a strange way of rising. According to this, all man's scrambling for place and power is really scrambling downward rather than upward. The real heights in human life are the heights of self-forgetfulness and service. We are to use all our redeemed powers in doing good to others in Christ's name. That is what Christ did with His blessed life, and we are to follow in His steps.

⬦

JESUS PASSING BY

⬦

When he heard that it was Jesus . . . he began to cry out.
Mark 10:47

No doubt the blind man had been wishing that Jesus would come to Jericho. He had grown to believe that if He would only come He could open his blind eyes. What a burst of joy filled the poor man when he learned that Jesus was passing by! Now was his opportunity. Instantly he began to cry out. The lesson here is that when Jesus is passing by all who need help should at once call upon Him.

But when may it now be said that Jesus is passing by? Of course He is always present everywhere. We cannot get out of His sight for a moment. Yet there are times when He seems especially to visit certain places. The day of Israel's visitation was when Jesus was going through the land teaching and healing. So times of revival in a church are times of peculiar visitation. When the Spirit is working mightily, when many hearts are bowing down in repentance, then Jesus of Nazareth is passing by, and then is the time to call upon Him. When conscience is tender, when the Spirit is silently striving, when some particular blessing has awakened the soul, again is Jesus passing by.

He passed by in youth. There is no other time when He is really so near. Then the heart is tender, the desires are committed, our life is flexible, and He comes especially close. There will never be a time in later life when it will be so easy to call upon Him and be saved as in youth. This blind man wisely seized the opportunity. Jesus was passing now, was close to him, could readily hear his call. Now was his time; if not now, perhaps never. Surely we ought to act as wisely in seeking Christ while He is near. It must not be forgotten that Jesus never passed through Jericho again. If Bartimaeus had said, "I will wait till he comes again," what would have been the result?

◇

FAITHFULNESS

◇

*Because thou hast been faithful in a very
little, have thou authority over ten cities.*
Luke 19:17

I t is remarkable how much the Word of God makes of faithfulness—simple faithfulness. It is not great things that God
requires of us unless our mission is to do great things; He asks
only that we be faithful in the duties that come to our attention
in our commonplace days. That means that we do all our work as
well as we can; that we serve well in the varied relationships of
life in which from time to time we find ourselves; that we stand
heroically in our calling, resisting temptation and continuing true
and loyal to God; and that we fulfill our mission in all ways
according to the grace given unto us, using every gift and talent
for the glory of God and the good of the world. The world crowns
"success"; God crowns "faithfulness."

Jesus tells us that faithfulness in this life lifts us to places of
authority hereafter. So, then, life here is only a trial to see what
we are capable of doing. It is after all a real trial period to find out
who may be set over large trusts. And the real life is to be begun
in the other world. Those who prove faithful here will have
places of responsibility in the kingdom of glory.

This ought to give a new and mighty motive to our living in
this world. Our eternal honor and employment will depend upon
the degree of our faithfulness here. Good men and women often
say at the close of their lives, "If I could only begin now, with all
my experience, I could live my life much better." Well, if they had
been faithful, that is the very thing they will be permitted to do in
the next world. A mother who had brought up a large family
said: "I have just learned now how to train children. I could do it
well if I could begin it again." If she has learned this, that is just
what Christ wanted her to learn. Now she is ready for full service
in His kingdom.

October 1

◇

HOUSEHOLD DUTIES

◇

They made him a supper; and Martha served.
John 12:2

There are certain Bible characters that we never fail to recognize. We know Martha by her busy serving. Each time we meet her we find her engaged in active duties. She represents those whose love for Christ takes practical form. Some people like to criticize Martha; but, after all, her type of piety is important in this world where there is so much need of her service. Beautiful as the Mary-spirit is, it would not do if all were Marys; for who would then do the work that needs so much to be done? A wife and mother, for instance, who should spend all her time in Bible-reading and prayer, giving no thought to her household duties, would not make a very happy home.

> *Yea, Lord!—Yet some must serve;*
> *Not all, with tranquil heart,*
> *Even at thy dear feet,*
> *Wrapped in devotion sweet,*
> *May sit apart.*
>
> *Yea, Lord!—Yet some must bear*
> *The burden of the day,*
> *Its labor and its heat,*
> *While others at thy feet*
> *May muse and pray.*
>
> *Yea, Lord!—Yet some must do*
> *Life's daily task-work; some*
> *Who fain would sing must toil*
> *Amid earth's dust and moil,*
> *While lips are dumb.*
>
> *Yea, Lord!—Yet man must earn,*
> *And woman bake the bread;*
> *And some must watch and wake*
> *Early for other's sake,*
> *Who pray instead.*

AT HIS FEET
◇

*Then took Mary a pound of ointment of spikenard,
very costly, and anointed the feet of Jesus.*
John 12:3

We see Mary three times in the gospel, and each time she is in the same posture—at Jesus' feet. When we have our first glimpse within the Bethany home, we find Martha in her characteristic attitude—serving; and Mary we see sitting at the Master's feet, eagerly listening to His words. Our next view of Mary is when Jesus came back to Bethany after the death of Lazarus, and the sisters went out to meet Him. Again she is at the feet of Christ, this time in deep sorrow, seeking comfort. Here a third time we find her at Christ's feet, and now it is in honoring her Lord.

We think of Mary, therefore, as a woman who was always at Christ's feet. In the pleasant, ordinary days, she sat there as a learner, looking up into His face, drinking in His words, and absorbing His spirit into her soul. When grief came she went to His feet for comfort, pouring out her sorrow there, looking up into His face for consolation. Then, when the trouble was over, and there were joy and victory instead, we find her again in her proper place, honoring Jesus with her heart's richest gifts. There is not a more proper place for the redeemed life than at the Savior's feet.

In Mary's gift she brought the best she had, the richest gift in all her possession. We should always bring our best to Christ. No ointment in the world is half so precious to Him as the love of human hearts; we should bring Him our best love, giving Him the first place in our affections. We should give Him the best of our lives, our youth in all its freshness and purity, our body and mind when they are at their best. We should give Him the best of our time, not the weary moments of fatigue only, but the hours when we are most alert. We should give Him the best of our services, doing our finest work of all kinds for Him.

October 3

❖

FLEETING OPPORTUNITIES

❖

Me ye have not always.
Mark 14:7

We ought to learn well the value of opportunities. They do not coincide with our convenience; but while we linger indecisively, they are gone. Then, when they are gone, they do not come again. Whatever was done for Jesus He said must be done at once, for they would not have Him always. To put off the act of love would be to miss doing it altogether; for when He was once away, however much they might want to do the kindness for Him, it would be too late. The poor they would always have— they might care for them at any time; but whatever act of love they would render to Jesus they must give at once.

There ought to be a deep lesson for us in our Lord's word in this place. There are certain things that we shall only have the opportunity to do once. Here is a mother in a home: for years she has given her life in loving, self-sacrificing service, poured it out like rich ointment for the good of her children. Now she is growing old, and as her children look upon her it is as if she said to them, "Whatever kindness you would do to me you must do now, for you will not have me always."

We hear of a neighbor who is sick. Now is the time to perform whatever act of love we desire to render, for we may not long have the friend. Tomorrow he may be gone. There have been tears shed over coffins and graves by those who would have given worlds to get their dead back again, to do for them the things that they neglected to do while they had them. The best time to do a kindness is now.

Someone has beautifully said: "I expect to pass through this world but once. If, therefore, there be any kindness I can do for any fellow-being, let me do it now. Let me not defer or neglect it, for I shall not pass this way again."

October 4

ACCEPTABLE OFFERINGS

She hath done what she could.
Mark 14:8

This was a wonderful compliment to come from the lips of the Christ. Mary could not have done better than this if she had been a thousand times as gifted. We receive two lessons. One is that all Christ wants is what we have the ability and opportunity to do. He asks no impossibilities of us. The poorest things, the smallest offerings, are acceptable if they are really our best in the circumstances.

A child in a mission school offered her teacher a handful of weeds and grass, wilted and soiled at that, which she called a bouquet. Did the teacher refuse the gift and criticize the poor withered weeds? No, she accepted them with as sincere gratitude and as many thanks as if some wealthy friend had offered her an elegant bouquet of flowers. The child did what she could; and the teacher looking behind the gift saw the love in the little heart, and that transfigured her poor gift. So it is that Christ accepts our poorest work or our humblest offering if it is our best.

But the lesson has another side. "She did what she could." It is this, then, that pleases Christ. Are we doing what we could do? Do we always bring to Him our very best gifts? Do we never put Him off with the faded flowers, keeping the fresh and fragrant ones for ourselves? Do we do for Him our very best work? Are we faithful? If we are only doing half what we might, we cannot take the comfort of this compliment. The widow's mites were very acceptable coming from her, because they were all she had; but they would not have elicited any such approval if one of the rich men had given them. A little child's ministry is very beautiful for a child, but it would not be as fitting in the father or mother. We must really do the very best we can if we would have this reward.

"Not Your Own"

The Lord hath need of him.
Mark 11:3

There seems to have been no formal request to the owner for the use of the colt. Jesus sent His disciples to take it by divine authority. So then the Lord has a right to anything we have. No property right that we can get takes the title out of His hands. We talk about our possessions as if they were ours indeed. Nothing is really ours except what is lent to us by the Lord to be used for Him.

There are practical inferences here which we must not overlook. Christ has a right to call for anything we have whenever He wants to use it. He has a right to ask for our money, for it is His far more than ours. When our property is taken away by some providential act, we should not murmur, but should remember that the Lord has a right to do as He will with His own. The same principle applies to the loss of friends by death. The Lord has a right to take them, for He only lends them to us; and when He wants them with Himself He has a right to call them home.

Another thought here is that Christ may sometimes have special use for even the humblest of our possessions. The Lord had need of the good Samaritan's beast to carry the wounded man to the inn. He had need of the boy's five loaves to feed the multitude.

A lady was trying to teach her child that she ought to give everything to Christ to be used in any way He might choose. "Why, Mother," she replied, "Jesus can never use my doll." Yet in an hour the child was letting a poor child that came to the door play with her doll. Was not the Lord using it then? The Lord may need our resources to carry burdens for others. He often has need of our money, our hands, our feet, our lips, our influence; and we do right when we hold all our possessions ready at any call of His to be used as He desires.

October 6

NOTHING BUT LEAVES

Seeing a fig tree afar off having leaves, he came,
if haply he might find any thing thereon.
                                                  Mark 11:13

There were many other fig trees in that region, but Jesus did not turn to any of them to look for food, because they gave no hope, made no display or pretense of having fruit. He went to this tree because by its early leaves it declared to all who saw it that it had also early fruit. Christ does not expect to find spiritual fruit in the life of the godless man or the worldly woman; but He does expect it on the life of the man or woman who professes to be a Christian.

As Jesus turned to that fig tree, drawn to it by the tree's profession of fruitfulness, so hungry souls turn to the church and to God's professed people to find spiritual food. What that tree with the leaves and no fruit was to Jesus, the Jewish hierarchy was to the people in their soul-hunger. With their burden of sin, with their deep heart-questions, with their sorrows, with their unsatisfied longings, with their yearnings for help and sympathy, they turned to the priests, the professed spiritual guides, if only they might get from them what they wanted. So the mission of every Christian church is to feed hungry souls. In the hour of remorse, when the soul is conscious of guilt; in the day of trouble, when the world has no more to give; in the shadow of death, in all the great crises of life, even the most worldly turn to the church for what they need.

A church is like a great tree in the desert which holds out the promise of fruit, and toward which all the spiritually hungry turn. There can be few sadder things in this world than a church, promising by its very name, by its spire pointing to heaven, by its open doors, by its songs and services, by its bells of invitation, to give food to the hungry, refreshment to the weary, comfort to the sorrowing, and then failing to keep its promise to the souls that come expecting.

BELIEVING PRAYER

—◇—

*And all things, whatsoever ye shall ask in
prayer, believing, ye shall receive.*
Matthew 21:22

There are other Scriptures qualifying this one. In the first place, it is not all asking that is really praying, and therefore not all asking that receives. James says, "Ye ask, and receive not, because ye ask amiss, that ye may consume it upon your lusts" (4:3). A man asks for money, not to use it for the glory of God and the good of others, but for his own glory and pleasure. Again, the psalmist says, "If I regard iniquity in my heart, the Lord will not hear me" (66:18). That is, if one is cherishing a secret sin in his heart while he is trying to serve God, no prayers that he offers will be heard or answered. So here are at least two kinds of asking that will not bring an answer.

Then there are conditions. One is that we must ask in Christ's name. *That implies that we believe in Christ as our Savior, and are His faithful friends, and therefore have a right to use His name.* This condition narrows down the promise to the true followers of Christ. Another condition is that we are abiding in Christ, and His words are abiding in us. So there is a double "if." Even a Christian who is following from afar does not come within the realm of this promise.

Then there is another qualification which belongs to all promises of prayer. God Himself must be the judge as to the things we ask, whether they would really be blessings to us or not. There may be things we desire very earnestly that it would be the greatest mistakes to grant us. Is God then bound by this promise to give us what we crave? By no means. "What is good the Lord will give." "No good thing will he withhold from them that walk uprightly" (Psalm 84:11). But He will withhold even from the most upright the things which in His divine wisdom He sees would not be good things. This is implied in every promise such as this.

October 8

A FORGIVING SPIRIT

When ye stand praying, forgive, if ye have ought
against any: that your Father also which is in
heaven may forgive you your trespasses.

Mark 11:25

It is told of a Christian woman that a friend entered her room and found her with bowed head, as if in prayer. At length the friend spoke to her tenderly, knowing that great sorrow was in her heart. "I have been trying to say the Lord's Prayer," she answered, "but I cannot get through it." She had said the words thousands of times, in happy childhood, in joyous youth, on her wedding day, and then along the glad years that followed, amid songs and flowers and prattling children's voices, and in the sweetness of an unbroken home-circle; and they had flowed from her lips like rippling music all the while. But now a great sorrow had come, and since that she had begun a hundred times, "Our Father who art in heaven, Hallowed be thy name. Thy kingdom come. Thy will—" But she could not get any further. She could not yet say, "Thy will be done."

A story is told of a nobleman in Alexandria, in ancient times, who complained bitterly to the bishop of his enemies. While in the midst of the recital of the wrongs done to him the bell rang for prayer, and bishop and nobleman dropped to their knees, the former leading in the Lord's Prayer, and the latter leaving his story unfinished for the time and joining in the prayer. When the bishop came to the words, "Forgive us our trespasses, as we forgive," he suddenly stopped and left the nobleman to go on alone. The nobleman attempted to say the words, but, startled by the sound of his own voice unaccompanied, and recalled by the bishop's silence to the meaning of the prayer, he stammered, ceased to pray, and rose in great despair; and it was only when he had learned to cherish a forgiving spirit toward others that he could say from his heart, "Forgive us our trespasses, as we forgive those who trespass against us."

October 9

THE CORNERSTONE

*The stone which the builders rejected, the
same is become the head of the corner.*
Matthew 21:42

Those to whom Christ first came did not think Him suitable to be their Messiah. So they refused to accept Him and nailed Him on a cross instead. But now what do we see? That same Jesus whom they thought unfit to be their king God has made King of glory, Lord of heaven and earth. All things are in His hands, all power, all mercy, all judgment. The very rulers who rejected Him and demanded His crucifixion, when they awake on the judgment morning, shall see as their Judge the same Jesus whom they thus despised and condemned to die.

A great many people now think Christ unsuitable to be their Master. They do not consider it an honor to be called Christians. They are embarrassed at His name or to include themselves among His followers. They do not care to model their life on His holy and perfect life. All these should remember that Christ has highest honor in heaven. No angel is ashamed to speak His name. Redeemed spirits praise Him day and night. God the Father has exalted Him to the throne of eternal power and glory. Why, then, should sinful men be ashamed to claim Him as Lord?

They should remember, also, that God has made Him the cornerstone of the whole building not made with hands. No life that is not built on Him can stand. There is no other rock on which to rest their hope. If they ever are saved it must be by this same Jesus whom they are now rejecting.

> *How can they live who, sinning, never seek*
> *To have their sins forgiven;*
> *Who, knowing that the strongest yet are weak,*
> *Ask not thy grace and never know thy peace—*
> *The gift unspeakable of thy release,*
> *The pardon sealed in heaven?*

◇

"LET HIM TAKE ALL"

◇

*Thou shalt love the Lord thy God with all
thy heart, and with all thy soul.*
Matthew 22:37

We are to notice, first, that *it is love God wants*. We may give Him our heart's highest honor, but He is not satisfied with honor. We ought to obey Him. He is our God and our King, and we owe Him the fullest obedience. But obedience is not enough. We owe Him service also, for we belong to Him, and we should pour out our lives for Him. But it is neither honor, obedience, nor service that this command requires. *We are to love God.* If it were possible for us to render such honor, obedience, and service as the angels give, and yet not love Him, He would not be satisfied. *Nothing but love will satisfy Him.*

We are told here also the degree of love that we are to give to God. It must be an all-absorbing love. God wants no half-hearts. He must be loved supremely—more than all tender friends, more than all worldly things. Then this love must draw the whole life after it—the mind, the soul, the strength; it must lead to true and entire consecration.

Suppose a mother gives her child a beautiful flower-plant in bloom and tells her to carry it to a sick friend. The child takes the plant away, and when she reaches the friend's door she plucks off one leaf and gives it to her, keeping the plant herself. Then afterward, once a week, she plucks off another leaf, or a bud, or a flower, and takes it to the friend, still keeping the plant. Has she obeyed? Nothing but the giving of the whole plant would be obedience. Yet God asks for all our life—heart, soul, mind, and strength; and we pluck off a little leaf of love now and then, a bud, a flower of affection, or one cluster of fruit, and give these little things to Him, keeping the life itself. Shall we not say, "Let Him take all"? This commandment requires the complete consecration of our whole life to God.

THE WIDOW'S MITE
◇

This poor widow hath cast more in, than all.
Mark 12:43

I t is good to recognize here our Lord's estimate of earth's gifts. We know that as He saw the offerings that day, and spoke of their worth, so He always sees how we give and always weighs our gifts in the same balances. It is most encouraging to us to note that it is not the earthly size of our offerings that makes them either great or acceptable in heaven's sight. The widow's mite outweighed the rich man's heavy coins.

No doubt this poor woman felt that her gift was so small that it was scarcely worthwhile to give it; but in the eyes of the divine Lord its value was very great. There are two scales weighing all human acts, and all human gifts and offerings. There are the earthly scales, which weigh in ounces and pounds; and there are the "balances of the sanctuary," which weigh spiritual values. In the latter scales this widow's mite weighed more than the great glittering coins of the rich which were given with so much ostentation.

This was not only because her gift was proportionally larger— the rich still had much left after giving, and she had nothing left— but also because of her motive and spirit in giving. She gave because she loved God's house and wished to do her part in maintaining its observances. She gave humbly, not to be seen of men, but to honor God and win His approval. She gave also largely according to her ability, putting to shame the rich men who gave so much and yet had riches left. Christ sees into the heart while we make our offerings; and if our heart is right, and we give as we are able, and give out of love for God and desire for His glory, even the smallest offering that we can bring will be acceptable in God's sight and will bring down heaven's approval. Gifts are not estimated in heaven by dollars and cents. Even a million dollars may be exceedingly small when the angels weigh it.

"Behold The Lamb Of God"

We would see Jesus.
John 12:21

These men had heard of Jesus, but they wanted to see Him for themselves. It does not suffice for us to see Jesus only through other people's eyes. No matter how vividly they may portray His beauty before us, it is not others seeing that blesses us and prints His image on our souls. We must encounter Him for ourselves. In those terrible days in the ancient camp when the people were bitten and the bronze image of a serpent was set up, a mother could not look at the serpent for her child, or a friend for a friend. It is so in gazing at Christ. No one can experience Him for another.

It is through seeing Christ that all spiritual blessings come to us. When we are burdened with sin, we are pointed to the Lamb of God who takes away sin. When we seek to grow stronger, we are exhorted to see as in a mirror the glory of the Lord, and thus be transformed into His image. When we ask for a model for our life, we are told to look to Jesus. Many a fleeing slave during the Civil War, by simply keeping his eye fixed on a star, was led away from bondage to liberty. Keeping our eye on Christ will lead us from chains to glory.

These Greeks came to a disciple and asked him to introduce them to Jesus. What nobler service can we render in this world than that of introducing people to Jesus? To do this we must know Him well ourselves. But let no one think that he really needs anyone to introduce him to Jesus.

A little child was dying, and she said she was not afraid to die, but she wished her mama could go with her to introduce her to Jesus. "For you know, mama," said the little one, "I was always afraid of strangers." But no one will find Jesus a stranger; He loves to be sought and to have people want to see Him, and He is always glad to reveal Himself to every seeker. He is not hard to find; He is near all the while, and we really need no one to take us to Him.

TWO WAYS OF LIVING

*He that loveth his life shall lose it; and he that hateth
his life in this world shall keep it unto life eternal.*
John 12:25

We have our choice. We may live for self, take good care of our lives, not exposing them to danger, not making sacrifices, and looking out for our own interests, and we may prosper in the world; people will commend our prudence and congratulate us on our success. We may reach old age hearty and well preserved and greatly enjoy our accumulated honors and possessions. This is one way of living. There seems to be something pleasant about such a life; but really it is only the grain of wheat preserved in the barn and kept from falling into the ground. The life dwells alone, well enough kept, perhaps, but with no increase. It has been no blessing in the world. It has done nothing for the glory of God. It has fed no one who hungers; it has won no reward. That is the whole outcome of selfishness. "He that loveth his life shall lose it."

The other way is to forget self—not to think of or care for one's own life, but to throw it away in obedience to God and in unselfish service. People will say you are foolish to waste your precious life, to sacrifice yourself for the sake of others or in Christ's cause. But was Christ Himself foolish when He went to His cross? Let the redeemed church be the answer. Were the martyrs foolish when they threw their lives away for Christ's sake? Ignatius said, when facing the fierce lions in the arena, "I am grain of God. Let me be ground between the teeth of lions if I may thus become bread to feed God's people." Were such martyred lives wasted, thrown away? Is any life wasted that becomes seed-corn to produce bread in due time for the world? The way to make nothing of our lives is to be very careful about them. The way to make our lives eternal successes is to do with them just what Christ did with His.

A SAVIOR FOR ALL

And I, if I be lifted up from the earth, will draw all men unto me.
John 12:32

A s we read the gospel story we are surprised to see how few persons were really drawn to Christ during His life. Crowds followed Him—many from curiosity—but very few were drawn to Him in heart and life. We see at the end how few; there were only a little handful of clinging friends about His cross.

It was not until He had made His great sacrifice, had been "lifted up" on the cross, that all men began to be drawn to Him. Why was the influence of a crucified Jesus so much greater than that of a living, miracle-working Jesus? For one reason, the death of Christ revealed the wonderful love of God. All His sweet, gentle, helpful life told of love, too; but it was when He went to His cross that the full, rich glory of the divine love was manifested. And love always draws. It is love that men need, and wherever they find it they want to come and rest in its warmth and tenderness.

Another reason that Jesus drew others in a powerful way after He had been lifted up was because after His death and resurrection the Divine Spirit was present to work on human hearts and lives. Without the drawing of the Spirit, no one would ever come to Christ. There was an old legend that when Jesus was dying a dove came and settled on His cross. It is only a legend; yet it suggests the truth that, even after the precious blood had been poured out, men would not have come to Christ had they not been drawn by the Holy Spirit. Keble writes—

> *Should'st thou not need some mighty charm*
> *To win thee to thy Savior's side,*
> *Though he had deigned with thee to hide?*
> *The Spirit must stir the darkling deep,*
> *The dove must settle on the cross,*
> *Else we should all sin on or sleep*
> *With Christ in sight, turning our gain to loss.*

---◆---

WATCHING AND PRAYING

---◆---

Take ye heed, watch and pray: for ye know not when the time is.
Mark 13:33

It is the time of our Lord's coming again to which these words refer. He is coming; but when, no one can know. He will come suddenly, without warning. Since, then, we cannot know what moment the Lord may appear, we must take heed, watch and pray, lest He comes and surprises us unprepared. This does not mean that we are always to be talking and thinking of the event and waiting for it in dreamy speculation and useless musings. What Christ wants us to do is to so live at all times that His coming at any moment of the day or night will not find us unready.

For one thing, we should be sure of our personal salvation. If we are not saved now, we should instantly see to the matter; for He may come the next hour, and there will be no time then to seek salvation. We should keep our work faithfully done, day by day, leaving nothing unfinished any evening; for before morning He may come. We should live at peace with all men, never allowing the sun to go down on our anger or on any enmity or bitterness; for before another day dawns He may come, and we would not want Him to come and find us in strife and bitterness. We should be careful about what we do any time; for He may come suddenly and find us in sin. We should watch where we go, so that His coming may not surprise us in some place where we would not want Him to find us.

This truth, kept always as a strong motivation in our consciousness, would be the strongest motive to faithfulness in every duty and vigilance against sin. His coming will be so sudden and so unexpected that there will be no time then to get wrong things right, to finish uncompleted tasks, to get sin-stains washed out, to undo evil deeds. The only safe way to live is to make each task complete—a fit ending for all of life.

MYSTERIOUS PROVIDENCE
◇

What I do thou knowest not now; but thou shalt know hereafter.
John 13:7

Like many other words of Christ, this saying of His has a much wider application than its primary reference to Peter's perplexity. It furnishes the key to much of the providence of all our lives. We do not understand them at the time. We do not see how they can have any blessing in them for us. They seem altogether mysterious. But we have no right to judge our Master's work in us or with us until it is finished. "What I do thou knowest not now." How could we be expected to understand all the Master's great thoughts?

Yet this is not the end of the matter. "Thou shalt know hereafter." This mystery is to be explained. This perplexity is to be resolved as clear as noonday. You do not understand now because you cannot yet see the end, cannot perceive the blessings and the glory of the future. The Master Himself knows just what He is going to bring out of each mysterious work of His, and so He is not perplexed. Then, He says that we also shall know later. We shall see the cloud as it departs, glorified by the rainbow arching its dark folds. We shall see the tangles resolving into revealed grace and beauty.

> *Some time, when all life's lessons have been learned,*
> *And sun and stars for evermore have set,*
> *The things which our weak judgments here have spurned,*
> *The things o'er which we grieved with lashes wet,*
> *Will flash before us, out of life's dark night,*
> *As stars shine most in deeper tints of blue;*
> *And we shall see how all God's plans were right,*
> *And how what seemed reproof was love most true.*

What is the lesson? That we should trust God when we cannot understand His ways with us. No doubt love has planned them all. No doubt there is blessing in the outcome as it lies now in God's mind. No doubt we shall see the blessing, too, hereafter.

LOWLY SERVICE

*If I then, your Lord and Master, have washed
your feet; ye also ought to wash one another's feet.*
John 13:14

Are we to take this literally? Some have understood it in this way. No, others say, He teaches us to do humble service for one another. Yes, but what kind of service? What did Christ's washing the feet of His disciples mean? It was more than a small meek act of service; He taught them that He would in this way cleanse their souls of remaining faults and blemishes of character, and of the stains gotten in the world as they passed through.

Our service to one another is to be of the same kind. We are to come to each other with basin and towel. We are to help each other to be pure Christians. We are to seek the sanctification, purification, and upbuilding in character of all our fellow disciples. Of course we cannot wash away sins—Christ alone can do that—but we can do something toward making others purer and holier. We can try to bring to Christ for salvation those who are not yet saved; then we can admonish others in love and humbly tell them of their faults, seeking the removal of the faults and blemishes.

This requires much grace and great wisdom; we need lowliness of heart and tenderness in our affection to complete a duty so delicate. We must be especially cleansed ourselves if we would seek the cleansing of others. What if our own hands, with which we would wash the feet of other disciples, are not clean, but are covered with sin? Instead of cleansing the lives we touch, we shall then leave stains upon them. So we must see that our own hands have been washed in the blood of Christ before we undertake to wash the feet of others. Then we must be willing to give over our own feet to the water. The washing is to go all around; we are to wash one another's feet. The secret of this must be genuine love for others.

RESTING ON JESUS

*There was leaning on Jesus' bosom one
of his disciples, whom Jesus loved.*
John 13:23

We are not told the name of this disciple, but we know him by his place and posture. What were the traits in John's character which made him the beloved disciple? One was his humility; another was his love. Artists always paint his face in features of gentleness and affection. Another of his winning traits was his trust. He never seems to have doubted.

When was it that he reclined on Jesus' bosom? It was in a time of great darkness. The Master was about to go away, and all the hopes of the disciples were being destroyed. But where was John in that darkness? Sorrow, instead of driving us into despair, should drive us nearer to Christ—to His bosom.

> *He's better to us than many mothers are,*
> *And children cannot wander beyond reach*
> *Of the sweep of his white garment.*
> *Touch and hold,*
> *And if you weep still, weep*
> *Where John was laid*
> *While Jesus loved him.*

Where was it that John leaned? On Jesus' breast. Not merely on His arm, the place of strength; nor upon His shoulder, the place of support; but on His breast, which is the place of love and tenderness. It is a great thing to know that the divine omnipotence is underneath us in all our weakness; but mere omnipotence is cold. How much better is it when omnipotence has the heart of love within it.

But what did John do? He leaned. He rested his weight on the omnipotent love of his Lord. Christ wants all His friends to lean upon Him. He wants to carry our burdens for us—He wants us to lay upon Him our sins and all our cares; but more than this—ourselves. He wants to bear us as well as our loads.

◇

THE LAST SUPPER

◇

Jesus took bread, and blessed it, and brake it,
and gave it to the disciples, and said, Take, eat.
Matthew 26:26

There was a meaning in every act. The bread itself is an appropriate symbol of Christ's body. Bread is food; Christ is food for our spirits. Something may be learned from the manner in which bread is prepared. The wheat is crushed and broken, and then the bread is baked in the fire before it is ready for use. So Christ died, His body was bruised and broken, and He was exposed to the fire of great sufferings before He could become food and life of our souls.

The breaking of the bread is also significant, pointing to the breaking of the body of Christ on the cross. We ought never to forget, in our sweet enjoyment of the blessings of grace, what it cost our Lord to provide them for us. Whenever we sit at our Lord's table and see the bread broken, we should remember the anguish and suffering endured by our Redeemer in saving us.

The giving of the bread to the disciples had also a deep meaning. It signified the freeness of Christ's offer of Himself to men. He is ever standing, reaching out His hands with the bread of life, imploring men to take freely of all the blessings of salvation.

The taking of the bread at the Lord's Supper is indicative of the act of faith by which Christ Himself is received. He offers; we receive. It is not enough that Christ gave Himself on the cross for sinners and now holds out in pierced hands the blessings of redemption. These stupendous acts of love and grace alone will not save us. There is a needed link which we must supply; we must reach out our hands and accept and take what Christ so graciously and lovingly offers to us. Then, since bread to nourish us must be eaten, we must receive Christ into our life as our soul's sustenance, feeding upon Him.

◇

REMEMBERING JESUS

◇

This do in remembrance of me.
Luke 22:19

There is something very moving in the thought of the Lord's Supper as a memorial. We all know the value of remembrances in keeping in mind one whose face we cannot see. A young man sat one morning in his pastor's study, and drew a letter from his pocket, saying that he had just heard from his sister away in the English home. Opening the letter, he showed the pastor some little pressed flowers and some dried grass-blades. The young man's voice choked with emotion as he said, "These flowers and grasses are from my mother's grave in England." The little memorials brought back the whole life of the mother, and the son sat there and spoke most affectionately of her love, her fidelity, her beauty of spirit, her sacrifices, then of her death. So it is that the memorials of the Last Supper recall to our forgetful hearts the sacred scenes and events of our Lord's passion and the love that led Him to such sacrifice.

But mere remembering is not enough; the remembering ought to kindle love and keep us faithful. A young man was about to go abroad for a long journey. Just before he set out, his father took his watch from his pocket. On the dial were the pictures of both his parents. "Take this watch," said the father, "and carry it with you in all your journeyings. Every time you look to see the hour the eyes of your father and mother will look up into yours. When you see these familiar faces, remember that we are thinking of you and praying for you. Go to no place where you would not want us to see you. Do nothing you would not want us to witness." In the Last Supper, Jesus has given us His own picture—His body broken, His blood shed; He wants us to remember Him and be faithful. Remembering Jesus should always keep us from doubting and sinning and inspire us to holiness and beauty.

THE REMISSION OF SINS

*This is my blood of the new testament, which
is shed for many for the remission of sins.*
Matthew 26:28

Right in the heart of the Lord's Supper we are reminded of two things—of the price paid for our redemption and of the deliverance that this redemption brings to us. The price paid was the precious blood of Christ; the deliverance is the remission of sins.

There is a particular Eastern custom which may help us better to understand the way Christ made atonement for our sins. "When a debt had to be settled," says Dr. A. J. Gordon, "either by full payment or forgiveness, it was the custom for the creditor to take the canceled bond and nail it over the door of him who had owed it, that all passers-by might see that it was paid. Oh, blessed story of our remission! There is the cross, the door of grace, behind which a bankrupt world lies in hopeless debt to the law. See Jesus, our bondsman and brother, coming forth with the long lists of our indebtedness in His hand. He lifts it up where God and angels and men may see it, and then, as the nail goes through His hand, it goes through the bond of our transgressions, to cancel it forever, blotting out the handwriting of ordinances that was against us. He took it out of the way, nailing it to the cross."

This is the marvelous act of redemption that is portrayed for us with such vividness in the cup of the Lord's Supper. The nail that went through those bonds and fastened them there on the cross went also through the body of the Lord Jesus. Blood flowed at the payment of our sins—the blood of the Son of God. The cup that is so sweet to us was emptied of terrible bitterness by the Lord Himself, then filled with heaven's choicest blessings and brought to us. While we rejoice at the remission, let us not forget what it cost our Redeemer; nor let us forget the abundant grace that puts all our sins away as far as the east is from the west.

THE HEAVENLY FEAST

I will not drink henceforth of this fruit of the vine, until that day when I drink it new with you in my Father's kingdom.
Matthew 26:29

The Lord's Supper points forward as well as back. It keeps the past in remembrance; we are to think of what happened more than nineteen hundred years ago. The Supper is a memorial. But it is also a prophecy. Christ pointed to the dawn of a blessed hope amid the mementoes of sorrow. He lifted the veil and gave a glimpse of a fulfillment very glorious beyond earth's shadows. Even the Holy Supper, precious as it is, is only a faint picture of something far better.

The disciples would not have Jesus with them at the table anymore. This was their "last supper" together. From here on His place would be vacant on earth. But in telling them this He gave them sweet comfort in the assurance that He would sit down with them again, by and by, not here, but in another kingdom. These words are full of luminous encouragement. They tell us of a supper in glory, of which the Lord's Supper on earth is but the shadow. In Revelation it is called "the marriage supper of the Lamb" (19:9). So it will be a memorial, too, of Christ's death and love.

That night when the Master and His disciples sat down together in the Upper Room, a great sorrow hung over their hearts and His; for Him it was the shadow of His Cross, with all its mystery of woe; for them it was the shadow of grievous loss and separation. But the other side of the cloud was very bright. Out of Christ's death came blessed and glorious salvation; now in heaven Jesus looks back on the anguish of His soul and is satisfied. Out of the brief separation there came to the disciples an abiding presence of Christ which filled their hearts full. Jesus went away from them for a little time that He might be with them forever. So out of these sad memories came great joys.

◇

COMFORT IN SORROW

◇

Let not your heart be troubled.
John 14:1

Jesus always loves to comfort. He loves to put little candles in the darkened chambers of sorrow. He loves to dry tears and change grief into joy. He is able to give comfort, because He has the comfort in Himself. We cannot give what we have not to give. We often say to one another in trial, "Do not worry! Do not be troubled!" when we have no comfort to give, nothing to cure the worry or brighten the darkness. Standing on the ship in the midst of a wild sea, Jesus said, "Peace!" and the winds and waves instantly became calm. He had the peace in Himself and could give peace to the sea. It is the same with His comfort; His words of consolation are not like so many of ours; they have power to quiet the troubled heart.

It was a time of the deepest grief and the sorest sorrow for the disciples when Jesus said this. Not only were they to lose their best Friend, but they were to lose Him in the saddest way— by death in the shame of the cross. Nor was that all of their sorrow. They had hoped He was the Messiah; now that hope was gone. They were in utter desolation—in a starless midnight. Surely there could be no comfort for such grief as theirs, they thought that night, as with breaking hearts they sat there in the darkness.

Yet right into the midst of this despairing grief came the words, "Let not your heart be troubled." Let us never say, therefore, that there is any, even the bitterest, grief for which there is no possible comfort. No matter how dark the night is, Christ can put stars into our sky and bring a glorious morning after the darkness. There is comfort for Christ's disciples in the most hopeless grief. We have but to look forward a few days to see the sorrow of these men turned to blessed joy. So it always is. However we may grieve, there is never any reason that we should lose our peace.

October 24

PEACE IN BELIEVING

Ye believe in God, believe also in me.
John 14:1

We should all learn how to comfort others. No duty of Christian love requires more sensitivity. We may study our Lord's way of comforting to learn to give comfort ourselves to those who are in trouble. We see that He did not go over the cold platitudes we are so accustomed to use when we try to console our friends in their grief.

> One writes that "Other friends remain,"
>   That "Loss is common to the race,"—
> And common is the commonplace,
>   And vacant chaff well meant for grain.
>
> That loss is common would not make
>   My own less bitter, rather more;
> Too common! Never morning wore
>   To evening but some heart did break.

But it is not in this empty way that Christ comforts His people. Here He offered no explanations, answered no questions, gave no reasons; He told His disciples simply to believe. They could not understand this terrible grief. They could see no star in the sky. But they did not need to understand, did not need to see any light. They were to do nothing but believe—just cling to Christ in the darkness and believe.

In all deep grief, this is the best way to find comfort. There is no use to ask questions, for no one can answer them. There is no use to strain our eyes trying to see the light, for as yet there is no light to see. All we can do is just to throw ourselves on our Savior's bosom and lie there till the light breaks. We may always be sure of the love and the faithfulness of Christ. We may nestle down, as John did that same night, upon the Savior's bosom, and be quiet and confident in the time of our worst calamities. "In the world ye shall have tribulations"—"In me ye shall have peace" (see John 16:33).

October 25

◇

THE WAY TO HEAVEN

◇

I am the way . . . no man cometh unto the Father, but by me.
John 14:6

A way always leads somewhere: Jesus is the way from earth to heaven, and also from heaven to earth. Through Him we get to God, and through Him God comes to us. He is the true and only ladder whose foot rests on the earth, and whose top reaches up to the very glory of God. In His humanity Jesus comes down to the lowest depths of human need and sorrow. Had He been God only, and not man, He could not have done this. The incarnation was the letting of the ladder down until it rested in the deepest valleys. There is now no spot of shame or guilt in this world from which there is not a ladder of light, with its celestial steps leading upward to God and heaven.

For while Christ's humanity brings the ladder down to earth's places of sorest need, His divinity carries the ladder up past the shining stars, into the very midst of the glory of God. On one page of the New Testament we find Jesus on a cross, dying in darkness and shame, between criminals. We open another page, and we see that same Jesus in the midst of the heavenly brightness, wearing still the wound-marks, but crowned in glory. Behold the ladder from earth to heaven!

A ladder is a way for feet to climb: Christ is the way, therefore, by which sinners can go up out of their sins to the purity and blessedness of heaven. One thing to note especially is that there is only one way. Christ is the only Mediator. We can enter the Father's family only through Him. Grace can come to us only through Him. There is, then, no choice of ways: if we do not go by this one way we can never reach home. Nor must we forget that a way is meant to be walked in. We must put our feet on this ladder and go up rung by rung until we reach the topmost step, which will be heaven.

KNOWLEDGE OF CHRIST

Have I been so long time with you,
and yet hast thou not known me?
John 14:9

There seems to be pain in the Master's question. This disciple had been with him for three years. He had seen His attractive and gentle life. He had witnessed His works of power. Surely by this time, after such long and close intimacy, the disciple ought to have known Jesus. Yet Jesus tells him here that he did not really know Him.

We understand this lesson—that it is possible to be with Christ a long time, and to know very much about Him, without knowing Him in the true sense of the word. Philip knew Jesus as a man, as a worker of miracles, as having a very exemplary character; but he seems never to have gone below the surface in understanding Him. He did not know Him as the revealer of the Father. He never saw divine glory in the radiance that streamed from that blessed life. And not to know Christ in this aspect, to know Him only as a man, is not to know Him at all. To leave out the divine in our thought of Christ is not to have any Christ at all.

We may be quite familiar with the facts of our Lord's life, from His birth in Bethlehem to His ascension from Olivet, and yet may not know anything of Him as a personal Savior, saving us from our sins, or as a Helper in our times of need. Such knowledge will do us no good unless it leads us to the true knowledge of Christ as Savior, Lord, and Friend.

There is something very touching in the thought that for so long the Son of God walked with His disciples, all the glory of divinity dwelling in His humanity, and yet they did not recognize Him. But is it any better with us? The divine love is close to us perpetually, flowing all about us, with all its infinite tenderness, but how unconscious we are of it! May our prayer be, "Lord, make thyself known to us."

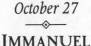

IMMANUEL

He that hath seen me hath seen the Father.
John 14:9

That was surely a very strange thing for a man to say. Can we imagine John, the beloved disciple, saying of himself that those who had seen him had seen the Father? The fact that Christ said it shows that He was conscious of divinity, that He really claimed to be the Son of God. So it is in all Christ's words: He speaks always as God. Wherever we turn in the gospel we find the evidence of Christ's divinity; it were easier to pluck the stars from the sky than to remove the truth of Christ's deity from the pages of inspiration. Everywhere it shines—its light the brightest beam in all the radiant splendor that blazes there.

What did Jesus mean when He said this? Evidently He meant that although He was a man, He was also the incarnation of God; that He was living out in a human life, which men could see, the invisible life of His Father. Men on earth could never see God. Then God sent His Son that He might veil His divine splendor in flesh and show people how the unseen God feels and acts as a human.

Thus, when we see Him taking little children in His arms, laying His hand on their heads and blessing them, we see how God feels toward children. When we see the compassion of Jesus stirred by human suffering, we learn how our heavenly Father is touched by the sight of earthly woe. When we see Jesus receiving sinners and eating with them, speaking forgiveness to penitents who sat at His feet, and making soiled, stained lives white and clean, we learn the mercy of God. When we follow Christ to His cross and see Him giving His life a willing sacrifice to make redemption for lost men, we see how God loves. So the meekness and patience and gentleness of Christ were mirrorings of the same traits in His Father. If we would see the likeness of God, we have but to turn to the story of the gospel. To know Christ is to know the Father.

October 28

---◆---

THE TRUE VINE

---◆---

I am the true vine, and my Father is the husbandman.
John 15:1

This is a wonderful Vine. It grew up at first like a root out of a dry ground, with no form nor attractiveness. The soil in which it was planted seemed too poor to produce anything good. But its origin was heavenly, and it grew into luxuriant beauty. By and by it seemed that men in their rage had altogether destroyed this Vine, which had in it so much blessing for the earth; however, it was not destroyed, but was only lifted away from earth and translated to heaven. There in the garden of God its roots were fixed, and the Vine itself dropped down to earth again and began to send out branches in all directions. Every poor human life which attaches itself to this Vine is grafted on it and becomes a branch in it, drawing life from the Vine's fullness and sharing its fruitfulness.

These branches are not left to grow wild and untended but have been given wise and skillful care. It ought to be a great comfort to us to know that as branches we are under the care of a gardener who is none other than our heavenly Father; "Your Father is the husbandman." We are very sure that His care will be both wise and tender. If an ignorant, inexperienced, unskillful man were to enter a beautiful vineyard and begin cutting away at the vines, he would soon destroy them. He does not know what he ought to prune off or what he ought to leave on the vines. But if the man who comes to tend the vineyard understands vines, has had long experience, and is skillful, there is no danger that he will do harm in his pruning. Sometimes, indeed, he may seem to be cutting the vine to death; but we know that he understands what he is doing, and that all his prunings are for the good of the branches. By and by we shall see increased fruitfulness as the result of his unsparing work.

October 29

◇

THE PRUNING KNIFE

◇

*Every branch in me that beareth not fruit he taketh
away: and every branch that beareth fruit,
he purgeth it, that it may bring forth more fruit.*
John 15:2

C hrist taught many lessons on the sin and doom of uselessness. One of His parables told of a tree that bore no fruit.
The soil was good, and the tree was carefully planted and well
tended; still, when the master came at the proper season, expecting to find fruit, he found none. Fruitlessness is cursed. The tree
with nothing but leaves is allowed to wither. There is no place in
the Lord's kingdom for uselessness.

We must notice here that it is the fruitful branch that is
pruned. The husbandman does not prune the unfruitful branch;
it would do it no good. It is the true Christian that the Father
chastens and causes sometimes to suffer under heavy discipline.
The wicked are not pruned, but in their bounty there is no spiritual fruit.

Another thing to be noticed here is that the object of the
Father's pruning is that the branch may be made to bear more
fruit. It seems sometimes as if the pruning were destructive; but
He who holds the knife knows that what He is doing will make
the vine far more productive in the end, and its fruit sweeter and
more luscious. The aim of God in all His pruning is greater fruitfulness.

> *Now the pruning, sharp, unsparing,*
> *Scattered blossom, bleeding shoot;*
> *Afterward the plenteous bearing*
> *Of the Master's pleasant fruit.*

If we would only remember that, when we find ourselves
suffering under God's chastening hand, it would help us to bear
the pain with patience and also to cooperate with God in His
design of blessing for us. Earthly prosperity often is to the Christian like the growth which the vine-dresser must cut away to
save the vine's life.

"ABIDE IN ME"

*As the branch cannot bear fruit of itself, except it abide
in the vine; no more can ye, except ye abide in me.*
John 15:4

As a truth in nature, the meaning of this is very plain. A branch torn off a vine or a tree, and lying on the ground, will not bear fruit. Indeed, it cannot even live, but soon withers. The analogy holds in spiritual life. It would be just as unnatural to expect the professing Christian who has given up praying, has ceased to read his Bible, and has withdrawn from loving and trusting Christ, to be really a fruitful Christian. The branch has no life but what flows into it from the vine or the tree; the Christian has no spiritual life but what comes from Christ's life, through faith and prayer and the Holy Word. We live as Christians only when Christ lives in us. Said St. Paul: "I live; yet not I, but Christ liveth in me; and the life which I now live in the flesh I live by the faith of the Son of God, who loved me, and gave himself for me" (Galatians 2:20). All spiritual life in us must be the life of Christ reproduced in us, just as the foliage and the fruit on a tree are produced by the tree's life flowing into the branches.

Mere Christian lip service will not therefore yield the fruits of a true Christian life. One might take a branch that had been torn off and with cords tie it on a green tree, but that would not make it a fruitful branch. It would draw no life from the tree and would soon be withered and utterly dead. One may be tied to Christ by the cords of belief, but if there is no real vital attachment of the life to Christ by faith and love, Christ's life cannot flow into it, and it is only a dead, withered branch. We must be truly in Christ and have Christ in us, or there can be no life in us and no fruitfulness. We must also abide in Christ, maintaining our communion and fellowship with Him year after year, or we cannot be fruit-bearing Christians.

October 31

FRUIT-BEARING

*Herein is my Father glorified, that ye bear
much fruit; so shall ye be my disciples.*
John 15:8

What is fruit in a Christian? We know what it is in the natural world, and we know its uses; what is it in the spiritual world? It is not merely Christian activities. True, important activities are fruits; but there is danger in these days, when work is so praised, that we overlook another kind of fruit which certainly is as essential as expending consecrated energy. In nature, fruit is part of the branch itself, not something apart from it. There are spiritual fruits that are part of the life and growth into holiness and Christlikeness.

Thus St. Paul says, "The fruit of the Spirit is love, joy, peace, longsuffering, gentleness, goodness, faith, meekness, temperance" (Galatians 5:22–23). These fruits are those that evidently appear in the character itself. The aim of Christ's religion is not merely to make workers of us, to send us out to do good in the world, to fight against evil, to help the weak, and to minister to the sorrowful and the suffering. Its first aim is to make us good, to transform our character, to produce in us the likeness of Christ. Then we shall be ready to minister. While, therefore, we are to be fruitful in every fruitful work, we are to seek also to be fruitful in the qualities of Christlike character.

In nature, the tree's fruits feed the hunger of men. No tree consumes its own fruits; it drops them for those who come to gather them. This suggests that we should not be selfish in our fruit-bearing. We should not seek the nurturance of our characters merely for our own sake. Our aim should be to provide something in our lives that will feed others and bless the world. All about us are hungry hearts. There are those who crave sympathy and love, those who yearn for comfort, those who desire to be saved. We are so to live that our lives shall yield life for these.

November 1

◇

LIGHT BEHIND THE CLOUD

◇

It is expedient for you that I go away.
John 16:7

The disciples thought that Christ's going away would be an irretrievable loss for them. It was the crushing of all their hopes. They thought they would be left in darkness and loneliness; for they had built up all their Messianic hopes on the idea of His remaining and ruling as a king over His people. Not only were they about to lose the dearest friend they had ever known, but they were to lose also the one in whom they had trusted as the promised Deliverer and Savior. They saw no silver lining whatever in the dark cloud that was gathering.

But now Jesus says to them, "It is expedient for you that I go away." There was a silver lining, after all, in that black cloud. What seemed an irreparable loss would in the end prove a gain. The disciples did not understand it then, but there was the Master's word for it.

The same is true now in the case of all the Master's disciples when He calls to Himself their human friends. We can readily see how it is well for our Christian friends when Christ takes them. They exchange earth for heaven, sin and sorrow for holiness and eternal joy. There is no doubt that death is gain for those who depart; but what about those who remain? What about the friends who are left with torn hearts to walk on lonely and sad over earth's ways? This word of Christ applies: "It is expedient for you that I go away." We cannot understand this; but neither could the disciples understand at the time how Christ's departure could be better for them than His staying with them would have been. Afterward they knew; and afterward we shall know how even for us the going away of our friends will become a blessing if we in faith submit ourselves to God. "We know that all things work together for good to them that love God" (Romans 8:28).

The Comforter

*If I go not away, the Comforter will not come unto
you; but if I depart, I will send him unto you.*
John 16:7

Why did the coming of the Comforter depend on Christ's going away? We may say, for one thing, that the Comforter could not come until the great offering for sin had been made. The Father sent the Son to be the propitiation for the sins of the world. Without shedding of blood there could be no remission of sins. There was, therefore, no redemption to be offered and applied until Jesus had made His great sacrifice. It was necessary, therefore, that He should die and that He should go away before the Comforter could come. The precious alabaster box of Christ's humanity must be broken open in order that the sacred ointment of His most blessed life might be poured out on the dead world.

It was necessary, also, that Christ should return to the Father as the Son of man, the representative of humanity, and be received into the Father's heart in this way. "Humanity was to ascend to heaven before the Spirit could be sent to humanity on earth." Christ also said that He would send the Comforter. He could not do this until He had returned to His glory and been exalted, in His humanity, to His throne of power.

These are hints of the reasons that Jesus had to go away before the Comforter could come. We live now under the blessed reign of the Holy Spirit. Sometimes we wish we had lived in the time of Christ's human presence in this world and we look back on the period of the Incarnation as earth's brightest and most glorious days; but really we have far richer privileges than those who knew Christ in the flesh. We have the same blessed Presence that they had, only without the limitations of flesh. Christ is now to millions everywhere far more than He was then to a few favored ones while in His fleshly body.

LIFE-GIVING KNOWLEDGE
◆

*And this is life eternal, that they might know thee the
only true God, and Jesus Christ, whom thou hast sent.*
John 17:3

Anyone, therefore, who truly knows God has eternal life.
Knowing God, however, is more than knowing about Him.
One may have all the doctrinal knowledge of God's character,
attributes, and works which the Bible reveals and yet not know
God at all in the way that gives life. We may know all about some
great man biographically and yet not know the man at all personally. But suppose we then meet him, become intimately associated with him, he becomes our dear friend, and we learn to love
him and trust him; then we really know him. It is this personal
knowledge of God that is meant in these words. We first learn
about Him, then seek Him and find Him; and He receives us into
His family, puts His divine love in our hearts, and gives us His
Spirit. Then we learn to trust Him and to love Him. This is the
knowing God which gives eternal life.

But how can we meet God, and get personally acquainted
with Him, and form this intimate friendship with Him? There is
another word in this verse which helps us to the answer. "That
they might know thee . . . and Jesus Christ." We are clearly
taught elsewhere that we can know God only through Jesus
Christ. "Neither knoweth any man the Father, save the Son, and
he to whomsoever the Son will reveal him" (Matthew 11:27).
Jesus Christ is the revelation of the Father to men: "He that hath
seen me hath seen the Father" (John 14:9). We can get acquainted with Christ in His humanity, and thus know God, and have
Him for our nearest friend. McCheyne said: "I seem to know
more of the Lord Jesus Christ than of the most intimate friend I
have on earth." Should we not all seek after Christ's personal
friendship? *The more we trust Him, the more shall we know of Him,
and the better shall we love Him.*

DIVINE PROTECTION

*Holy Father, keep through thine own name those whom
thou hast given me, that they may be one, as we are.*

John 17:11

There is matchless tenderness in the picture which these words in our Lord's intercessory prayer suggest. We think of a dying mother about to leave her children behind her in this world, exposed to all the world's dangers. During her own life she has cared for them with all tenderness and faithfulness. Now, however, she is going away and can guard them no more. But she cannot leave them without securing for them shelter and protection. Looking up to God, therefore, she commends them to His care. She knows that He never goes away, that He is present everywhere, and that He will look after her motherless children.

In the same way Jesus, about to go away and leave His disciples, places them in their peril and need in His Father's care. The prayer suggests two things. It gives us a glimpse of the heart of our Savior, and of His deep, tender, yearning love for His disciples. It ought to be a great comfort to us to know that He has just the same love for us if we are His. When we are going into any danger, He looks down upon us with deep affectionate longing, and intercedes for us as He did here for His disciples.

The other suggestion here is that if we belong to Christ we are divinely sheltered and kept. We cannot protect ourselves, but we have the Lord for our keeper; the wings of the Almighty cover us wherever we go. I have slept in camps in war times, when hostile forces pressed close upon the lines; but we all lay down at night in quiet confidence and peace, without fear, because all around the camps sentinels waked and watched. So God's angels encamp around His children, and so always the Lord keeps those who trust in Him. To have Christ for our Savior is to have His divine protection and guardianship.

November 5

◆

LIFE WORTH LIVING

◆

I pray not that thou shouldest take them out of the world.
John 17:15

It would be a great deal safer, in one sense, for believers to be taken at once to heaven as soon as they begin to follow Christ. They would then have no temptations, no enemies to fight, no conflicts and struggles to pass through. But who would then do Christ's work in the world? There would be no one to tell sinners about the Savior, none to show to men the beauty of Christ in a holy life, none to witness for God and to fight His battles.

There is another reason that Christians are left here. They are not the majestic trees that grow in the sheltered valleys, where no storms break, but those rather which are found upon the hilltops and on the mountains, where they must encounter the fierce gales. It is so with men; the greatest are grown amid difficulties and hardship, not in pampered ease. Even Jesus Himself was trained in the school of conflict and struggle. It may be the easiest thing to have no battles in life, to grow in some sheltered plain where the storms never blow, to meet no hardships, to have no burdens to carry; but what sort of life comes in the end from such a career? If we would reach the heights of blessedness, we must be content to pass through the fields of struggle.

When armies return from victorious war, the loudest cheers are not for those who have fought the newest battles, nor for the flags which are cleanest, but for the regiments which are cut down to a few men, and for the flags that are shot to pieces. So it will be in heaven when the redeemed are welcomed home; those who have fought the most battles and bear the most "marks of the Lord Jesus" will receive the highest honors. It is better, then, for Christians to stay in this world and to grow in strength through duty and conflict.

OUR GREAT INTERCESSOR

Neither pray I for these alone, but for them also
which shall believe on me through their word.
John 17:20

In this wonderful intercessory prayer our Lord reached out beyond the little circle of imperiled disciples that stood around Him that night and gathered in His arms all those who to the end should believe on Him. It embraced us, therefore, who in these days believe on Christ. He looked down along the ages and saw us and our dangers, and amid the deepening shadows of His cross He prayed for us. How sweet to be prayed for by Christ!

Even that is not all, precious as it is; for we are told elsewhere that Jesus ever lives to make intercession for His people. We are not to think of Him as losing interest in this earth when He went away. This intercessory prayer, whose profundity we observe as we read this chapter, is but a momentary revealing to us of Christ's continual pleading for us within the veil. We are to think of Him as in heaven watching us perpetually and praying for us in every time of danger. He sees each stealthy temptation as it approaches and asks, "Father, keep Thy imperiled child."

It is a very precious comfort even to know that a dear human friend is praying for us. Many a time in my youth was I kept from doing wrong things by the thought that in my quiet home far away my father and my mother, every morning and every evening, stretched out holy hands in earnest, loving prayer that God would keep their boy. I could not do the wrong thing with this vision in my mind. Still more powerful in its restraining influence upon us should be the assurance that day and night Jesus in heaven is thinking of us, watching us from His holy height in glory, and at every appearance of evil He prays for us. How could we do the evil thing if we but stopped long enough to think of this divine intercession for us?

"SONGS IN THE NIGHT"

*And when they had sung an hymn,
they went out into the mount of Olives.*
Matthew 26:30

This is the only record of our Lord's singing when He was on the earth. It is worthy of special notice that it was just as He was starting out to Gethsemane that He sang a hymn with His disciples. It would not have seemed so strange to us if He had sung that night on the Transfiguration Mount, or on the day He entered Jerusalem amid the people's hosannas, or on some other occasion of great gladness and triumph; but that the only time we hear Him singing should be in the darkest night of His life is very suggestive.

It tells us of the deep gladness that was in the heart of Christ under all His griefs and sorrows. He knew the agony into whose black shadows He was about to enter. Yet He went out toward the darkness with songs of praise on His lips. There is a Scripture word which tells us that "for the joy set before him [he] endured the cross, despising the shame" (Hebrews 12:2). This was the joy that broke forth here in a hymn of praise. It was the joy of doing the Father's will and of saving lost souls. We see here another glimpse of Christ's great heart of love.

We learn a lesson, too, for ourselves. We should go forward with joy to meet sorrow and sacrifice when we are doing our Father's will. We should learn to sing as we enter life's valleys of shadow. It is a great thing to be able to sing as we work and sing as we suffer. The secret of Christ's song here was His looking beyond the garden and the cross; He saw the reward, the glory, the redemption accomplished. If we look only at the sorrow before us, we cannot sing; but if we look on to the joy of victory, and the blessedness of the reward, and the ripened fruits that will come from the suffering, we can sing too as we enter the sorest trial.

November 8

---◇---

THE BAFFLED TEMPTER

---◇---

Satan hath desired to have you, that he may sift you as wheat.
Luke 22:31

Peter was put through Satan's winnowing; but only the chaff in him was blown out. He was a smaller man after the winnowing, just as the bulk of the wheat pile is reduced when the chaff is blown out; but he was a better man. He lost his rashness, his self-confidence, his pride, and he came again a humble man, but stronger, majestic—a power to bless the world.

Thus through the grace of Christ even the failures of believers are made to work for their good. Much of the grandeur and power of Peter's later life came out of that costly lesson. "The oyster mends its shell with a pearl." Where the ugly wound was there comes a gem, hiding the scar and making it a spot of lustrous beauty. So true repentance of sins changes the weakness of our lives into strength. If we are Christ's true followers, even our defeats become blessings. Longfellow says of Peter's sifting—

> *One look of that pale, suffering face*
> *Will make us feel the deep disgrace*
> > *Of weakness;*
> *We shall be sifted till the strength*
> *Of self-conceit be changed at length*
> > *To meekness.*
>
> *Wounds of the soul, though healed, will ache,*
> *The reddening scars remain and make*
> > *Confession;*
> *Lost innocence returns no more;*
> *We are not what we were before*
> > *Transgression.*
>
> *But noble souls through dust and heat*
> *Rise from disaster and defeat*
> > *The stronger;*
> *And conscious still of the Divine*
> *Within them, lie on earth supine*
> > *No longer.*

STRENGTH OUT OF WEAKNESS

When thou art converted, strengthen thy brethren.
Luke 22:32

Peter was not to be lost in the terrible experience through which he was to pass. Christ had made intercession for him, and he would emerge again from the trial humbled, bruised, defeated, but saved, and a better man. Our Lord tells him here that after his restoration he should turn his experience to account in helping other souls. "Do thou, when once thou hast turned again, stablish thy brethren." He would be able then to warn others of the dangers in which he had suffered so terribly. We can imagine Peter in later days counseling Christians against self-confidence and the other false steps which led to his own fall, thus strengthening or establishing them in God's ways. Then there is no doubt that his experience of penitence, and of the grace and love of Christ in that experience, enabled him to be a wise and safe guide to many another disciple who had fallen into sin and was seeking to be restored.

The lesson is important. All the lessons that God teaches us we should teach others. When we are helped, it is that we may then help others. When God comforts us in any sorrow, He therefore ordains us to go forth to comfort others with the comfort wherewith we ourselves have been comforted of God. When we fall in temptation, and God lifts us up and restores us, He wants us to use our experience in helping other weak ones in their temptations.

> *Oh lead me, Lord, that I may lead*
> *The wandering and the wavering feet;*
> *Oh feed me, Lord, that I may feed*
> *Thy hungering ones with manna sweet.*

> *Oh strengthen me, that while I stand*
> *Firm on the rock, and strong in thee,*
> *I may stretch out a loving hand*
> *To wrestlers with the troubled sea.*

---◇---

THE MAN OF SORROWS

---◇---

My soul is exceeding sorrowful, even unto death.
Matthew 26:38

We should often sit down with our Lord in Gethsemane and look upon Him while He suffers. We never can understand more than a very little of the anguish of that hour in the garden, yet we should often study it. Some hints of its meaning may be reverently mentioned.

Before our Lord there lay the betrayal, the arrest, the trial with all its mockery and humiliation, then death amid the shame of the cross. These physical sufferings alone made an anguish that was terrible to endure. Another element of our Lord's suffering was the falseness of the human hearts about him. There were the traitorous kiss of Judas, the sad denial of Peter, the flight and desertion of the other disciples, the rejection and crucifixion by the people He had come to save. All this He foresaw from Gethsemane.

But the very essence of the anguish of Gethsemane was the fact that Jesus was bearing our sins. What that meant to Him we can never know. We know only what is most dimly prefigured for us in the profound words of Holy Scripture, which speak of His vicarious sacrifice. They are such words as these: "Behold the Lamb of God, which taketh away the sin of the world."(John 1:29)—"The Lord hath laid on Him the iniquity of us all" (Isaiah 53:6)—He "bare our sins in His own body on the tree" (1 Peter 2:24)—He "hath redeemed us from the curse of the law, being made a curse for us" (Galatians 3:13). We are sure, at least, that the death of Jesus was not like the death of any other man, even though the other could endure all the physical sufferings that were included in our Lord's agony. In some way, though innocent and holy Himself, and without sin, He died for sin. We never can fathom the mystery, but the fact we must remember as we watch with our Lord in Gethsemane.

November 11

◇

"WATCH WITH ME"

◇

Tarry ye here, and watch with me.
Matthew 26:38

This request shows the humanness of our Lord. As He entered the darkness, He craved sympathy. He wanted His dearest friends near to Him. It was not because of anything they could really do to help Him. They could not lighten the awful load by so much as a feather's weight. They could not in any way share the burden. But their presence would make Him stronger to endure. The consciousness of tender love close beside Him would sustain Him in the fearful anguish.

We all understand this from personal experience. A little child's terror in the darkness is instantly soothed by a word from the mother or by her touch. A sufferer can endure his pain better if a friend sits beside him and holds his hand. We all crave companionship in life's great trials. These are hints of our Lord's feeling and desire that night when He asked His three best beloved disciples to accompany Him and begged them to watch with Him while He entered into His agony.

Jesus no longer suffers in any Gethsemane, yet He still calls us to watch with Him. Many of His people suffer, and He wants us to come up close beside them and by loving sympathy and tenderness sustain and strengthen them. He who watches with one of the least of Christ's brethren in time of pain or sorrow watches with Christ Himself.

We can also watch with Christ by being loyal and devoted to Him in every dark hour when His cause falters and when many are proving shallow and untrue. The time to be faithful to one's friend is when the popular clamor is against him. Our loyalty to Christ, likewise, should be most emphatic when His enemies are most active and when His friends are fewest. He wants us then to be faithful. He wants us to keep near Him. Surely we should never offend Him by coldness or lack of interest.

November 12

◆

"THY WILL BE DONE"

◆

O my Father, if it be possible, let this cup pass from me:
nevertheless not as I will, but as thou wilt.

Matthew 26:39

Among other lessons which we learn from our Lord's prayer in Gethsemane is this: that all our crying to God should close in acquiescence to the divine will. It is right to plead earnestly for what we want—earnestly, but never unsubmissively. We should recognize the fact that our Father has a plan for our lives, and that what we crave may not be in accordance with His plan. We should never want, therefore, to press our will against God's will.

There was a man who wished to pray, but did not know what he needed. Taking the letters of the alphabet, he laid them down and said: "Lord, I do not know what I need, or ought to ask for. Take these letters and arrange them into the prayer I ought to make, and give me that."

The best thing possible for us is always what God wills for us. Sometimes it may be pain or worldly loss or painful grief; yet His will is always love, and in simple submission to this will we shall always find our highest good. No prayer, therefore, is pleasing to God which does not end with this refrain of Gethsemane. This is the way also to peace; as we yield with love and joy, and merge our own will in our Father's, the peace of God flows like a river into our souls.

> *Not as I will!—the sound grows sweet*
> *Each time my lips the words repeat.*
> *"Not as I will!"—the darkness feels*
> *More safe than light when this thought steals*
> *Like whispered voice to calm and bless*
> *All unrest and all loneliness.*
> *"Not as I will," because the One*
> *Who loved us first and best has gone*
> *Before us on the road, and still*
> *For us must all his love fulfill—*
> *"Not as we will."*

November 13

◆

"Watch Unto Prayer"

◆

Watch and pray, that ye enter not into temptation:
the spirit indeed is willing, but the flesh is weak.
Matthew 26:41

We must learn both to watch and pray. It is good to watch. There is danger everywhere. An army in an enemy's country never rests a moment without its encircling line of pickets, keeping watch against danger at every point, and reporting instantly any hostile movement. We are living in the enemy's country and cannot safely pass an hour without watching. But watching is not enough; for we are not able to keep ourselves when the danger comes. We need to pray also, asking God to protect us. But as watching without praying is not enough, neither is praying without watching. God expects us to use our eyes and to keep our wits about us, as well as to cry to Him for help.

We must not say that everyone who makes a good profession, and then fails, is insincere or a hypocrite. Peter was neither when he made his bold avowal that he would never deny Christ, and that he could die with Him. He loved Christ and meant to be true to Him. His spirit was eager and earnest, but he was weak in himself; and because he relied only on himself, he was not able to hold out against the strong temptations which came upon him.

We are all just like Peter. If we are true Christians we mean to be faithful to our Lord. But sincerity is not enough. "The flesh is weak," and we need to rest continually upon God for help to be true and faithful. If young Christians would learn this lesson, they would not fall so easily. If the drunkard who resolves to reform learned it, he would be safer and stronger. No matter how good his intentions are, he is not able of himself to fulfill them. None of us are as good as we want to be and strive to be; and only through the mighty help of Christ can any of us live a true and holy life amid all the world's temptations and dangers.

LOST OPPORTUNITIES

He cometh the third time, and saith unto them, Sleep on now, and take your rest: it is enough, the hour is come.

Mark 14:41

The time for watching was past. Jesus had now passed through His agony, and on His face was the radiance of peace. He did not need any longer the help of the sympathy which in vain He had craved in the darkness. He looked toward the city gate, and there was the traitor coming. There was neither need nor use now for the disciples' waking and watching, and they might as well sleep on.

The lesson is clear. Whatever we do for our friends we must do when they are in need of our help. If one is sick, the time to show our sympathy is while the sickness continues. If we allow him to pass through his illness without showing him any attention, there is little use when he is healthy again for us to offer kindness.

If one of our friends is passing through some deep struggle with temptation, then is the time for us to come up close alongside him and put the strength of our love under his weakness. If we fail him then we may almost as well let him go on alone after that. Of what use is our help when the battle has been fought through to the end and won without us? Or suppose the friend was not victorious; that he failed—failed because no one came to help him—is there any use in our rushing to him then to offer assistance? Let us not fail to act at the right time.

> We might have lent
> Such strength, such comfort and content
> To you out of our ample store;
> We might have hastened on before
> To lift the shadows from your way,
> Darkened, ere noon, to twilight's gray;
> With earth's chilled air love's warm heart-scent
> We might have blent.

NEVER DESPAIR

Rise up, let us go.
Mark 14:42

There seems to be a voice of hope in this call. The disciples had sadly failed in one great duty; they had slept when the Master wanted them to watch with Him. He had just told them that they might as well sleep on, so far as the prayer was concerned, for the time to render it was gone forever. Yet there were other duties before them, and Jesus called them to arise and meet these. Because they had failed in one hour's responsibility, they must not sink down in despair. They must arouse themselves to meet the responsibility just before them.

Again the lesson is plain. Because we have failed in one duty, we must not give up in despair. Because a young man has wasted his youth, he must not therefore lose heart and think all is lost. There are other opportunities waiting for him. The loss of youth is irreparable. The golden years can never be gotten back. The innocence, the energy, the power, are gone forever. Yet why should a person squander all because he has squandered the best? Because the morning has been thrown away, why should all the day be lost?

The lesson is for all of us who have failed in any way. Christ ever calls to hope. He bids us rise again from the worst defeat. In the kingdom of grace there is always margin enough to start again and to build a holy life. Even down to life's latest hour this remains true. The door of opportunity opened to the penitent even on the cross in his dying hour; there was no time to make anything good or attractive of his life on the earth, except in his dying confession and testimony; but the eternity into which he passed is very long, with time enough for a glorious career. So it is the same now. In this world, blessed by divine love and grace, there is never any need for despair. The call after any defeat or failure still is, "Rise up, let us go."

November 16

◇

"PRAY WITHOUT CEASING"

◇

Jesus oftentimes resorted thither with his disciples.
John 18:2

These words give us a glimpse of our Lord's devotional habits. The deep quiet of the olive garden was His closet. Here He had been regularly going for seasons of prayer. There were other places, too, which were sacred retreats to Him. There were mountaintops where He often spent whole nights in communion with His Father.

Our Lord's example teaches us that we should spend much time in devotion. Some people manage to get along without much praying; but it is always at the expense of their spiritual lives. Not feeding their souls, they grow very lean. There really can be no beautiful, strong, helpful Christian life without much quiet prayer. Every tree has a root, which people do not see, which has no beauty, but which in secret, in the darkness, performs service for the tree, without which the tree could not live. What the root is to the tree, that is the Christian's secret devotional life to the external and visible life which the world sees. *We shall flourish and be fruitful in spiritual life just in proportion to the earnestness, the reality, and the intensity of our devotional life.* A great deal of praying needs to go with a very little working.

Our Lord's example teaches us also the importance of regular habits of praying. Some people say that praying should be spontaneous and that stated times and places make it formal and take the spirit out of it. But we are such creatures of habit that if we do not pray at regular times each day, we shall very soon not pray at all. But if we always go to our prayer closet at the same time, our devotions will become part of our daily life, and we shall never live a day without its moments of prayer. If our Lord's holy life required regular habits of prayer and communion, much more do our broken, imperfect lives require the same.

November 17

THE TRAITOR

Judas also . . . knew the place. . . . Judas then,
having received a band of men . . . cometh thither.
John 18:2–3

Every new line in the story of the betrayal shows greater darkness in the heart of Judas. Leaving from the supper table he hastened to the priests and was quickly under way with his band of soldiers. He probably first hurried back to the Upper Room, where he had left Jesus; not finding Him there, he knew well where the Master had gone and hastened to the sacred place of prayer. Then the manner in which he let the officers know which of the company was Jesus shows the deepest hypocrisy of all: he went up to Him as a dear friend and kissed Him, with outward warmth and affection.

Let us remember how this treason grew in the heart of Judas, beginning with greed for money, growing into theft and deception, ending at last in the worst crime the world ever saw. The lesson is that we should watch for the beginnings of evil in our hearts before it is too late.

A picture in the royal gallery of Brussels represents Judas wandering about on the night after the betrayal. He comes by chance upon the workmen who have been making the cross on which Christ shall be crucified tomorrow. A fire near by throws its light full on the faces of the work-men, who are sleeping peacefully while resting from their labor. Judas' face is somewhat in the shade; but it is wonderfully expressive of awful remorse and agony as he catches sight of the cross and the tools used in making it—the cross which his treachery made possible. But still, though in the very torments of hell, as it appears, he clutches his money-bag, and seems to hurry on into the night. That picture tells the story of the fruit of Judas's victory—the money-bag with the thirty pieces of silver in it (and even that he could not long keep), carried off into the night of fiendish despair: that was all.

November 18

◇

THE TRAITOR'S KISS

◇

He came to Jesus, and said, Hail, master; and kissed him.
Matthew 26:49

The very reading of the words makes us shudder. A kiss has always been the token of affection and the seal and pledge of fidelity. Judas's going up to Christ and kissing Him was a solemn sign of sincere friendship. Yet the kiss was not only false, but was the sign of betrayal. No words are strong enough to characterize this crime. We remember the fable of the poisonous reptile taken into the bosom of a kindly man to be warmed, rewarding the benefactor by striking its deadly fangs into his flesh. But even this does not illustrate the evil quality of Judas's act. It is no wonder that he is the lowest of the world. A poet represents him as placed in the lowest circles of the lost, as the sole sharer with Satan himself of the very uttermost punishment and shunned even there and even by the guiltiest.

In studying the character and the sin of Judas, the following lessons may be brought out: (1) We must not be surprised if some bad men enter the church, for even among the twelve was Judas himself. (2) It is no proof that Christianity is untrue when some of its professors prove hypocrites. The defection of Judas did not leave a stain on the name of Christ, nor did it disprove the loyalty and fidelity of the other disciples. (3) One may be very near to Christ and not be made holy in character. Judas was three years with Christ, heard His words, lived in the atmosphere of His love, and remained unchanged. An empty bottle, hermetically sealed, may lie long in the ocean and continue perfectly dry within. A heart sealed to Christ's love may lie in His bosom for years and not be blessed. Only when the heart is opened to receive His grace does closeness to him sanctify. (4) Sin grows, and we never can know to what terrible extent a wicked thought or desire may reach.

November 19

◇

GOD'S WILL IS BEST

◇

The cup which my Father hath given me, shall I not drink it?
John 18:11

The "cup" is our portion, embracing all the experiences of our earthly lives. Our Father gives us the cup, therefore it must be the very best that the wisest love can provide. When death enters a Christian home there is sweetest comfort in the thought that God has really done the best possible for the friend whom He has taken away. We asked Him to crown our loved one with His richest blessings, and is that not just what He has done? Here is a little poem which in a beautiful way illustrates this. There is first a prayer for a friend:

> *"Give her, I pray, all good:*
>   *Bid all the buds of pleasure to grow*
> *To perfect flowers of happiness*
>   *Wher'er her feet may go;*
> *Bid Truth's bright shield and Love's strong arm*
>   *Protect her from all earthly harm.*

> *"Lest there should be some other thing*
>   *Better than all the rest,*
> *That I have failed to ask," I said,*
>   *"Give thou the very best*
> *Of every gift that thou dost deem*
>   *better than aught I hope or dream."*

Then here is the answer which came:

> *"Better than I can ask or dream!"*
>   *This was my prayer, and now*
> *That she is lying still and pale,*
>   *With God's peace on her brow,*
> *I wonder, sobbing, sore dismayed,*
>   *If this be that for which I prayed.*

PETER'S FALL

And Simon Peter stood and warmed himself. They said therefore unto him, Art not thou also one of his disciples?
John 18:25

For our own sakes we should regard the steps which led to Peter's fall. One was his self-confidence. When forewarned, he resisted the Master's prophecy and declared that though others might deny Christ, he never would. When we grow boastful we are in great peril. Safety lies in a consciousness of our own weakness and in implicit trust in God.

The next step toward Peter's fall was his sleeping in the garden when he should have been watching and praying. That hour was given for preparation for temptation but was not taken advantage of.

Another step was his rashness in drawing his sword in the garden. This act made him liable to arrest, and this fact made him nervous and afraid of recognition. He tried to hide his connection with Jesus, lest he should be arrested for his assault in the garden. Rash acts are sure to make trouble for us afterward.

Another step toward denial was Peter's following Christ from afar. This showed timidity and failing faith. His courage was leaving him. Following Christ at a distance is always perilous. It shows a weakening attachment and a trembling loyalty. It is in itself partial denial. The only worthy and the only safe discipleship is thorough, unwavering devotion and whole-hearted consecration.

This apostle took another step toward his fall when he sat down among the servants of the high priest. He went among them to hide his relationship to Jesus. The only safe thing for a Christian is unequivocally to declare his discipleship wherever he goes.

When Peter had taken these steps he could scarcely do otherwise than openly deny his Lord. The time for us to guard ourselves is at the beginning of separation.

THE GREAT DENIAL

He denied before them all.
Matthew 26:70

One thing that made Peter's denial so peculiarly sad was that he had received so many marks of special favor from Christ. He was one of three disciples who had been taken into the inner circle of friendship. The more Jesus has done for us, the worse it is for us to prove unfaithful to Him.

Another thing was that Peter had so boldly confessed Christ. It was he who said, when Jesus asked the disciples whom they believed Him to be, "Thou art the Christ, the Son of the living God" (Matthew 16:16). It was he who, just a few hours before his denial, so vehemently avowed his loyalty and his readiness to die with his Lord. These repeated protests of fidelity made the evil of denial more grievous. It is a greater sin for one who has publicly declared his love for Christ to prove disloyal to Him than for one who has never made such confession.

Another thing that made the sin worse was the fact that Jesus had forewarned Peter. We say "forewarned is forearmed"; but it did not prove so in this instance, because the disciple utterly disregarded the Master's warnings. We are all warned of danger; do we heed the signals?

Still another aggravation was that it was in our Lord's hour of deepest need that the disciple denied Him. Had it been in some time of popular favor, the denial would not have been so serious; but it was when Jesus was deserted and was in the hands of His enemies. Was that a time for the bravest disciple, the most honored friend, the noblest adherent, to turn his back on his Master? When the shadow falls on your friend, when the tide has turned against him, when others fall away from him, is that the time for you, his long-time closest companion, the recipient of his favors, to turn and desert and deny him?

THE HOLY ONE
—◇—

What accusation bring ye against this man?
John 18:29

That was a fair question. The Jews wanted Pilate to put Jesus to death; but Pilate had a right to ask why such sentence should be pronounced. No man should ever be condemned without a trial.

We have a right to ask the same now of those who condemn and reject Christ. What wrong thing has He done? What flaws are there in His character? Whom has He injured? The Jews attempted no answer to Pilate's question; indeed there was no answer possible, for no accusation could be brought against Jesus. He had never sinned against anyone. A little girl kissed her young brother's hand as he lay in the coffin, and said, "Mama, this little hand never struck me." It could well have been said of Christ when He lay in death, "This hand never struck anyone. These lips never spoke a word that gave unnecessary pain. This heart never cherished an unkind thought or feeling."

On the other hand, the life of Christ was a perpetual blessing to all who loved Him. His hands were ever stretched out in healing—until finally they were stretched out on the cross and fastened back there, but outstretched still in blessing. His lips were ever speaking words of comfort, of love. His heart was ever full of love and grace. Who could ever bring any accusation against Him? In truth no one ever did; He was hurried to death by men's hate, without reason or charge of any kind.

This same Jesus stands now before men, asking for their love and their faith. What reason is there that He should not be received? What has He ever done to discredit His own claims? What charge of evil can anyone, the worst enemy, bring against Him? Has He ever led a confiding soul into wrong paths? Has He ever disappointed the hopes of any heart that has trusted in Him? Why, then, should any reject Him?

PILATE'S INDECISION

Then said Pilate unto them, Take ye him,
and judge him according to your law.
John 18:31

Pilate wanted to evade the responsibility of trying and sentencing Jesus. But instead of honestly refusing to have anything to do with His condemnation, Pilate sought by evasion simply to get clear of the case. He could not do it, however; for each time Jesus came back and stood before him waiting for his decision.

One of Pilate's questions a little later than this was, *"What shall I do with Jesus?"*—a question he was compelled to answer in the end. Jesus stands before every human soul, as He stood before Pilate, demanding reception or rejection, and every one of us must answer this same question. The question may be postponed, but we cannot get it off our hands. We may send Jesus away, but soon we find Him back, standing again at our door. Every soul must judge Christ's claims and give a decision for or against.

Look on a little later. We see Pilate on the judgment seat and Jesus standing before him to be judged. "Knowest thou not that I have power to crucify thee, and power to release thee?" (John 19:10). Immense power for any man to hold! The scene closed, and Jesus went to His cross. Pilate soon fell into disgrace, and in a few years he committed suicide. When he stood before the throne of the divine Judge, into whose eyes did the poor guilty Roman look? What a reversal occurred here. Once Pilate was judge, and Jesus stood at the bar; now Jesus is judge, and Pilate is before Him.

Jesus stands now before sinners, meek and lowly, asking to be received; but the scene will soon be changed for those who reject Him—they will be hurried away into eternity, and the Judge before whose bar they shall find themselves will be the same One who stood so long, patient and loving, waiting to save them.

November 24

CHRIST OUR KING

The governor asked him, saying, Art thou the King of the Jews?
Matthew 27:11

Jesus did not look much like a king as He stood there, His hands bound, a cord about His neck. Pilate's questions sound ridiculous. Yet Jesus answered, "Yes, I am a king." Strange answer! Where, then, was His power? Where were His throne, His crown, His scepter, His royal robes? Who recognized His majesty? Pilate probably looked at Him with mingled contempt and pity.

But to us today how different does it all appear! He is throned now "far above all principality, and power, and might, and dominion, and every name that is named, not only in this world, but also in that which is to come" (Ephesians 1:21). In heaven He is honored as King of kings and Lord of lords. On His head are many crowns. All over the earth, too, His rule is felt. Wherever His gospel has gone, with its revelation of divine love and grace, the influence of His kingdom has reached.

And Jesus was as truly a king when He stood before Pilate that day, to human eyes bound and powerless, as He is now, exalted on heaven's throne. His kingdom was spiritual: it was a kingdom of truth, of righteousness, of holiness, of grace, and of love. He seemed the weakest of all men that morning; but in reality He was the mightiest, the grandest, the most kingly. What, then, is greatness? What is power? What is kingship? Not anything external, not anything that our eyes can see. The world bows down before thrones that glitter and crowns whose jewels flash in sunlight, and it worships power whose majesty is expressed in material splendor. But the real power of the world is Christ's power—the kingdom whose sway is over human hearts and lives. It is spiritual. It makes men better and lifts them up into noble life, into purity, holiness, and divine beauty.

"BEHOLD THE MAN!"

Pilate saith unto them, Behold the man!
John 19:5

We cannot do better than obey Pilate's word, "Behold the man!" and fix our eyes in loving gaze upon Jesus as He is led out from the palace and stands before the multitude. On His head He wears a crown of thorns; around His bleeding body is thrown a purple robe, a mock emblem of royalty. He had been called King of the Jews, and the cruel soldiers tried to carry out what appeared to them to be a farce.

Behold the man! Behold the man enduring shame and contempt, set forth before the people as a spectacle of mockery, in order that at last we may be presented in glory and honored before angels and the Father. Behold the man wearing a crown of thorns, that we may wear a crown of glory and of life, robed in mocking purple, that we may wear the white garments of righteousness. Behold the man in the majesty of meekness—reviled, yet reviling not again; hated, yet still loving on; wronged, yet speaking no resentful word. We should study the character of our Lord as revealed amid the terrible scenes of that morning. How His sublime patience shames our miserable impatience!

We fret and worry ourselves with inexcusable discontentment over the smallest discomforts; let us see the blessed peace of Jesus in the midst of the worst trials. We fly into anger and cherish bitter resentments when others slight us or wrong us in merest trifles; let us understand the sweet spirit of Jesus—loving, gentle, meek, under the greatest cruelties and wrongs ever inflicted on any life.

Behold the man, the God-man, divinity manifested in humanity, humbling Himself and becoming obedient unto shame and death that He might save our souls. Behold the man, holy, undefiled, separate from sinners, yet bearing upon His own head, as the Lamb of God, the sin of the world. Let us look and weep, and love and trust, and rejoice.

POWER BELONGS TO GOD

◇

*Knowest thou not that I have power to crucify thee, and
have power to release thee? . . . Thou couldest have no power
at all against me, except it were given thee from above.*

John 19:10–11

Authority is one of the entrusted talents. Men talk very boast-
fully of their power, forgetting that it is delegated power
which they hold, and that they must wield it for God and must
give account to Him for their use of it. No man's power belongs to
himself to do with as he pleases; it is given him from God, the
source of all power. This is true of the authority of parents and
teachers, of the power possessed by judges, and of all power
whatsoever.

Men are eager to obtain offices in the city or nation, and
they do not always realize the responsibility which attaches to
such positions. Power belongs to God, and must be used for God,
or its misuse will bring a serious penalty. It is a talent which is
given to us to be accounted for, and no treason is worse than
abuse in the wielding of power. This is true all the way from the
power of the child on the playground to the power of the president of the nation or the king on his throne. "Thou couldest have
no power . . . except it were given thee from above."

A comforting thought is suggested by the words in this sentence, "Thou couldest have no power against me." Christ in this
world was under the protection of His Father, and no one on
earth could lift a finger against Him except by divine permission.
What was true of Him, the Son of God, is true of each one of the
sons of God in all their earthly lives. Each believer, the humblest,
the weakest, is kept in this world as the apple of God's eye. No
one can touch one of God's little ones except by divine permission. This shows how safe we are, amid all the world's dangers
and enmities, while we trust ourselves to our Father's keeping.

FATAL DECISION

◇

Then delivered he him therefore unto them to be crucified.
John 19:16

So we see the sad and terrible end of Pilate's weak struggles with his conscience and his sense of right. He first tried every way to avoid the issue; then he delayed, hoping in some way to get free from responsibility. At last he gave in; and his name goes through history stigmatized forever as the man who delivered Jesus to be crucified. He is known by no other deeds. It had been a thousand times better for him if he had remained forever in obscurity, instead of going to that high place of power where he had to meet and deal with this momentous question of history.

We read that Pilate took water in the presence of the Jews and washed his hands—thus by a symbol declaring that he was not responsible for the sentencing of Jesus to die. But the water did not wash away one particle of the stain of the guilt of that terrible sin. Pilate had the misfortune to be the only man in all the province who could send Jesus to the cross. Upon him, therefore, the final responsibility rested, regardless of the pressure that was brought to bear upon him by the enemies of Jesus. The fact that others urge us to sin does not take away our guilt for that sin. No being in the universe can compel us to do wrong; if, then, we do wrong, the sin is our own.

Pilate was using his position for purposes of political advancement, thinking to make a great name for himself. Yet he was forced to reject Jesus in order to do that—the worst mistake anybody can make. The leaders and people in the crowd who did the same suffered similar consequences. What is our decision? We, too, have put Jesus to death by our sins. Would we crucify the Son of God afresh by rejecting Him in our own self-interest? Let us repent of our sins today and choose life in Him rather than our own way.

---◇---

"TAKE UP THY CROSS"

---◇---

And he bearing his cross went forth.
John 19:17

At first there was no one to help Jesus to bear His cross; though fainting from loss of rest and from the gashing and laceration of His body by the scourge, and still more from the untold anguish through which He had been passing, He yet had to carry His cross for Himself until His frailty gave way. Yet we must remember that while Jesus had to bear the cross unaided, it really was not for Himself that He bore it, but for us. He endured the shame and pain, and staggered beneath the awful burden, that He might set us free from the burden of sin's curse. John the Baptist said, when Jesus passed by him at the beginning of His ministry, "Behold the Lamb of God, which taketh away the sin of the world!" (John 1:29). We may say the same words as we see Jesus bearing His cross. That is what He is doing. It was not the mere wood that was so heavy; the real load which Jesus bore that day was the mountain of our sins. It was this that made Him faint and sink down by the way and that wrung from Him such cries and tears in Gethsemane and on Calvary.

A little later He sank down under the burden, and then the officers compelled a passerby to help Him. After that this scene emerged—Jesus and Simon of Cyrene together carrying the cross, Jesus in advance carrying the heavy end, and Simon coming behind bearing the lighter end. Here again the picture is very suggestive in two ways: We must share the cross with Christ before we can be saved; that is, we must accept our place with Him under the cross and follow Him. Then we can view the picture another way, and we see Jesus helping His people to bear their crosses. Every cross we have to bear, His shoulder is also beneath it, and He always bears the heavy end of it. No believer ought to be unable to bear any cross with Jesus. No load that He shares could crush us.

November 29

THE PERFECT SUFFERER

*They gave him vinegar to drink mingled with gall:
and when he had tasted thereof, he would not drink.*
Matthew 27:34

The offer was kindly meant. There was a group of women at Jerusalem, a compassionate sisterhood, whose work was to provide such sedative drinks for those who were crucified. The object was to produce partial unconsciousness, so that the terrible agonies might not be so keenly felt. It is good to know that such a profession existed at that early day, and that it was found among the Jewish people. True religion always yields such fruits. Christianity has filled the world with just such kind ministries. Wherever there is pain, Christian women go to alleviate it.

But it must be noticed that Christ did not accept this drug. He tasted it, showing His recognition and appreciation of the kindness that offered it, but He did not drink it. One reason probably was that He would not seek to lessen in any way the bitterness of the cup which His Father had given Him to drink. He would drink it to its last drop and not dull the sense of suffering in Himself to make the draught any less bitter.

Doubtless another reason was that He would not cloud His mind in the least degree as He entered the last experiences of life. He would not dim the clearness of His communion with His Father by any medication that should impair His full consciousness. The example of Christ does not teach that it is wrong in ordinary cases to use anesthetics to deaden the sense of pain. There were peculiar reasons why our Lord would lessen nothing of the bitterness of His suffering. Anesthetics have been wonderful agents of mercy and blessing in the world. But Christ died without them.

THE CRUCIFIXION

◇

They crucified him.
Mark 15:25

Here we come to the mount of our Redeemer's sorrow, and we should bare our heads in holy reverence as we stand in the silence of wondering love and gaze upon Him on His cross. Many thoughts will come to us as we contemplate this scene.

What a terrible thing sin is, that its expiation required such a sacrifice! Shall we go on carelessly sinning when we see what our Savior suffered to save us from our sins? What wonderful love there must be in the heart of God to cause Him to give His Son to endure such a death to save sinners!

What worth there must be in human souls, under all the ruin of sin, that Jesus was willing to make such a sacrifice of His own precious and glorious life to redeem the lost!

What a pattern for all life have we here! The cross is Jesus giving Himself to bless and save others. The more completely we forget ourselves and live for others, the nearer do we get to the example of Christ. How can we ever complain again of our little deprivations and sacrifices for the sake of others? The cross, where Christ is giving all, should make us ashamed even to mention again any little thing that we have done or suffered for another.

Crucifixion was such a blot at that time, associated in name with such terror and scorn, that one who died this way was buried forever in shame. That person could never be mentioned except with dishonor. But Jesus, instead of being shamed and weighed down forever by the cross, in the black waters of guilt, lifted the cross itself to glory, until today it is the emblem of hope, of victory, of blessedness, and of joy wherever the gospel has gone. Let no one be afraid to endure for Christ's sake, for when the cross is taken up in His name it becomes a "weight of glory."

December 1

◇

THE SACRED GARMENTS

◇

*They parted his garments, casting lots upon
them, what every man should take.*
Mark 15:24

We love to think of those sacred garments which our Savior had worn. Perhaps they had been made by His mother's hands, or maybe by the hands of some of the other women who followed Him from Galilee, ministering unto Him. They were the garments, too, that the sick had touched in reverent faith, receiving instant healing. We treasure the garments of those we love when they have left us. How sacred they are! How it would pain us to see them divided among rude enemies and worn by them about the streets! A peculiar sadness clings to everything that Jesus ever touched; and what desecration it appears to our hearts to see these scoffing heathen soldiers take His garments and divide them among themselves as booty! Then what terrible sacrilege it seems to see them throwing dice and gambling under the very cross while the Savior hangs there in agony!

Why was Jesus stripped of His garments? Was there no meaning in it apart from the mere custom? Was it not that He might prepare garments of righteousness for us in our spiritual nakedness?

One night of bitter cold and pitiless storm, a mother was out in the wilds with her child in her arms. Unable to carry her precious burden and find a shelter, she took off her own outer clothing, and wrapping it about her little one she laid him in a cleft of the rock, and hastened on, hoping to find help. The next morning shepherds heard the cry of a child and found the babe safe and warm in the rock's cleft. Then, not far away in the snow, they discovered the mother—dead. She had stripped off her own garments and died in the cold to save her child. Did not Jesus do the same? He took off His clothing and hung naked on His cross, that we may stand in the final judgment arrayed in robes of beauty.

December 2

---◇---

THE KING OF THE JEWS

---◇---

And set up over his head his accusation written,
This is Jesus the King of the Jews.
Matthew 27:37

There was no other crime charged. He had done nothing wrong. Pilate had satisfied himself of that. He had examined Him and could find no fault in Him, so he would not write any charges on His cross but this, that He was the King of the Jews. The rulers objected to this and wanted him to write that *He said* He was King of the Jews; but Pilate would not change a word, and there it stood above His head during all the agony and all the darkness—the King of the Jews.

And He was. The tablet told the truth, though erected to mock the people. He was the Messiah who had been promised all through the centuries. He was the King of whom David was only a shadow. He was the Christ who had been foretold by prophets and waited for age after age by the nation. At last He came. Angels sang at His birth. His life had been one of great blessing and power. He had completed miracles of mercy over all the land. He had taught, speaking as no other man spoke. He had fulfilled all the Messianic conditions. Yet His enemies had rejected Him; and at last they led Him out to Calvary and nailed Him on the cross. Still He was their King—their King rejected, their King crucified. His throne was His cross; His crown was the circle of thorns that the soldiers had twisted and wound around His head.

It does not seem to us a kingly hour in our Lord's life when He hangs on His cross dying, yet really it was the time of His highest earthly exaltation. He spoke of going to His cross as going to be glorified. He was indeed King of the Jews. They crucified their King. He is our King too. How are we treating Him? Are we obeying Him? Are any of us rejecting Him? Are any of us crucifying Him afresh? We need to answer these questions.

DIVINE FORGIVENESS

◇

Father, forgive them; for they know not what they do.
                                                    Luke 23:34

This was the first word spoken by our Lord on His cross. It was uttered just when the soldiers were in the act of crucifying Him—driving the terrible nails through His hands and feet. It was a moment of excruciating, inconceivable anguish. Yet He uttered no cry of pain, no word of judgment upon those who were causing Him such suffering, but calmly prayed for His brutal, pitiless murderers—"Father, forgive them; for they know not what they do."

The moment the sacred blood began to flow, the intercession for sinners began. The pleading was first for the ignorant heathen soldiers who were acting as executioners; but it was not for these alone. It certainly spread further and took in all who had been involved in the condemnation and crucifixion of Jesus. It was for the Jewish rulers and people who had rejected their Messiah. Should we not believe that many of those who on the day of Pentecost and afterward were brought to repentance were forgiven and saved because on His cross Jesus made intercession for them?

The prayer also went beyond the people who had a direct part in the crucifixion. From His cross Jesus saw the lost world down to the extremities and prayed for all humans. We know, too, that that work of prayer was but the beginning of an intercession that is going on even now in heaven, where Jesus pleads the merits of His own sacrifice for the salvation of sinners.

This word of Jesus teaches us a great lesson on Christian forgiveness. He prayed for His murderers. We should pray for those who injure us. There are some fragrant trees which bathe in perfume the axe that gashes them. So should it be with Christ's people. Instead of resentment and injury for injury, we should show only sweet, tender love to those who harm us.

December 4

SELF-SACRIFICE

*The rulers . . . derided him, saying, He saved
others; let him save himself, if he be Christ.*
Luke 23:35

I t was because He chose to save others that He could not save
Himself. The soldier in the battle cannot save himself and save
his country. The mother cannot spare herself and save her child.
Jesus could have saved Himself; but what would have been the
fate of sinners?

Three little children wandered from home one afternoon.
Evening found them playing by the seashore. It grew suddenly
dark and cold, and they could not return. In the morning they
were found, the two youngest sleeping warm and safe under cov-
erings of garments and seaweed, and little Mary, the elder, lying
cold and dead, with her arms still full of seaweed. She had taken
off nearly all her own warm clothing to cover the younger children, and then carried grass and seaweed to pile upon them, until
she died in her loving devotion. She did not save herself, because
she wanted to save the little ones entrusted to her care.

During a plague in Marseilles, the physicians decided that
nothing could be done to save the people unless a victim could be
dissected and the nature of the disease then learned. But who
would do such a perilous work? One physician arose and said he
would do it. Saying his farewell to his family, he entered the hos-
pital, made the dissection, wrote out the results, and in a few
hours was dead. But now the physicians could treat the disease,
and the plague was checked.

These incidents illustrate Christ's devotion to death for sinners. Men could not be saved unless someone could suffer and
die in their place, and Jesus became the propitiation for sins. In
one sense He could have saved Himself, but then the world
would have been lost. His death was voluntary. He gave His life
for the sheep. We are saved because He did not save Himself.

December 5

◇

"AT HOME WITH THE LORD"

◇

To day shalt thou be with me in paradise.
Luke 23:43

This was the second word on the cross. Something touched the heart of one of the robbers—perhaps it was the Savior's prayer for His murderers?—and he became penitent in his dying hour and cried to Jesus for mercy: "Lord, remember me when thou comest into thy kingdom" (v. 42). Quickly from the lips of the dying Redeemer came the gracious response, "To day shalt thou be with me in paradise." The words are full of meaning, of which only partial hints can here be given.

Though in the agony of death, Jesus could yet give life to a dead soul. Though draining the dregs of the cup of woe, He could give a cup of blessing to a penitent sinner. Though His hand was nailed to the cross, it yet carried the key of paradise and opened the gate to allow a repentant soul to enter. Surely there was no more royal moment in all Christ's life than this.

The promise itself tells us what death is for the believer. "To day shalt thou be with me." There is no long, dark passage, therefore, through which the freed soul must go to reach blessedness. There is no purgatory in which it must wait to be prepared for glory. At once the spirit goes into the presence of Christ. St. Paul teaches us the same truth when he describes death as departing to be with Christ and says that to be absent from the body is to be at home with the Lord. That same day, said Jesus, this penitent soul should be in paradise. We ought not then to be afraid to die if we are of Christ's redeemed ones.

The words tell us also in what heaven's blessedness really consists. "Thou shalt be with me." Being with Christ is glory. No sweeter, more blessed heaven can be conceived of. We know only little about heaven as a place—where it is, what it is like; but this much we know—there we shall be with Christ. Is not that enough to know?

December 6

◇

THE DIVINE LEGACY

◇

When Jesus therefore saw his mother, and the disciple standing by, whom he loved, he saith unto his mother, Woman, behold thy son!
John 19:26

This was the third word spoken by our Lord from the cross. Not far away, in some quiet spot amid the multitude, stood a little group of His dearest friends. Most of them were women. As His eye looked down upon them He saw among them His own mother. Truly a sword was piercing through her heart as she beheld her divine son on His cross.

As Jesus saw His mother in her deep grief, though suffering untold anguish Himself, His heart went out in compassion and love for her. He thought of her unsheltered, as she would be, when He was gone. He remembered what she had been to Him in His tender infancy and defenseless childhood as she had blessed Him with her rich, self-forgetful love.

"Stripped of everything," says Godet, "Jesus seemed to have nothing more to give. Nevertheless, from the midst of this deep poverty He had already made precious gifts; to His executioners He had bequeathed the pardon of God; to His companion in punishment, paradise. Could He find nothing to leave to His mother and His friend? These two beloved persons, who had been His most precious treasures on earth, He commissioned to one another, giving thus at once a son to His mother and a mother to His friend."

In this beautiful act of our Lord we have a wonderful commentary on the fifth commandment. Every young person, or older one, with parents yet living, who reads this fragment of the story of the cross should remember the lesson and pay love's highest honor to the father or the mother to whom he owes so much. No suffering or pain of our own should ever make us forgetful of our parents, and we should honor them to the last moment of their lives.

THE DARK VALLEY
◇

It was about the sixth hour, and there was a
darkness over all the earth until the ninth hour.
Luke 23:44

It was a mysterious and supernatural darkness. We may say, and we can say no more, that it was nature sympathizing with the crucifixion of its Lord. How dense it was we cannot tell; but it must have filled the hearts of the multitude about the cross with awe.

There was also a still deeper darkness around the soul of Him who hung on that central cross. It was so dark that He even seemed forsaken of God. We can never understand it, although we know that it was the sin of the world that made the darkness. Jesus wrapped the glooms of death about Himself that we might be clothed in garments of light. He died this way in darkness that we might walk into the valley amid the splendors of heavenly light. He experienced agony in His last hour that we might have joy. His head wore the crown of thorns, and He had no place to rest in dying, that under our heads might be the pillow of peace.

It is profitable for us to contrast the death of Christ with that of His disciples in all ages since. He shrank from the "cup"; they are eager to drink it. He seemed forsaken of God; they look with ecstasy and unclouded vision into the Father's face. Why did death mean so much to Him, and why is it such a peaceful experience to them? It is easy to answer this question. Death has no bitterness for the Christian, because it was so bitter to the Redeemer. He drew the curse from it, and now it has in it only the sweetness of blessing. Indeed, there is no death anymore for the Christian. Jesus abolished death. What we now call death is death no longer, since He passed through it. It is now only the shadow of death, and even the shadow is lighted up with the beams of divine glory bursting from heaven. Let us never forget that we have light in our dying because Jesus had darkness.

CHRIST'S CRY ON THE CROSS

◇

My God, my God, why hast thou forsaken me?
Matthew 27:46

This was the fourth word on the cross. It is too mysterious for explanation, and we may only ponder it with hushed hearts for a little.

"Why has Thou forsaken Me?" It was not the nails in His flesh, nor the insults of scoffing enemies, nor the shame of the cross, but the fact that Jesus for the time had lost the sense of the Father's presence that caused the grief of the hour.

"Why hast Thou forsaken Me?" What had He, the beloved Son, done that the Father should forsake Him? It would not have seemed so strange if He had forsaken the angels or the saints living in glory; but why should He forsake His own Son?

"My God!" Why does He not say "My Father"? He said "Father" in the first word on the cross, and in the very last; why is it "My God" here? Has He in the darkness lost the consciousness of sonship? Does He seem removed far from home, from the Father's heart, from the bosom where from all eternity He had resided? So it seems. Yet mark how His faith clings in the darkness; it is still "My God!" He has not lost faith even in the darkness. His faith holds, though He cannot see God's face. No matter how dark the night about us, how heavy the cross that weighs us down, how lonely and deserted we may feel, we should never lose faith in God. Behind the blackest clouds His face ever beams with love. He is still our God, though for the time He may have left us alone.

"Why hast Thou forsaken Me?" Can we answer this "why"? We know only that Jesus was bearing our sins, and that it was for our sake He had to endure this hiding. He was forsaken then for a small moment that for all eternity we might enjoy the favor of God and dwell in communion with Him.

December 9

DIVINE THIRST

*After this, Jesus knowing that all things
were now accomplished . . . saith, I thirst.*
John 19:28

Here we have our Lord's fifth word on the cross. It was just before the end. All things belonging to His work as Redeemer were now finished. He had suffered from thirst all the terrible six hours that He hung on the cross, but He restrained His anguish until His task was done. Now He gave expression to His desire for drink, the only word on the cross that referred to His physical sufferings.

Someone reached up to Him on a stem of hyssop a sponge which had been moistened in the sour vinegar that stood there. It was an act of kindness and pity, and it was the only mark of human tenderness shown to Jesus in those hours. We cannot but be thankful for this small ministry which must have given momentary relief to the holy Sufferer.

Earlier in the day, at the moment of crucifixion, He was offered drink which He refused. That was a numbing drug, a deadening wine mingled with myrrh or wormwood. It was offered with the intention of dulling His senses, that He might not be conscious of His great suffering. He refused it because He wished to preserve the clearness of His mind in the hours when He was making atonement for the world. This drink offered now by the soldier was not medicated wine and was not a sedative in its effects. He needed refreshment to strengthen Him for the great final act—the giving of His soul up to God.

All the experiences of Jesus Christ which reveal human need and suffering bring Him very near to us. Since He suffered hunger and thirst, and pain and weariness and sorrow, He is able to sympathize with us in all our human experiences. He knows what we feel, for He has not forgotten even in heaven what He Himself endured in His incarnation.

"It Is Finished"

◇

He said, It is finished.
John 19:30

T his was our Lord's sixth word on the cross. His allotted life-work was done; His entire task was ended, all things appointed for Him to do were done, and nothing more remained for Him but to die. Many men come to the end even of long lives and find their work far from finished when the call comes to leave this world; but though the life of Jesus had been so short, He was ready to go. He had each day done the work given Him that day to do, and when the last hour of the last day came, there was nothing that He had left undone. We ought to learn the lesson for ourselves and live as Jesus lived, so as to have every part of our work finished when the end comes. We can do this only by taking our allotted duty each day from God's hand and doing it faithfully. Then when the last day comes we shall leave nothing unfinished.

But what was it that was finished when Christ bowed His head on the cross? The work of redemption was done. The atonement for sin was made. As Jesus died, the veil of the temple was rent in two from top to bottom, and access was made into the holiest for all who would enter. A famous picture represents Christ lifted up and beneath Him an innumerable procession of the saints advancing out of the darkness and coming into the light of His cross. There can be no doubt that He had such a vision of redemption while He hung there; for we are told that He "endured the cross, despising the shame" (Hebrews 12:2), because of the joy set before Him—that is, the joy of receiving home the souls He had redeemed.

"It is finished" was, therefore, a shout of victory as He completed His work of suffering and sacrifice. Death seemed like defeat, but it was not defeat. He went down into the grave, but not to stay there. He came again, like a glorious conqueror, and because He lives all His people shall live also.

December 11

◇

LAST WORDS

◇

Father, into thy hands I commend my spirit.
Luke 23:46

This was the seventh and last of the words spoken on the cross. Christ's work as Redeemer was now altogether done; His last word, "finished," marked its completion. Now He is ready to go back to His Father. Before Him now lies the mystery of death. He is about to lose consciousness; His spirit is about to escape from His body. Here we see His calm, trustful faith. The terrible struggle is over, and He is at perfect peace. The word "Father" which He here uses shows that His soul has recovered its serenity. A little while ago He was in the darkness and felt Himself forsaken; now the darkness is gone, the full light shines again, and the Father's face beams upon Him in loving approval. It is the first experience of the glorious joy of redemption, breaking over the Redeemer's soul, as He emerges from the shadows of His cross.

The words are peculiarly instructive to us as a picture of Christian dying. It is but a breathing of the spirit into the hands of the heavenly Father. It is natural to regard death as a strange and mysterious experience, and to think of it with shrinking, if not with fear. We are leaving behind everything with which we are familiar—the friends, old scenes, familiar paths, our lives—and are going out into an untried way, into what seems to us darkness, a valley of shadows. What is death? Where shall we be when we escape from the body? Will it be dark or light? Shall we be alone or accompanied?

Here comes this word of our Lord, and we learn that the believing soul when it leaves the body passes at once into the Father's hands. Surely that is enough for us to know. We shall be perfectly safe eternally if we are in our Father's hands. If we think this way of death it will have no terrors for us. No child is ever afraid to go into its father's hands, and that is all of dying for a believer.

December 12

◇

THE RENT VEIL

◇

The veil of the temple was rent in
twain from the top to the bottom.
Matthew 27:51

The veil was the symbol of separation from God. In the Holy of Holies behind it was the place where God's presence dwelt. Men could not pass the veil. The teaching was that God could not be approached by sinners; the way was not yet opened. Once a year the high priest went behind the veil, implying that there was access to God, but only through a priest. He went with blood—never without it—signifying that only by blood, by sacrifice, could God be approached. The priest was a type of Christ, and his yearly entrance with blood into the Holy of Holies was a constant prefigurement of Christ's once entering with His own blood to make atonement.

The rending of this veil at the time of Christ's death was not an accident caused by the earthquake. It was part of the symbolism—the end, the completion of it. Men were no longer to be excluded from God's presence, since the great sacrifice had now been made. The separating wall had been broken down by Christ's death. So the symbol of this separation was also removed. This rending of the veil was therefore a supernatural act, teaching that the way of access to God was now and forever open to all.

The fact that the veil was rent from top to bottom (that is, torn in two pieces) signifies that the way is entirely opened—the veil is clean gone; the Holiest of all stands wide open with its mercy-seat accessible to every sinner, without the intervention of any earthly priest. The time at which this rending took place is important. It was just after Christ had died—after He had cried, "It is finished." It was because the great atonement was now made that the way was opened; as soon as the sacrifice had been made, the way to God was thrown open to all.

MINISTERING WOMEN

◇

And many women were there beholding afar off.
Matthew 27:55

These were the earliest of a great and noble army of holy women, attached to Christ by deep, personal love, following and ministering to Him. In all the ages since, Christian women have shown like devotion and constancy to Christ and like heroic love in serving Him. The record of women's ministry to Christ is one of the brightest in all the world's history. Women owe an incalculable debt to Christ. He has lifted them up from base slavery and from the degradation of ancient cultures.

Women have always been grateful, too, and have served Christ with great devotion. Women are found in every sickroom, bending over the sufferer with unwearying care, with matchless tenderness ministering to bodily comfort, and pouring the warmth of affection upon feverish spirits. They are found in the wards of hospitals, and upon battlefields, moving like God's angels in blessed, loving ministry. Christian mothers are following the Master and doing work which will shine forever in glorious luster. Christian teachers are doing in lowly paths quiet service which in God's sight is nobler than that of many of the world's famous saints.

Everywhere, too, there is field for women's ministry. Christ is no longer here in person to be served as He was served by these women who followed Him from Galilee; but in His needy and suffering followers He is ever present, and whosoever will may minister to Him; for He said that in doing acts of kindness to the least of His we do them unto Him.

The practical teaching is in the picture which is here held up before every woman, inspiring her to follow Christ. Why will so many young girls choose a life of idle pursuits of aimless, purposeless existence, of mere show, outer display, when such a life of glorious service is open to them?

◇

JOSEPH OF ARIMATHAEA

◇

*Joseph of Arimathea . . . went in boldly unto
Pilate, and craved the body of Jesus.*
Mark 15:43

Joseph had been a disciple of Christ for some time before, but he had lacked the courage to come out boldly. He was rich and influential and had feared the consequences of a public identification with Jesus. But now he threw away his timidity and came out boldly as a friend of Jesus. He did it at a time when all the other disciples, even the apostles, were paralyzed with fear and afraid to speak. He did it, too, at a time of greatest peril, when shame covered the name of Jesus and the bitterness against Him was most intense. He did it also at a time when faith had died in the hearts of all Christ's friends, and when there could be no hope of personal preference or gain as a reward for his act.

There were several reasons that Joseph made this bold confession at this time. One was that he was a true disciple, and true love for Christ cannot always hide itself. Then, when he saw Christ suffering so at the hands of His enemies, the loyalty of his own heart was strengthened, and he felt that he must confess it. When he saw Jesus dead, all the warm and long pent-up affection in his soul awoke. Then he saw how unworthy his conduct had been in hiding his friendship for Christ at a time when confession would have done him good. It looks as if his act were an effort to atone for the imperfectness of his former discipleship.

We must ever be grateful that Joseph gave Jesus such noble burial. Yet we cannot but remember that his love blossomed too late. It is evident that his discipleship was incomplete, that it missed much of the blessing of open discipleship, and that even to himself it was far from satisfactory when the great crisis came. Secret discipleship cannot always remain secret; it must at some time and in some way confess itself, regardless of what it may cost.

◆

THE DESCENT FROM THE CROSS

◆

*When Joseph had taken the body, he wrapped it in a
clean linen cloth, and laid it in his own new tomb.*
Matthew 27:59–60

According to the Roman custom, the bodies of those who
were crucified were left hanging until they were eaten by
birds and wild beasts. This barbarous custom being revolting to
the Jews, an exception was made in their favor and burial was
permitted. If relatives or friends made application, the body of a
crucified man would be given to them to be interred as they saw
fit; but if none came it was thrown into a pit. Had it not then
been for Joseph and Nicodemus, the body of Jesus would have
been cast, with the bodies of the robbers by His side, into the
common graves for criminals. Thanks to the love of these previ-
ously secret disciples, though He died on a cross, our blessed Lord
was buried like a king.

We may dwell with loving thought upon the scenes of this
hour. First, the body was taken down, not by the rude, unfeeling
soldiers, but by Joseph himself, aided by Nicodemus, and probably by some other friends. How tenderly this would be done we
can imagine when we think of the love that was in the hearts of
these friends. The blood was washed from the face, hands, feet,
and side. Next, the body was wrapped in the linen, with the
spices and the ointments. Then, with farewell kisses impressed on
the silent lips by the loving, sorrowing friends who stood by, the
face was covered with the cloth, and the cold form was tenderly
taken to the sepulchre near at hand, amid garden plants and
flowers, and was laid away to rest.

We cannot study this scene of the burial of our blessed Lord
without rich spiritual profit. Shall we not, for one thing, seek to
carry away a spirit of loving gentleness which shall make our love
deeper and our touch softer as we go out among sorrowful ones?

*In the place where he was crucified there was a garden; and
in the garden a new sepulchre. . . . There laid they Jesus.*
John 19:41–42

As we stand by this garden tomb many thoughts are suggested. Christ lived life at every point. Beginning at infancy, He went through every phase, finally lying down in a grave. There is no path on which His footprints are not seen. There is no place any of us shall have to stand in of which we may not say, "Jesus was here. He went through this experience; therefore He knows all about it." We dread the grave; we think of its darkness; but since Jesus has lain there, why should we fear its effects?

Another idea comes from the fact that this tomb was provided for Jesus by His friends. Writers have noted this as another mark of His humiliation. When He was born His cradle was a borrowed manger. During His ministry He had nowhere to lay His head. When He died He was buried in a borrowed grave.

Another thought, as we look at the sepulchre, is how hopeless everything seemed for the time. He on whom the disciples had leaned as the Messiah is now silent in death, His work apparently finished. All their expectations based on Him depended on His living to ascend a throne. It certainly seemed now to His friends that all was over. Yet the grave was simply the humble gateway to glory. As we see it now, in the light that streams from the gospel, it interrupted no plan, quenched no light, destroyed no hope. When shall we learn to bring the truth of immortality into our own faiths and hopes? We stand by the graves of our Christian friends almost as sad as were these friends of Jesus about His grave. Why shall we not learn faith? Death ends nothing for those who die in the Lord—nothing but struggle, sorrow, and sin. No hopes perish when a Christian is buried. Just beyond is glory.

December 17

❖

LOVE AND SORROW

❖

*Mary Magdalene and Mary the mother
of Joses beheld where He was laid.*
Mark 15:47

I t was a loving watch, but a hopeless one, which those devoted
women kept. No stars shone through their cypress trees that
afternoon. To their faith their Christ was lost, because their faith
had taken in only an earthly idea of Messiahship. Death was the
end of all the hope they had yet learned to cherish.

It surely was a dark hour for the disciples when that Friday's
sun sank in the west. Satan seemed to have conquered and utterly to have destroyed the good seed of life which God had sent
down from heaven. A Persian fable says that the earth was created with a great barren plain, without tree or plant. An angel was
sent to scatter the choicest seeds on every spot. Satan, seeing the
seeds on the ground, supposed that the sowing of the seeds was
God's work and determined to destroy it. So he buried all the
seeds in the soil, and summoned the sun and rain to make them
rot away. But while with malicious feeling of triumph he smiled
on the ruin he had created, the seeds which had been buried
away to rot germinated and sprang up, clothing all the earth with
plants and flowers, and in beauty undreamed of before. It was as
if a voice said from heaven, "Thou fool, that which thou sowest is
not quickened except it die."

The application is obvious. The burial of Christ was thought
by His enemies to be the end; but in truth this was the very way
to the glory of Christ. He Himself had said, "Except a corn of
wheat fall into the ground and die, it abideth alone; but if it die, it
bringeth forth much fruit." Christ's burial in the grave was but
the necessary way to His final and glorious victory. So now when
we lay our beloved Christian dead in the tomb it is in the assured
hope of blessed resurrection. The grave is only the dark way to
glory.

December 18

THE FIRST AT THE SEPULCHRE

Mary Magdalene, and Mary . . . and Salome . . . very early in the morning . . . came unto the sepulchre.
Mark 16:1–2

Nothing shines more brightly in the story of our Lord's cross and tomb than the loving fidelity of His female friends. They were last at His cross and first at His tomb when the Sabbath was past. They came very early in the morning, while it was still dark and the day was only dawning. They must have been up much of the night preparing their spices and ointments. Hope had died in their hearts when they saw Jesus dead and laid away in the tomb; but love had not died. They had not forgotten the blessings they had received from His hand; and though they had been disappointed in their Messianic expectations, they were eager to do all that could be done to honor His memory.

There are lessons in this picture that are so obvious that they need scarcely be written about. One is that no matter how dark the hour, our love for Christ should never fail. Though our expectations fail to be realized, though our blossoms of hope fade and fall and yield no fruit, still let us cling to Christ. Our disappointments often prove the richest blessings in the end. It was so with these faithful women. Their Messianic hopes were buried and never rose, but the true Messianic hopes came in full glory from the grave's despair. So it is always with faith's hopes that seem to perish; they come again in immortal beauty.

Another lesson is that in the expression of our love for Christ we should bring to Him the very richest and best that our hearts can find or our hands can prepare. Still another insight is that we ought always to come early in our service of love for Christ. We ought to come to Him in life's morning, while youth's purity and freshness are unspoiled. We ought also to seek Him in the morning of each day, so that not one golden moment may be lost.

December 19

THE STONE ROLLED AWAY

*Who shall roll us away the stone? . . . They
looked . . . the stone was rolled away.*
Mark 16:3–4

We are all alike. Even these holy women on this most sacred errand went forward only to find difficulty. There was a stone in the way that must be rolled aside, and they had not the strength to do it. Naturally enough, they began to be anxious as to the removal of this obstacle. When they came near they saw that the obstacle had been already removed. The divine love had been there beforehand in preparing the way for them. Angels had rolled the stone aside. The lesson is very simple and beautiful. We go forward worrying about the difficulties that lie before us, wondering how we can ever get through them or who will remove them out of our way. Then when we come up to them we find that they are manageable. Someone has been there before us and has taken them away. God always opens the way for us if we quietly move on in our duties.

This applies to one beginning a Christian life. Many persons shrink from it. They say: "I never can be faithful. I never can do the duties. I never can bear the burdens." But as they enter and go on they find that an unseen and mighty Helper goes on before and prepares the way. The hard tasks become easy, and the heavy burdens grow light. It is so all through the Christian life. God's commandment seems impossible in terms of obedience. Walls of stone seem built across the path we are required to walk over. But as we go on the commandment is easy, and a gateway is opened in the wall. Love and faith always have an advance of angels to roll away stones. The practical lesson is that we are never to hesitate or shrink back because obstacles seem to lie before us; we are to go right on, and God will take them away for us. When He wants us to go anywhere He will open the path for our feet. Knowing this, we may go on feeling confident of our own safety.

THE EMPTY TOMB

Fear not ye: for I know that ye seek Jesus.
Matthew 28:5

I t must have been a glad errand to the angels who were sent to minister at the grave of the Redeemer, to roll the stone away, to keep watch at the empty sepulchre, and to tell the good tidings to the disciples who came with such heavy hearts. Their message was one of great joy. Jesus, whom His friends sought dead, was alive again forevermore. He had been in the grave, but He was not there now.

The empty tomb has many glorious voices. It tells us first that Jesus actually died. He was buried here, just in this place. His head lay there, His feet here. Here are the grave clothes, the pieces of fine linen which gentle hands wound around Him. Here is the napkin that covered His face. He lay just here. Look at the place and mark it well, and never forget that He actually was dead. This is important, for upon His death your acceptance with God depends.

But look again. The grave is empty now. He was here, but He is not here now, for He is risen. The grave is empty. Here are the grave clothes, but there is no body. He is gone. The empty tomb tells, then, of resurrection. Death could not hold the Christ. He burst its bands and conquered the grave's power. This is important, for a dead Christ could not have saved us. Had He never risen, how could He have stood for us before God? How could He be our help in weakness, our support in trial, our Comforter, our Friend, if His dust lay yet in the grave? Therefore He is alive to intercede for us, to help us, to save us.

Still another truth which the empty tomb teaches us is that all who sleep in Jesus shall rise too. One precious word of Scripture says: "For if we believe that Jesus died and rose again, even so them also which sleep in Jesus will God bring with him" (1 Thessalonians 4:14). So let us learn to see through the grave to the life beyond.

GO AND TELL PETER

Go your way, tell his disciples and Peter.
Mark 16:7

Why "and Peter"? Why was Peter named, and none of the other disciples? Had Peter been the most loyal and faithful of all the Master's friends, that he deserved such a mark of distinction as this? Oh no, we remember how Peter had fallen. The last word that had dropped upon the ear of Jesus from his lips was a bitter word of denial. Peter had acted worse than any other of the disciples.

Why, then, did Jesus send this special word to Peter? It was just because he had sinned. That last look of the Savior broke Peter's heart, and he went out into the night a penitent man, weeping bitterly. Those had been dark days for him since Jesus died. Not only was he overwhelmed with sorrow at the death of his Lord, whom he truly and most dearly loved, but his grief was made bitter beyond endurance by the remembrance of his own sinful denial at the very end. Deep must his sorrow have been, and all the deeper because he would never be able to ask forgiveness. How he must have longed to have Jesus back, if but for one moment, to confess his sin and seek pardon!

Jesus left this special word for Peter with the angel at the tomb because He knew of the bitterness of His disciple's sorrow. Peter might have been saying, when he heard Jesus had risen, "Perhaps He will not own me anymore," and so Jesus sent this message with Peter's name in it personally, just to let him know that he was forgiven and would not be cast away. What a world of comfort there is in this inclusion of Peter for any who have sinned and are penitent! Those who have fallen are the very ones who receive the deepest, tenderest compassion from Jesus, because they need it most, and because He would help them to rise again. The gospel always has its special word for the penitent; Christ still comes to call the sinner.

—◇—

MARY MAGDALENE

—◇—

*She turned herself back, and saw Jesus
standing, and knew not that it was Jesus.*
John 20:14

The story of Mary of Magdala is one of very tender interest. Jesus had given her a wonderful deliverance, casting out the seven demons that possessed her. From that time her devotion to Him was such that she followed Him wherever He went, ministering to Him. She was one of those who watched by His cross and tomb and came early to do honor to His body. In return for her loving devotion, Jesus appeared first to her the morning He arose.

But when she saw Him she did not know Him, though her heart was crying out for Him with intense yearning. As she stood talking with the angel she heard a step behind her, and turned, and there Jesus stood. Yet she did not recognize Him, though she loved Him so much, and though her heart was hungering for Him. She was thinking He was dead, and she did not know Him when He stood before her alive. Another reason she did not know Him was that her eyes were so full of tears she could not see Him. Many a time it is the same with us; we need Christ, and our hearts are crying out for Him, yet when He comes to us we do not know Him, and we therefore fail to receive comfort from His presence.

There is a picture which represents a mother in deep distress; yet close by her is an angel bending over her to comfort her, his fingers touching at the same time the strings of the harp in his hands. But she is so absorbed in her own grief that she neither sees the angel nor hears his celestial music. So her heart goes uncomforted and still breaking while the comfort is so close at hand. We should look up when we are in sorrow; if we only look down we shall never see the beauties and glories of the face of Jesus, and our hearts shall be uncomforted though He is close beside us.

◇

"Why Weepest Thou?"

◇

Jesus saith unto her, Woman, why weepest thou?
John 20:15

There really was no cause for tears; for Jesus, whom she mourned as dead, was living. Does not Jesus ask the same question now of many a mourner: "Why weepest thou?" We cannot restrain our tears when a dear friend is taken from us; and there is nothing wrong in such tears. Jesus Himself wept beside the grave of His friend whom He was about to raise to life.

But sometimes the grief at loss of dear ones is selfish, unbelieving, even rebellious. When a Christian dies he only departs to be with his Lord; can we therefore weep for him? Surely not; death to him is glorious gain. We weep for ourselves, for our own loss. But those tears of grief and sadness are to be mixed with joy for the believer who has died. He is with Christ, in eternal blessedness; he is past all pain and trial; he has been exalted to a place in the King's palace.

Shall we blame God, and weep bitter, rebellious tears, because He has taken one of His own children away from us? Does God make mistakes? Are we not sure of His love? Was it in anger that He came and caused us such grief? May we not be sure that the sorrow which came with such heavy pain was really God's best kindness for us, as well as for the beloved one He took to Himself? Can we not, then, learn through our tears to give the person back to God? Can we weep with sweet and loving submission to the will of Him who loves us?

> Mother, I see you with your nursery light,
> Leading your babies, all in white,
>   To their sweet rest;
> Christ, the Good Shepherd, carries mine tonight,
>   And that is best.

"RABBONI"

Jesus saith unto her, Mary.
John 20:16

Jesus had not forgotten Mary's name in His experience of death. It was the ancient heathen belief that death washed from the soul all memory of the earthly life—its loves, its sorrows, all its recollections. But here we see Jesus on the other side of death, and the old affections are found unchanged in Him. He met Mary and His other friends, and He took up the threads of the tender story of love just where they had been broken off three days before, when He died. This fact ought to be very comforting. Love is stronger than death. When our friends pass through death, whatever changes may be brought about in them or upon them, we know that there will be no change in their love for us. Death will not sever the ties that bind Christian hearts together on the earth. We shall meet again in the afterlife and remember each other and love each other as before, and take up the old bonds of affection and go on weaving love's web forever.

When Jesus had called Mary and she recognized Him by His voice, she at once answered Him in the one word "Rabboni!"—"My Master!" This name by which she called Him showed the loyalty of her heart and the consecration of her life to Him. Many people get only a half-conception of Christian faith. They believe in Christ as a Savior, but do not think of Him as Lord—their own personal Lord. They think of faith only as trusting for salvation, and do not understand it also as obedience and service. Mary had the true concept. Her answer to Christ's call implied the surrender of herself to Him. All true faith accepts Christ in two ways and under two names. First, it receives Him as Savior, Jesus, trusting in Him alone for salvation. "Simply to Thy cross I cling." Next, it accepts Him as Lord, Rabboni, yielding the life to Him. The saved soul owes obedience, submission, loyalty, service.

December 25

◇

TRUE CHRISTMAS JOY

◇

Mary Magdalene came and told the
disciples that she had seen the Lord.
John 20:18

On this Christmas day we come to the hour of restored joy, which is even richer and deeper because it is fuller than the joy of the Savior's birth. Christmas tells of the first coming of Christ to earth, with blessings for a lost world. But Jesus was lost to His disciples when He went down into the darkness of death. Mary's message is of a Savior returning from the darkness, and from beyond death in immortal life. Only part of the joy came with the birth; here we have the full joy, telling of accomplished redemption and glorious victory over death and the grave. Hope was lost on the Friday of Christ's death; now the stars are shining again, never again to be eclipsed.

So this really is the full Christmas message. It tells not merely of a Savior born, but also of a Savior who has lived, obeyed, suffered, died, and risen again, and is able therefore to save unto the uttermost all who come unto God by Him. The shepherds and the Magi found only a little babe when they came to see the newborn King. We see a Savior with the print of the nails in His hands and feet, who has accomplished a full and glorious redemption for the world.

Jesus appeared to Mary after He had come again from death; yet death had not extinguished one beam of His brightness. The resurrection was a foretaste and prophecy of the future resurrection of all who believe in Him and sleep in Him. It shows us therefore that death does not mean destruction, is not the end of life. It is but a brief event, an experience, and life goes on afterward without loss or corruption. We ought to try to learn this blessed truth. A life is not worth living which is limited by earth's small horizon and does not reach out toward immortality. Indeed we do not really begin to live until we are living for immortality.

◆

THE WALK TO EMMAUS

◆

While they communed together and
reasoned, Jesus himself drew near.
Luke 24:15

These two friends, as they walked along with heavy hearts, had only one theme: they were talking of their heavy loss and of Him whom they had lost. They were so intensely absorbed in their sorrow as they talked of it that they were not aware of the near approach of a stranger until He had drawn up to them and joined them. Jesus always draws near today when His friends are talking of Him. In the Old Testament it was said that when the Lord's people come together and speak of sacred things, the Lord listens and keeps a book of remembrance.

There is something more to this. Two of Christ's friends talk of Him, and He comes and joins them. How much those Christian people miss who meet and pass time together, if they have no theme of conversation but the silly gossip of society, filled with backbiting and bits of malicious criticism and mischievous scandal, but without one single word about Christ! Does anyone suppose that the Lord hearkens to such conversation or puts it down in His book of remembrance? Of course He hears every word of the talk, and every word goes down in the book of remembrance, and we must give account for every idle word. But He does not listen and record the conversation in the sense the prophet meant, with loving pleasure. Does anyone think Christ will draw near and become one of any such group of Christians as often gather in homes, deliciously feeding on every bit of fresh gossip, but with never a word about their Redeemer?

What a blessing every hour of conversation would bring if we would only talk together of Christ and His kingdom! He would then draw near and join us, adding the joy of His presences to our hearts. Shall we not talk together more of our Lord?

◇

"ABIDE WITH US"

◇

They constrained him, saying, Abide with us.
Luke 24:29

I f the two disciples had not convinced Jesus to stay with them, He would have passed on, and they would have missed the blessed enjoyment of His company and the disclosure of Himself which He made to them at the end. The lesson is for us. No doubt we miss many rich comforts and blessings because we do not earnestly seek Jesus to tarry with us. He loves to be pursued. He does not go where He is not really and earnestly desired, where His presence is not eagerly sought after. Only love in us can receive and enjoy Christ's love.

The only reason we do not have more of the blessed fellowship with Christ is that we really do not want more. He is willing to be our abiding guest, entering into every experience with us in our work, in our pleasures, in our social life, in our temptations and trials; but many of us do not want Him always with us. His presence would interfere with our methods of business, or with our way of living, or with our enjoyments and amusements. We do not then approach Him to abide with us. He passes on, and we miss the blessing He would bring.

If we were truly to desire Christ to abide always with us, He would never go away. What a life of benediction and joy we should live if He were indeed always here with us! Unbroken communion with Him would hold heaven close about us all the while, and thus these mundane earthly lives of ours would be permeated and shot through with the sweetness and fragrance of holiness and transformed into the likeness of Christ Himself. Then all life's experiences would be transfigured. Joy would be purer, and even sorrow would be illumined. All through life this should be our continual prayer; then in death our earthly communion shall brighten into heavenly glory.

◇

PRIZE PRESENT BLESSINGS

◇

*Their eyes were opened, and they knew
him; and he vanished out of their sight.*
Luke 24:31

All along the way Jesus had walked with these disciples, pouring the light of His spirit upon them; but they did not recognize Him until the moment of His vanishing out of their sight. It is the same with us and many of our best blessings. We do not recognize them till they are taking their flight. We do not prize health till it is broken. Our common privileges we do not value till something deprives us of them. Our homes appear ordinary till we are thrown upon the world homeless.

It is the same with our friends. We do not see the beauties of their character, nor perceive their real worth, until in some way we have lost them. This is especially true of the friends who are nearest to us in our own households. They seem to us commonplace, because they are always there with us. Their help is so regular and their ministry is so continual that we do not realize their value to us. But one day one of these friends vanishes out of our sight. The familiar form is seen no more. The voice of tender love is heard no more. The quiet, gentle ministry ceases. Tomorrow we miss the friend; then in his vanishing we learn what he was to us. Very sadly one has sung—

> *And she is gone, sweet human love is gone!*
> *'Tis only when they spring to heaven that angels*
> *Reveal themselves to you; they sit all day*
> *Beside you, and lie down at night by you,*
> *Who care not for their presence; muse or sleep,*
> *And all at once they leave you. Then you know them!*
> *We are so fooled, so cheated.*

Should we not receive a lesson here in these closing days of the year? Shall we not try to prize our blessings while we have them? The vacant chair should not be the first revelation of a loving friend.

"REJOICE IN THE LORD"

Then were the disciples glad, when they saw the Lord.
John 20:20

Christ's death has caused them great sorrow; to have Him back again from death gave them unspeakable joy. Indeed there never would have been any Christian joy if Jesus had not risen from the dead. It was necessary that He should die for our sins; but if He had died and remained in the grave, no benefit could have come to us from His dying.

A dead mother cannot do anything for her children; nor could a dead Savior have helped those who trusted in Him. We need a living Savior, to whose feet we can fall with our remorse when we have sinned, and in whose hands we can be kept in safety until we reach glory. We need a living Friend, who will bless us by His rich love; whose strong arm will hold us up in weakness and defend us in temptation; whose presence will restrain us from sin and inspire in us all good thoughts and holy desires and aspirations. We want a living Comforter, who will stand for us in heaven, plead our cause there, and stand by us on the earth in all our imperiled life. We want a living personal Caretaker, who will look after all our interests, plan for our lives, order our steps, and provide for all our wants. We want a Prince who has won for us the battle over death and the grave and is able therefore to bring us also from under the power of death.

No wonder, then, that the disciples were glad when they saw the Lord, when they had Him back again from the dead. We should be glad too, and rejoice in the glorious truth of Christ's resurrection. We have a living Savior. We have One in heaven who loves us. Our Redeemer holds the keys of death. No dark grave can hold us or any of ours who sleep in Jesus. We can enjoy as real communion with Jesus as did His first disciples, because He lives and is one with us.

"LOVEST THOU ME?"

*Simon, son of Jonas, lovest thou me? . . . Feed my
lambs. . . . Feed my sheep. . . . Feed my sheep.*
John 21:15–17

There are several great lessons which we should learn from Peter's restoration. One is that the first essential in a Christian worker is love for Christ Himself. Wisdom will not do. Eloquence will not do. We may delight in the work itself. People sometimes talk about a "passion for souls" as essential in one who would work for Christ; but this is not enough. Nothing less than a passion for Christ Himself will do to fit one for labor for souls. "I have but one passion, and that is He," said a great missionary. When we love Christ with all our heart, and not till then, are we ready to do His work. He will not entrust the care of His flock to any who are not loyal to Him and do not love Him. "Lovest thou Me?" comes before "Feed my lambs."

Another thought here for workers is that they must feed the souls entrusted to their care. Entertainment is not the object, but feeding, spiritual feeding. What is food for souls? Nothing but Christ Himself; and the way to feed others on Christ is to open up for them the holy Word, that they may see Christ and learn to love Him and trust Him and do His will. We must be sure that we give true soul-food, the pure Word of God, to those whom we undertake to feed.

After that more than mere feeding is commanded. The Master's words vary here: He told Peter to feed the lambs and tend the sheep; that is, give them all shepherd-care—love, protection, guidance, provision. The most important and responsible work in all this world is caring for souls. The responsibility rests not on pastors alone, but upon all parents, all teachers, all Christians. We dare not do this work carelessly. It would be a terrible thing if through our negligence any soul should be wounded or lost. They are Christ's lambs and Christ's sheep that we are to begin to shepherd; we must be faithful.

December 31

◇

"FOLLOW ME"

◇

When he had spoken this, he saith unto him, Follow me.
John 21:19

We have now come to the last day of the year. For a whole year in these daily readings we have been walking with Christ. Is there any better message with which to close this book and close the year than this last invitation of Jesus—"Follow Me"? This is the true outcome of all learning of Christ. Mere knowledge, though it be of spiritual things, amounts to nothing, except as it leads us to follow Christ.

We have seen Jesus in all the different phases of His life. We have heard many of His words. Now it remains only for us to follow Him. The outcome of seeing and knowing should be living and doing. The last day of the year suggests also the same duty. Who is satisfied with his life as it appears in retrospect from these evening shadows? The past, however blotted, must remain as it is; we cannot change it, and we need not waste time in regretting it. But the new year is before us, and if we would make that better than the guilt of the past, it must be by following Christ more closely.

To follow Christ is to go where He leads, without questioning or hesitating. It may be to a life of trial, suffering, or sacrifice—but no matter; we have nothing whatever to do with the kind of life to which our Lord calls us. Our only simple duty is to obey and follow. We know that Jesus will lead us only in right paths, and that the way He takes slopes upward and ends at the feet of God.

The new year on which we are about to enter is unopened, and we know not what shall befall us; but if we follow Christ we need have no fear. So let us leave the old year with gratitude to God for its mercies, with penitence for its failures and sins, and let us enter the new with earnest resolve in Christ's name to make it the best and most beautiful year we have ever lived.